普通高等教育系列教材

电子商务英语教程

张强华　郑聪玲　周先武　司爱侠　编著

机械工业出版社

本书选材广泛，覆盖了电子商务的类型、电子商务解决方案、B2B、B2C、在线销售、电子商务网站建设与营销、电子商务网站的 SEM 和 SEO、O2O、电子商务支付系统、电子商务安全技术、移动电子商务、电子商务与大数据、电子商务与云计算、购物车软件、计算机网络、无线网络、互联网、物流以及利用社交媒体营销等内容。

本书每一个单元都由以下几部分组成：课文——选材得当、面广实用；单词——给出课文中出现的新词，读者由此可以积累电子商务专业的基本词汇；词组——给出课文中的常用词组；缩略语——给出课文中出现的、业内人士必须掌握的缩略语；注释讲解——进一步讲解课文中出现的疑难知识，扩大读者的阅读面；习题——既有针对课文的练习，也有针对行业考试的练习；阅读材料——进一步扩大读者的视野；参考译文（Text A）——供读者对照学习。本书课文配有音频材料，扫描二维码即可收听；扫描相应的二维码还可以免费获得本书的词汇总表，既可用于复习和背诵，也可作为小词典随时查阅。另外，本书还配有 PPT、参考答案等资料。

本书既可作为高等院校本、专科电子商务相关专业的专业英语教材，也可供从业人员自学，还可作为培训班的培训用书。

图书在版编目（CIP）数据

电子商务英语教程 / 张强华等编著. —北京：机械工业出版社，2018.1
（2024.1 重印）
普通高等教育系列教材
ISBN 978-7-111-60212-5

Ⅰ. ①电⋯ Ⅱ. ①张⋯ Ⅲ. ①电子商务－英语－高等学校－教材
Ⅳ. ①F713.36

中国版本图书馆 CIP 数据核字（2018）第 128532 号

机械工业出版社（北京市百万庄大街 22 号　邮政编码 100037）
责任编辑：郝建伟　杨　洋　　责任校对：张艳霞
责任印制：单爱军

北京虎彩文化传播有限公司印刷

2024 年 1 月第 1 版 • 第 11 次印刷
184mm×240mm • 16.5 印张 • 404 千字
标准书号：ISBN 978-7-111-60212-5
定价：49.00 元

电话服务　　　　　　　　　网络服务
客服电话：010-88361066　　机　工　官　网：www.cmpbook.com
　　　　　010-88379833　　机　工　官　博：weibo.com/cmp1952
　　　　　010-68326294　　金　书　网：www.golden-book.com
封底无防伪标均为盗版　　　机工教育服务网：www.cmpedu.com

前　言

　　电子商务的极速发展需要从业人员掌握许多新技术和新方法，因此对他们的专业英语水平要求较高。而跨境电子商务的激增，更凸显了专业英语的重要性。具备相关职业技能并精通外语的人员往往能赢得竞争优势，成为职场中不可或缺的人才。本书就是为帮助读者提高专业英语水平而编写的。

　　本书具有如下特色：

　　（1）本书选材广泛，覆盖了电子商务的类型、电子商务解决方案、B2B、B2C、在线销售、电子商务网站建设与营销、电子商务网站的 SEM 和 SEO、O2O、电子商务支付系统、电子商务安全技术、移动电子商务、电子商务与大数据、电子商务与云计算、购物车软件、计算机网络、无线网络、互联网、物流以及利用社交媒体营销等内容。

　　（2）体例创新，适合教学。本书内容设计与课堂教学的各个环节紧密切合。每一单元都包含以下部分：课文——提供选材广泛、风格多样、切合实际的两篇专业文章；单词——给出课文中出现的新词，读者由此可以积累电子商务专业的基本词汇；词组——给出课文中的常用词组；缩略语——给出课文中出现的、业内人士必须掌握的缩略语；注释讲解——进一步讲解课文中出现的疑难知识，扩大读者的阅读面；习题——既有针对课文的练习，也有一些开放性的练习；阅读材料——进一步扩大读者的视野；参考译文（Text A）——让读者对照理解和提高翻译能力。**本书课文配有音频材料，扫描每单元的课文的二维码下载后即可收听（音频建议用耳机收听）**；扫描封底的二维码还可以下载本书的词汇总表，既可用于复习和背诵，也可作为小词典随时查阅。

　　（3）教学资源丰富，教学支持完善。本书有配套的 PPT、参考答案、音频文件等资料。另外，书中的习题量适当，题型丰富，难易搭配，便于教师组织教学。

　　本书编者具有 20 多年的行业英语教学与图书编写经验，使本书更符合教学要求，让教师和学生使用本书时更得心应手。在本书使用过程中，有任何问题，读者都可以通过电子邮件与我们交流，我们一定会给予及时答复。我们的 E-mail 地址如下：zqh3882355@sina.com；zqh3882355@163.com。教师也可到机工出版社网站免费下载课件。

　　本书既可作为高等院校本、专科电子商务相关专业的专业英语教材，也可供从业人员自学，还可作为培训班的培训用书。

编　者

目 录

前言

Unit 1 ················ 1
  Text A
    What Is E-commerce? ············ 1
      New Words ············ 5
      Phrases ············ 8
      Abbreviations ············ 9
      Exercises ············ 9
  Text B
    E-commerce and Selling Online ············ 11
      New Words ············ 14
      Phrases ············ 15
      Abbreviations ············ 16
      Exercises ············ 16
    Reading Material ············ 16
    E-commerce Advantages and Disadvantages ············ 16
  参考译文：什么是电子商务？············ 19

Unit 2 ················ 23
  Text A
    How to Choose an E-commerce Business Model ············ 23
      New Words ············ 27
      Phrases ············ 28
      Abbreviations ············ 29
      Exercises ············ 29
  Text B
    Business-to-Business ············ 31
      New Words ············ 33
      Phrases ············ 35
      Abbreviations ············ 35
      Exercises ············ 35
    Reading Material ············ 35
    About E-commerce ············ 35
  参考译文：如何选择电子商务商业模式 ············ 40

Unit 3 ················ 44
  Text A
    What Is a Computer Network? ············ 44
      New Words ············ 46
      Phrases ············ 47
      Abbreviations ············ 47
      Exercises ············ 48
  Text B
    A Basic Guide to the Internet ············ 49
      New Words ············ 53
      Phrases ············ 54
      Abbreviations ············ 55
      Exercises ············ 55
    Reading Material ············ 56
    Network Security ············ 56
  参考译文：什么是计算机网络？············ 60

Unit 4 ················ 62
  Text A
    How to Build an E-commerce Website ············ 62
      New Words ············ 65
      Phrases ············ 66
      Abbreviations ············ 67
      Exercises ············ 67
  Text B
    Website Navigation and Its Impact on E-commerce ············ 70
      New Words ············ 72
      Phrases ············ 73
      Exercises ············ 74
    Reading Material ············ 74
    Shopping Cart Software ············ 74
  参考译文：如何建立电子商务网站 ············ 77

Unit 5 ················ 80
  Text A
    Five Ways to Market Your E-commerce Site ············ 80

  New Words ·············· 83
  Phrases ·············· 85
  Abbreviations ·············· 85
  Exercises ·············· 86
Text B
 E-commerce Supply Chain Management:
  Reducing Cost and Inefficiency ········ 88
  New Words ·············· 92
  Phrases ·············· 93
  Abbreviations ·············· 94
 Exercises ·············· 94
 Reading Material ·············· 95
 Online Advertising ·············· 95
 参考译文：电子商务网站营销的五种
  方法 ·············· 99

Unit 6 ·············· 102
 Text A
 Web Traffic ·············· 102
  New Words ·············· 105
  Phrases ·············· 107
  Abbreviations ·············· 107
 Exercises ·············· 107
 Text B
 Conversion Rate Optimization ·········· 109
  New Words ·············· 112
  Phrases ·············· 113
  Abbreviations ·············· 114
 Exercises ·············· 114
 Reading Material ·············· 114
 PageRank ·············· 114
 参考译文：网络流量 ·············· 118

Unit 7 ·············· 121
 Text A
 Essential SEO Strategies for E-commerce
  Sites ·············· 121
  New Words ·············· 123
  Phrases ·············· 125
  Abbreviations ·············· 125
 Exercises ·············· 126
 Text B

 Best Practices That Could Double
  E-commerce Sales ·············· 128
  New Words ·············· 132
  Phrases ·············· 133
  Abbreviations ·············· 133
 Exercises ·············· 134
 Reading Material ·············· 134
 Top Ten SEM Optimization Tips for
  E-commerce Sites ·············· 134
 参考译文：电子商务网站的基本 SEO
  策略 ·············· 137

Unit 8 ·············· 140
 Text A
 The Ways to Track Online to Offline
  Conversions (and Vice Versa) ········ 140
  New Words ·············· 143
  Phrases ·············· 144
  Abbreviations ·············· 144
 Exercises ·············· 145
 Text B
 Benefits of Social Media Marketing ······ 147
  New Words ·············· 150
  Phrases ·············· 151
 Exercises ·············· 151
 Reading Material ·············· 152
 E-commerce Legals and Law ·············· 152
 参考译文：跟踪线上到线下（反之亦然）
  的转化方法 ·············· 156

Unit 9 ·············· 159
 Text A
 E-commerce Payment System ·············· 159
  New Words ·············· 161
  Phrases ·············· 163
  Abbreviations ·············· 163
 Exercises ·············· 164
 Text B
 Understanding Online Payment Services ···· 166
  New Words ·············· 171
  Phrases ·············· 171
 Exercises ·············· 172

Reading Material ·············· 172
 Safe Online Payment Methods ·············· 172
 参考译文：电子商务支付系统 ·············· 175

Unit 10 ·············· 177
Text A
The Basics of Website Security for E-commerce Retailers ·············· 177
 New Words ·············· 180
 Phrases ·············· 181
 Abbreviations ·············· 182
Exercises ·············· 182
Text B
How to Stay Safe When Shopping Online ·············· 185
 New Words ·············· 188
 Phrases ·············· 190
 Abbreviations ·············· 190
Exercises ·············· 190
Reading Material ·············· 191
 Ways to Protect Your E-commerce Site from Hacking and Fraud ·············· 191
参考译文：电子商务零售商网站安全的基础 ·············· 195

Unit 11 ·············· 198
Text A
Mobile Commerce ·············· 198
 New Words ·············· 201
 Phrases ·············· 203
 Abbreviations ·············· 203
Exercises ·············· 203
Text B
Mobile Marketing ·············· 205
 New Words ·············· 209
 Phrases ·············· 210
 Abbreviations ·············· 210
Exercises ·············· 211
Reading Material ·············· 211
 Mobile Payment ·············· 211

参考译文：移动商务 ·············· 216

Unit 12 ·············· 219
Text A
A Guide to Using CRM in E-commerce ·············· 219
 New Words ·············· 222
 Phrases ·············· 223
 Abbreviations ·············· 224
Exercises ·············· 225
Text B
Reverse Logistics in E-commerce ·············· 227
 New Words ·············· 230
 Phrases ·············· 231
Exercises ·············· 232
Reading Material ·············· 233
 Electronic CRM ·············· 233
参考译文：电子商务中使用 CRM 的指南 ·············· 237

Unit 13 ·············· 241
Text A
Benefits of Big Data for E-commerce Companies ·············· 241
 New Words ·············· 243
 Phrases ·············· 244
 Abbreviations ·············· 245
Exercises ·············· 245
Text B
Cloud Computing and Its Effect on E-commerce ·············· 247
 New Words ·············· 250
 Phrases ·············· 251
 Abbreviations ·············· 251
Exercises ·············· 252
Reading Material ·············· 252
 The Benefits of Cloud Computing to the E-commerce Industry ·············· 252
参考译文：大数据对电子商务公司的益处 ·············· 255

Unit 1

Text A

What Is E-commerce?

扫一扫，听课文

Electronic commerce or e-commerce refers to a wide range of online business activities for products and services. It also pertains to "any form of business transaction in which the parties interact electronically rather than by physical exchanges or direct physical contact".

E-commerce is usually associated with buying and selling over the Internet, or conducting any transaction involving the transfer of ownership or rights to use goods or services through a computer-mediated network. Though popular, this definition is not comprehensive enough to capture recent developments in this new and revolutionary business phenomenon. A more complete definition is: E-commerce is the use of electronic communications and digital information processing technology in business transactions to create, transform, and redefine relationships for value creation between or among organizations, and between organizations and individuals.

The major different kinds of e-commerce are: Business-to-Business (B2B); Business-to-Consumer (B2C); Business-to-Government (B2G); Consumer-to-Consumer (C2C); and Mobile Commerce (M-commerce).

1. What Is B2B E-commerce?

B2B e-commerce is simply defined as e-commerce between companies. This is the type of e-commerce that deals with relationships between and among businesses. About 80% of e-commerce is of this type, and most experts predict that B2B e-commerce will continue to grow faster than the B2C segment. The B2B market has two primary components: e-infrastructure and e-markets.

E-infrastructure is the architecture of B2B, primarily consisting of the following:

- logistics—transportation, warehousing and distribution (e.g., Procter and Gamble);
- application service providers—deployment, hosting and management of packaged software from a central facility (e.g., Oracle and Linkshare);
- outsourcing of functions in the process of e-commerce, such as web-hosting, security and customer care solutions (e.g., outsourcing providers such as eShare, NetSales, iXL Enterprises and Universal Access);
- auction solutions software for the operation and maintenance of real-time auctions in the

Internet (e.g., Moai Technologies and OpenSite Technologies);
- content management software for the facilitation of website content management and delivery (e.g., Interwoven and ProcureNet); and
- Web-based commerce enablers (e.g., Commerce One, a browser-based, XML-enabled purchasing automation software).

E-markets are simply defined as websites where buyers and sellers interact with each other and conduct transactions.

Most B2B applications are in the areas of supplier management (especially purchase order processing), inventory management (i.e., managing order-ship-bill cycles), distribution management (especially in the transmission of shipping documents), channel management (i.e., information dissemination on changes in operational conditions), and payment management (e.g., Electronic Payment Systems[1] or EPS).

2. What Is B2C E-commerce?

Business-to-Consumer e-commerce, or commerce between companies and consumers, involves gathering customers information; purchasing physical goods (i.e., tangibles such as books or consumer products) or information goods (or goods of electronic material or digitized content, such as software, or e-books); and, for information goods, receiving products over an electronic network.

It is the second largest and the earliest form of e-commerce. Its origins can be traced to online retailing (or e-tailing). Thus, the more common B2C business models are the online retailing companies such as Amazon.com, Drugstore.com, Beyond.com, Barnes and Noble and ToysRus. Other B2C examples involving information goods are E-Trade and Travelocity.

The more common applications of this type of e-commerce are in the areas of purchasing products and information, and personal finance management, which pertains to the management of personal investments and finances with the use of online banking tools.

B2C e-commerce reduces transactions costs (particularly search costs) by increasing consumer access to information and allowing consumers to find the most competitive price for a product or service. B2C e-commerce also reduces market entry barriers since the cost of putting up and maintaining a website is much cheaper than installing a "brick-and-mortar" structure for a firm. In the case of information goods, B2C e-commerce is even more attractive because it saves firms from factoring in the additional cost of a physical distribution network. Moreover, for countries with a growing and robust Internet population, delivering information goods becomes increasingly feasible.

3. What Is B2G E-commerce?

Business-to-Government e-commerce or B2G is generally defined as commerce between companies and the public sector. It refers to the use of the Internet for public procurement, licensing procedures, and other government-related operations. This kind of e-commerce has two features: first, the public sector assumes a pilot/leading role in establishing e-commerce; and second, it is

---

[1] Electronic Payment System—the system of non-cash transactions, placement of contracts and money transfers between sellers and purchasers, banks and their clients, with the help of means of electronic communications using information encoding and its automatic processing.

assumed that the public sector has the greatest need for making its procurement system more effective.

Web-based purchasing policies increase the transparency of the procurement process and reduces the risk of irregularities. To date, however, the size of the B2G e-commerce market as a component of total e-commerce is insignificant, as government e-procurement systems remain undeveloped.

4. What Is C2C E-commerce?

Consumer-to-Consumer e-commerce or C2C is simply commerce between private individuals or consumers. This type of e-commerce is characterized by the growth of electronic marketplaces and online auctions, particularly in vertical industries where firms/businesses can bid for what they want from among multiple suppliers. It perhaps has the greatest potential for developing new markets.

This type of e-commerce comes in at least three forms:

- auctions facilitated at a portal, such as eBay, which allows online real-time bidding on items being sold in the Web;
- peer-to-peer systems, such as the Napster model (a protocol for sharing files between users used by chat forums similar to IRC) and other file exchange and later money exchange models; and
- classified ads at portal sites, such as Excite Classifieds and eWanted, Pakwheels.com (an interactive, online marketplace where buyers and sellers can negotiate and which features "Buyer Leads & Want Ads").

There is little information on the relative size of global C2C e-commerce. However, C2C figures of popular C2C sites such as eBay and Napster indicate that this market is quite large. These sites produce millions of dollars in sales every day.

(1) Advantages of C2C Sites

Consumer to Consumer e-commerce has many benefits. The primary benefit to consumers is reduction in cost. Buying ad space on other e-commerce sites is expensive. Sellers can post their items for free or with minimal charge depending on the C2C website. C2C websites form a perfect platform for buyers and sellers who wish to buy and sell related products. The ability to find related products leads to an increase in the visitor to customer conversion ratio. Business owners can cheaply maintain C2C websites and increase profits without the additional costs of distribution locations. A good example of a C2C e-commerce website is Esty, a site that allows consumers to buy and sell handmade or vintage items and supplies including art, photography, clothing, jewelry, food, bath and beauty products, quilts, knick-knacks, and toys.

(2) Disadvantages of C2C Sites

There are a couple of disadvantages to these type of sites as well. Doing transaction on these type of websites requires cooperation between the buyer and seller. It has been noted many times that these two do not cooperate with each other after a transaction has been made. They do not share the transaction information which may be via credit or debit card or Internet banking. This can result in online fraud since the buyer and seller are not very well versed with each other. This can lead to lawsuit being imposed on either ends or also on the site if it has not mentioned the disclaimer in it's terms and conditions. This may also hamper the C2C website's reputation. Companies which handle consumer to consumer e-commerce websites seem to have becoming very cautious to prevent online scams.

5. What Is M-commerce?

M-commerce (mobile commerce) is the buying and selling of goods and services through wireless technology—i.e., handheld devices such as cellular telephones and personal digital assistants (PDAs).

As content delivery over wireless devices becomes faster, more secure, and scalable, some believe that m-commerce will surpass wireline e-commerce as the method of choice for digital commerce transactions. This may well be true for the Asia-Pacific where there are more mobile phone users than there are Internet users.

Industries affected by m-commerce include:

1) Financial services, including mobile banking (when customers use their hand-held devices to access their accounts and pay their bills), as well as brokerage services (in which stock quotes can be displayed and trading conducted from the same hand-held device).

2) Telecommunications, in which service changes, bill payment and account reviews can all be conducted from the same hand-held device.

3) Service/retail, as consumers are given the ability to place and pay for orders on the fly.

4) Information services, which include the delivery of entertainment, financial news, sports figures and traffic updates to a single mobile device.

6. Is E-commerce the Same as E-business?

While "e-commerce" and "e-business" can be used interchangeably, they are distinct concepts. In e-commerce, Information and Communications Technology (ICT) is used in inter-business or inter-organizational transactions (transactions between and among firms/organizations) and in business-to-consumer transactions (transactions between firms/organizations and individuals).

In e-business, on the other hand, ICT is used to enhance one's business. It includes any process that a business organization (either a for-profit, governmental or non-profit entity) conducts over a computer-mediated network. A more comprehensive definition of e-business is:

"The transformation of an organization's processes to deliver additional customer value through the application of technologies, philosophies and computing paradigm of the new economy."

Three primary processes are enhanced in e-business:

1) Production processes, which include procurement, ordering and replenishment of stocks; processing of payments; electronic links with suppliers; and production control processes, among others.

2) Customer-focused processes, which include promotional and marketing efforts, selling over the Internet, processing of customers' purchase orders and payments, and customer support, among

others.

3) Internal management processes, which include employee services, training, internal information-sharing, videoconferencing, and recruiting. Electronic applications enhance information flow between production and sales forces to improve sales force productivity. Workgroup communications and electronic publishing of internal business information are likewise made more efficient.

New Words

e-commerce	*n.*	电子商务
activity	*n.*	行动，行为，活跃，活动性
transaction	*n.*	交易，事务，办理，处理
interact	*v.*	互相作用，互相影响
Internet	*n.*	互联网，因特网
conduct	*v.*	实施，执行，引导，管理
	n.	行为
comprehensive	*adj.*	全面的，广泛的，能充分理解的，包容的
capture	*n.*	捕获，战利品
	v.	捕获，夺取
phenomenon	*n.*	现象
communication	*n.*	通信
digital	*adj.*	数字的，数位的
	n.	数字，数字式
transform	*v.*	转换，改造，使……变形，改变，转化，变换
redefine	*v.*	重新定义
relationship	*n.*	关系，关联
individual	*n.*	个人，个体
	adj.	个别的，单独的，个人的
expert	*n.*	专家，行家
	adj.	老练的，内行的，专门的
predict	*v.*	预知，预言，预报，做出预言
segment	*n.*	段，节，片断
	v.	分割
e-infrastructure	*n.*	电子基础设施
e-market	*n.*	电子市场
architecture	*n.*	体系结构
logistics	*n.*	物流，后勤
transportation	*n.*	运输，运送
warehousing	*n.*	仓库储存

distribution	*n.*	分配，分发，发送
deployment	*n.*	展开，配置
hosting	*n.*	托管
facility	*n.*	便利，敏捷，设备，工具
outsourcing	*n.*	外部采办，外购，外包
software	*n.*	软件
maintenance	*n.*	维护，保持
real-time	*adj.*	实时的
facilitation	*n.*	简易化，助长
browser-based	*adj.*	基于浏览器的
enabler	*n.*	赋能者，使能者，使能器，推动者
automation	*n.*	自动控制，自动操作
supplier	*n.*	供应者，补充者，厂商，供给者
dissemination	*n.*	传播，分发
payment	*n.*	付款，支付，报酬
tangible	*adj.*	切实的
search	*n.*	搜寻，查究
	v.	搜索，搜寻，探求，调查
cost	*n.*	成本
barrier	*n.*	障碍物，栅栏，屏障
brick-and-mortar	*adj.*	实体的
firm	*n.*	公司，(合伙)商号
	adj.	结实的，坚固的，稳固的，严格的
	v.	使牢固，使坚定，变稳固，变坚实
	adv.	稳固地，坚定地
attractive	*adj.*	吸引人的，有魅力的
robust	*adj.*	稳健的，坚固的，强壮的，精力充沛的
procedure	*n.*	程序，手续
establish	*v.*	建立，设立，安置
transparency	*n.*	透明，透明度
irregularity	*n.*	不规则，无规律
component	*n.*	成分
	adj.	组成的，构成的
insignificant	*adj.*	无关紧要的，可忽略的，无意义的
undeveloped	*adj.*	不发达的，未开发的
marketplace	*n.*	市场，集市，商场
online	*n.*	联机，在线式
potential	*adj.*	潜在的，可能的

	n. 潜能，潜力
portal	*n.* 入口，门户
protocol	*n.* 协议
classified	*v.* 分类
	adj. 机密的
interactive	*adj.* 交互式的
negotiate	*v.* 买卖，商议，谈判，磋商
indicate	*v.* 指出，显示
ad	*n.* 广告
item	*n.* （可分类或列举的）项目，条款
profit	*n.* 利润，益处，得益
	v. 得益，利用，有益于，有利于
handmade	*adj.* 手工的，手制的
cooperation	*n.* 合作，协作
fraud	*n.* 欺骗，诡计，骗子，假货
lawsuit	*n.* 诉讼（尤指非刑事案件）
disclaimer	*n.* 放弃，拒绝，不承诺
condition	*n.* 条件，情形，环境
	v. 以……为条件
hamper	*v.* 妨碍，牵制
reputation	*n.* 名誉，名声
cautious	*adj.* 谨慎的，小心的
scam	*n.* 诡计，故事
secure	*adj.* 安全的，可靠的
	v. 保护
scalable	*adj.* 可升级的
surpass	*v.* 超越，胜过
wireline	*n.* 有线线路
telecommunication	*n.* 电讯，无线电通信，电信学
e-business	*n.* 电子业务
enhance	*v.* 提高，增强
philosophy	*n.* 哲学，哲学体系
paradigm	*n.* 范例
ordering	*n.* 排序，分类
replenishment	*n.* 补给，补充
stock	*n.* 库存，股票，股份
	adj. 常备的，存货的
	v. 进货，采购
link	*n.* 链接

employee	n.	职工，雇员，店员
videoconference	n.	视频会议
productivity	n.	生产力
workgroup	n.	工作组

Phrases

electronic commerce	电子商务
pertain to	属于，关于，附属，适合
associate with	联合
transfer of ownership	所有权转让
mobile commerce	移动电子商务
deal with	安排，处理，涉及
consist of…	由……组成
Procter and Gamble	宝洁公司
interact with…	与……相互作用，与……相互影响，与……相互配合
purchase order	订单
inventory management	库存管理
shipping document	货运单据
channel management	渠道管理
information dissemination	信息传播
trace to	上溯
online retailing	在线零售
personal investment	个人投资
online banking	在线银行
transactions cost	交易成本
competitive price	竞争价格，公开招标价格
factor in	考虑，把……计算在内，包括
distribution network	配送网络
public sector	公共部门，公共成分
be characterized by…	……的特点在于，……的特点是
bid for	投标，许诺以获支持
peer-to-peer system	对等网系统
classified ads	分类广告
a couple of	两个，几个
debit card	借记卡
result in	导致
impose on	利用，欺骗，施加影响于
handheld device	手持设备
cellular telephone	移动电话

mobile banking	移动银行
brokerage service	经纪服务，佣金服务
on the fly	在百忙中；急忙地；直接地
financial news	财经新闻；交易所新闻，股票消息
on the other hand	另一方面
information flow	信息流

Abbreviations

B2B (Business-to-Business)	企业对企业
B2C (Business-to-Consumer)	企业对消费者
B2G (Business-to-Government)	企业对政府
C2C (Consumer-to-Consumer)	消费者对消费者
XML (eXtensible Markup Language)	可扩展标记语言
EPS (Electronic Payment Systems)	电子支付系统
IRC (Internet Relay Chatting)	互联网在线聊天系统
PDA (Personal Digital Assistant)	个人数字助理，掌上电脑
ICT (Information and Communications Technology)	信息与通信技术

Exercises

[Ex. 1]　Answer the following questions according to the text.

1. What does electronic commerce refer to? What is it usually associated with?
2. What are the major different kinds of e-commerce mentioned in the text?
3. What is B2B e-commerce defined as? What does it deal with?
4. What is the definition of e-market?
5. How does B2C e-commerce reduce transactions costs (particularly search costs)?
6. What are the two features B2G has?
7. What are the three forms C2C comes in?
8. What is m-commerce?
9. What industries are affected by m-commerce?
10. What are the three primary processes which are enhanced in e-business?

[Ex. 2]　Translate the following terms or phrases from English into Chinese and vice versa.

1. transportation
2. competitive price
3. electronic commerce
4. inventory management
5. online retailing
6. 通信

1. _____
2. _____
3. _____
4. _____
5. _____
6. _____

7. 基于浏览器的 _____   7. _____
8. 传播，分发 _____   8. _____
9. 电子基础设施 _____   9. _____
10. 可升级的 _____   10. _____

[Ex. 3] Translate the following passage into Chinese.

What Is E-commerce?

Electronic commerce or e-commerce is a term for any type of business, or commercial transaction, which involves the transfer of information across the Internet. It covers a range of different types of businesses, from consumer based retail sites, through auction sites, to business exchanges trading goods and services between corporations. It is currently one of the most important aspects of the Internet to emerge.

The history of e-commerce dates back to 1970, when for the first time, Electronic Data Interchange (EDI) and electronic fund transfer were introduced. Since then, a rapid growth of e-commerce has pervaded almost every aspect of business such as supply chain management, transaction processing, Internet marketing, and inventory management.

E-commerce allows consumers to electronically exchange goods and services with no barriers of time or distance. It has expanded rapidly over the past five years and is predicted to continue at this rate, or even accelerate. In the near future the boundaries between "conventional" and "electronic" commerce will become increasingly blurred as more and more businesses move sections of their operations onto the Internet.

[Ex. 4] Fill in the blanks with the words given below.

online	account	make	consideration	business
want	site	need	e-commerce	research

To start an online business it is best to find a niche product that consumers have difficulty finding in malls or department stores. Also take shipping into ___1___. Pets.com found out the hard way: dog food is expensive to ship FedEx! Then you need an e-commerce enabled website. This can either be a new ___2___ developed from scratch, or an existing site to which you can add e-commerce shopping cart capabilities.

The next step, you need a means of accepting ___3___ payments. This usually entails obtaining a merchant ___4___ and accepting credit cards through an online payment gateway. Some smaller sites stick with simpler methods of accepting payments such as PayPal.

Lastly, you ___5___ a marketing strategy for driving targeted traffic to your site and a means of enticing repeat customers. If you are new to ___6___ keep things simple—know your limitations.

E-commerce has proved to be a suitable alternative for people who ___7___ to shop and transact from the confines of their home. It can be a very rewarding venture, but you cannot ___8___ money overnight. It is important to do a lot of ___9___, ask questions, work hard and make on business decisions on facts learned from researching e-commerce. Don't rely on "gut" feelings. We hope our online e-commerce tutorial has helped your ___10___ make a better decision in choosing an online shopping cart for your e-commerce store.

Text B

E-commerce and Selling Online

1. Overview

E-commerce plays an increasingly important role in the way in which products and services are purchased. Selling products and services online can help your business become more profitable and lower your costs. E-commerce can also strengthen and improve the efficiency of your relationships with suppliers and other key trading partners.

扫一扫，听课文

It's important to plan for the ongoing development and maintenance of any e-commerce system from the start. You also need to be aware of your legal obligations when selling online.

2. Get Started with E-commerce

Investigate your options for getting online. Make sure you choose the right website and e-mail addresses so your customers and suppliers can find you quickly and easily.

Consider the different ways to connect your business to the Internet. A range of options are available including ADSL, dial-up, cable and satellite.

Pay attention to the design of your site. The overall look and feel will play an important role in its usability. There are also legal issues to consider in the design of the website. For example, you must ensure it's accessible for disabled people.

If you want to sell directly through your website, you'll need to have the infrastructure in place to showcase your products and services and process orders electronically.

To complete your e-commerce solution, you'll need to set up the facility to accept payment through your website.

Once your shop is online, consider how to monitor its effectiveness, make it more powerful and ultimately sell more through it. Think about how you can drive traffic to your site.

3. Maintain and Develop Your E-commerce Services

Your work doesn't end once your initial e-commerce system is up and running. You need to maintain the site, constantly review how well it is operating and consider new opportunities and ways of working that it may present to you.

(1) Maintaining Your E-commerce Site

You must ensure that the content of the site is accurate and updated regularly. This will help to promote a positive image for the business, attracting and retaining visitors to the site.

As your e-commerce presence grows, you must protect yourself against the threats posed by hackers, viruses and fraudsters. Identify the risks they pose and implement appropriate security controls to counter them.

(2) Identifying New Opportunities

Mobile commerce (m-commerce) is a type of e-commerce using mobile devices such as mobile phones, smart-phones, tablet computers and other devices with a wireless connection. M-commerce brings new opportunities to small businesses both to sell new services and to operate existing businesses more efficiently.

Extranets enables your business to communicate and collaborate more effectively with selected business partners, suppliers and customers. They can play an important role in enhancing business relationships and improving supply chain management. Intranets are an invaluable way to communicate with employees, especially for businesses with multiple locations and staff who work remotely or from home.

An e-marketplace allows you to use a variety of online services such as electronic catalog, business directory listings and online auctions to sell your goods and services more effectively to other businesses.

4. Selling Online: the Advantages

Selling online has a number of advantages over other selling methods, including:

- Savings in set-up and operational costs. You don't need to rent high street premises or pay shop assistants.
- Reducing order processing costs. Customer orders can automatically come straight into your orders database from the website.
- Reaching a global audience, increasing sales opportunities.
- Competing with larger businesses by being able to open 24 hours a day, seven days a week.
- Quicker payments from online transactions.
- Improving your business using data gathered from tracking customer purchases.
- Using your online shop as a catalog for existing customers.

Online selling will work best if you have:

- well-defined products or services that can be sold without human involvement in the sales process;
- fixed prices for all types of potential customers;
- products or services that can be delivered within a predictable lead time.

5. Selling Online: the Disadvantages

Selling online also has a number of disadvantages over other selling methods, including:

- Authenticity and security. Due to the lack of trust, a large number of people do not use the Internet for any kind of financial transaction. Many people have reservations regarding the requirement to disclose personal and private information for security concerns. Some people simply refuse to trust the authenticity of completely impersonal business transactions, as in the case of e-commerce.
- Time-consuming. The time period required for delivering physical products can also be quite significant in case of e-commerce. Hence it is not suitable for perishable commodities like food items. A lot of phone calls and e-mails may be required till you get your desired

products.
- Inconvenient. People prefer to shop in the conventional way than to use e-commerce for purchasing food products and objects that need to be felt and touched before actually making the purchase. So e-commerce is not suitable for such business sectors. However, returning the product and getting a refund can be even more troublesome and time-consuming than purchasing, in case you are not satisfied with a particular product.

6. Selling Online: Types of Shops

(1) Basic Online Shops

Basic online shops allow you to sell a small range of products, providing photos, descriptions and prices as well as accept orders online.

Most customers shopping online will want to pay by debit or credit card. You can create electronic mail-order forms using web authoring software packages. These order forms let customers e-mail their orders to be processed offline. You'll need a more sophisticated online shop if you want to accept card payments online.

A basic site is of low cost and easy to create for a limited product range. But it might have restricted design and functionality and might be less secure than more sophisticated options.

(2) Intermediate Online Shops

An intermediate online shop is typically an e-commerce package and should include catalog management, enhanced order processing and a broader range of design templates.

It should also include encryption for secure ordering. Using Secure Socket Layer[1] technology to collect card details (noted by the "golden padlock" symbol in your browser's status bar) is key to encouraging online sales.

Some e-commerce packages may offer back end systems integration, i.e. they connect to your product database and accounts systems.

An intermediate-level site might not be suitable if you want to offer more complex products and services.

(3) Sophisticated Online Shops

Sophisticated online shops should provide a range of options, including cutting-edge design and functionality, personalized pages and product news.

Software can be integrated to trigger order confirmations and automatically dispatch goods and replenish stocks.

You may need a design and development company to help define your technical requirements and integrate the website with your existing systems.

You could also consider free, open source[2] shopping cart software packages. This should allow

---

1 SSL (Secure Socket Layer) is the standard security technology for establishing an encrypted link between a web server and a browser. This link ensures that all data passed between the web server and browsers remain private and integral. SSL is an industry standard and is used by millions of websites in the protection of their online transactions with their customers.

2 In general, open source refers to any program whose source code is made available for use or modification as users or other developers see fit. Open source software is usually developed as a public collaboration and made freely available.

you to set up a sophisticated e-commerce website that has a wide range of options, features and support, even if you have only basic computer skills.

7. Selling Online: Common Mistakes

Customers will be put off by:

- out-of-date or incorrect information;
- difficult site navigation and purchasing processes;
- poor customer fulfillment and late delivery;
- lack of customer support;
- lack of business information;
- poor visual design.

To make customers feel secure about buying from your site, you should:

- make your site easy to navigate and user friendly;
- make sure photographic images on your site are accurate and show products in their best light;
- hire a customer service representative who can give advice on the phone to customers on more complex or expensive products;
- make ordering procedures straightforward and quick;
- confirm orders immediately by e-mail;
- be honest—i.e. tell the customer if you can't deliver on time;
- provide a way for customers to track down the progress and availability of their order.

New Words

increasingly	*adv.*	日益，愈加
strengthen	*v.*	加强，巩固
trading	*n.*	贸易
investigate	*v.*	调查，研究
dial-up	*n.*	拨号（上网）
cable	*n.*	电缆
usability	*n.*	可用性
accessible	*adj.*	易接近的，可到达的，可理解的
showcase	*v.*	展现，在玻璃橱窗陈列
effectiveness	*n.*	效力
accurate	*adj.*	正确的，精确的
regularly	*adv.*	定期地，有规律地，有规则地
retain	*v.*	保持，保留
hacker	*n.*	计算机黑客
extranet	*n.*	外联网
intranet	*n.*	内联网

invaluable	*adj.*	无价的，无法估计的
remotely	*adv.*	远程地，遥远地
catalog	*n.*	目录，目录册
	v.	编目录
database	*n.*	数据库，资料库
predictable	*adj.*	可预言的
authenticity	*n.*	确实性，真实性
disclose	*v.*	揭露，透露
refuse	*v.*	拒绝，谢绝
perishable	*adj.*	容易腐烂的
commodity	*n.*	日用品
inconvenient	*adj.*	不便的，有困难的
mail-order	*adj.*	邮购的
e-mail	*n.*	电子邮件，电子信函
restricted	*adj.*	受限制的，有限的
template	*n.*	(=templet) 模板
padlock	*n.*	挂锁
confirmation	*n.*	证实，确认，批准
dispatch	*v.*	分派，派遣
	n.	派遣，急件
replenish	*v.*	补充
out-of-date	*adj.*	过时的，落伍的
visual	*adj.*	视觉的，形象的
confirm	*v.*	确定，批准
honest	*adj.*	诚实的，正直的

Phrases

be aware of	知道，明白，意识到
legal obligation	法律义务(如合同契约等)
pay attention to	注意
think about	考虑，回想
tablet computer	平板电脑
business partner	业务伙伴
play an important role in…	在……中起重要作用
a number of	许多的
operational cost	运营成本，运作成本
high street	大街，主要街道

shop assistant	店员
fixed price	固定价格
financial transaction	金融业务，财务事项，财务往来
suitable for…	适合……的
be satisfy with…	对……感到满意，满足于……
order form	订货单
Secure Socket Layer	安全套接层协议
back end	后端，后台
replenish stock	补充库存，补货
open source	开放资源，开源
customer service representative	客服代表
track down	追寻，追踪，追到

Abbreviations

ADSL (Asymmetrical Digital Subscriber Line)　　非对称数字用户线路

Exercises

[Ex. 5]　Answer the following questions according to the text.

1. What can selling products and services online do for your business?
2. Once your shop is online, what should you do?
3. What must you do as your e-commerce presence grows?
4. What do extranets enable your business to do?
5. What should you have if you want your online shopping works best?
6. What disadvantages does online shopping have?
7. How will most customers shopping online want to pay?
8. What may some e-commerce packages offer?
9. What should sophisticated online shops provide?
10. What should you do to make customers feel secure about buying from your site?

Reading Material

E-commerce Advantages and Disadvantages

　　E-commerce is business transactions through electronic means, including the Internet, telephones, televisions and computers. As the number of Internet users grows, many believe e-commerce will soon be the main way to complete business transactions. There are purchasers and business alike that are affected by e-commerce. Let's take a look and see the main e-commerce advantages and disadvantages.

1. E-commerce Advantages

(1) E-commerce Advantages for Customers

1) Convenience. Every product is at the tip of your fingers on the Internet, literally[1]. Type in the product you are looking for into your favorite search engine and every option will appear in a well organized list in a matter of[2] seconds.

2) Time saving. With e-commerce there is no driving in circles while looking and digging in hopes of finding what you need. Stores online offer their full line as well as use warehouses instead of store fronts[3]. Products are easy to locate and can be delivered to your door in just days.

3) Options, options, options! Without driving from store to store the consumer can easily compare and contrast products. See who offers the best pricing and have more options to choose from. While a physical store[4] has limited space, the same store on the Internet will have full stock.

4) Easy to compare. Side by side[5] comparisons are readily available and easy to do. When products are placed online, they come with all the specifics, and they want you to compare them with others, know they have the best options and come back for more!

5) Easy to find reviews. Because the competition[6] is high, companies online want you to look at other consumer reviews. Good and bad reviews are on every site, not only can you see if the product is liked, you can also see the reasons behind the thumbs up[7] or down.

6) Coupons[8] and deals. With every online business wanting you, more and more coupons and deals can't be avoided, which are totally great for customers. With major sites that act as department store, you may find items up to 80% off! Take advantage of the competition and find the best price available.

(2) E-commerce Advantages for Businesses

1) Increasing customer base. The customer base is every business's main concern, online or off. When online, a business doesn't have to worry about getting the best property[9] in town, people from around the world have access to their products and can come back at anytime.

2) Rise in sales. By not managing a store front, any business will have more sales online with a higher profit margin. They can redistribute[10] money to make the consumer shopping experience faster and more efficient. While being available to international markets, more products will sell.

3) 24/7, 365 days. If it's snowing and the roads are closed, or it's too hot and humid to even step outside in the summer, or a holiday that every store in town closes, your online business is open

---

1　literally　　　*adv.*　照字面意义，逐字地
2　a matter of　　　大约，大概
3　store front　　　店面
4　physical store　　实体店
5　side by side　　　并排，并肩
6　competition　　*n.*　竞争，竞赛
7　thumbs up　　　竖大拇指，赞许
8　coupon　　*n.*　优惠券
9　property　　*n.*　财产，所有物，所有权
10　redistribute　　*v.*　重新分配，重新分布

for consumers 24/7 every day of the year. The doors never close and profits will keep rising.

4) Expand business reach. A great tool on the Internet is…translation! A business online does not have to make a site for every language. With the right marketing, every consumer around the globe can find the business site, products and information without leaving home.

5) Recurring payments made easy. With a little research, every business can set up recurring payments. Find the provider that best suits your needs and billing will be done in a consistent manner; payments will be received in the same way.

6) Instant transactions. With e-commerce there is no more waiting for the check to clear, or a 30-day wait for certain other types of payment. Transactions are cleared immediately or at most two to three days for the money to clear through the banking system.

2. E-commerce Disadvantages

(1) E-commerce Disadvantages for Customers

1) Privacy and security. Before making instant transactions online, be sure to check the sites certificates of security. While it may be easy and convenient to shop, no one wants their personal information to be stolen. While many sites are reputable[1], always do your research for those with less than sufficient security.

2) Quality. While e-commerce makes everything easily accessible, a consumer cannot actually touch products until they are delivered to the door. It is important to view the return policy before buying. Always make sure returning goods is an option.

3) Hidden costs. When making purchases, the consumer is aware of the product cost, shipping, handling and possible taxes. Be advised: there may be hidden fees that won't show up on your purchasing bill but will show up on your form of payment. Extra handling fees may occur, especially with international purchases.

4) Delay in receiving goods. Although delivery of products is often quicker than expected, be prepared for[2] delays. A snow storm in one place may throw off the shipping system across the board. There is also a chance that your product may be lost or delivered to the wrong address.

5) Need access to Internet. Internet access is not free, and if you are using free Wi-Fi, there is the chance of information theft over an insecure site. If you are weary of your public library, or cannot afford the Internet or computer at home, it may be best to shop locally.

6) Lack of personal interaction. While the rules and regulations[3] of each e-commerce business is laid out for you to read, there is a lot to read and it may be confusing[4] when it comes to the legalities. With large or important orders, there is no one you can talk to face to face[5] when you have questions and concerns.

---

1 reputable   *adj.*   著名的
2 prepare for   准备
3 rules and regulations   规章制度
4 confuse   *v.*   搞乱，使糊涂
5 face to face   面对面地

(2) E-commerce Disadvantages for Businesses

1) Security issues. While businesses make great efforts to keep themselves and the consumer safe, there are people out there that will break every firewall possible to get the information they want. We have all seen recently how the biggest and most renowned business can be hacked online.

2) Credit card issues. Many credit card businesses will take the side of the consumer when there is dispute[1] about billing. They want to keep their clients, too. This can lead to a loss for e-commerce business when goods have already been delivered and the payment is refunded back to the consumer.

3) Extra expense and expertise for e-commerce infrastructure. To be sure an online business is running correctly, money will have to be invested. As an owner, you need to know transactions are being handled properly and products are represented in the most truthful[2] way. To make sure you get what you need, you will have to hire a professional to tie up any loose ends.

4) Needs for expanded reverse logistics. The infrastructure of an online business must be on point. This will be another cost to the business because money will need to be invested to ensure proper handling of all aspects of buying and selling, especially with disgruntled[3] consumers who want more than a refund.

5) Sufficient[4] Internet service. Although it seems that everyone is now on the Internet all the time, there are still areas in which network bandwidth[5] can cause issues. Before setting up an e-commerce business, be sure your area can handle the telecommunication bandwidth you will need to run effectively.

6) Constant upkeep[6]. When a business has started as e-commerce, they must be ready to make changes to stay compatible. While technology grows, the systems that support your business must be kept up to date or replaced if needed. There may be additional overhead[7] in order to keep databases and applications running.

参考译文

什么是电子商务？

电子商务是指各类产品和服务的在线商业活动。它也适用于"当事人以电子方式进行交互而不是通过实际交换或直接物体交换的任何形式的商业交易"。

电子商务通常与通过互联网进行的购买和销售相关，或者与通过计算机中介网络进行转

1　dispute　　　*v.* 争论，辩论，怀疑
2　truthful　　　*adj.* 诚实的
3　disgruntled　　*adj.* 不满的，不高兴的
4　sufficient　　*adj.* 充分的，足够的
5　bandwidth　　*n.* 带宽
6　upkeep　　　*n.* 维持，维修费
7　overhead　　*n.* 企业一般管理费用

让商品或服务的所有权或使用权的任何交易相关。虽然这个定义很流行，但是不够全面，不足以捕捉这种新的和革命性的商业现象的最新发展。更完整的定义是：电子商务是在商业交易中使用电子通信和数字信息处理技术来创建、转换和重新定义组织之间，以及组织和个人之间的创造价值的关系。

电子商务的主要类型有：企业对企业（B2B）；企业对消费者（B2C）；企业对政府（B2G）；消费者对消费者（C2C）以及移动商务（M-commerce）。

1. 什么是 B2B 电子商务？

B2B 电子商务被简单地定义为公司之间的电子商务。这类电子商务涉及企业之间的关系。大约 80% 的电子商务属于这种类型。并且大多数专家预测，B2B 电子商务将继续增长，其速度会超过 B2C 市场。B2B 市场有两个主要组成部分：电子基础设施和电子市场。

电子基础设施是 B2B 的结构，主要包括以下内容：

- 物流——运输、仓储和分配（如宝洁公司）；
- 应用服务提供商——从中央设施部署、托管和管理软件包（如 Oracle 和 Linkshare）；
- 在电子商务过程中外包功能，例如网络托管、安全和客户服务解决方案（如 eShare，NetSales、iXL Enterprises 和 Universal Access 等外包供应商）；
- 用于互联网的实时拍卖操作和维护的拍卖解决方案软件（如 Moai Technologies 和 OpenSite Technologies）；
- 内容管理软件，用于促进网站内容管理和交付（如 Interwoven 和 ProcureNet）；
- 基于 Web 的商业提供者（如 Commerce One，基于浏览器，支持 XML 的采购自动化软件）。

电子市场被简单地定义为买方和卖方交互并进行交易的网站。

B2B 大多数应用于供应商管理（特别是采购订单处理）、库存管理（即管理订单——交货单循环）、配送管理（特别是运输单据的传输）、渠道管理（如运营时渠道中信息的传播）和支付管理（如电子支付系统）。

2. 什么是 B2C 电子商务？

B2C 是企业对消费者的电子商务，或公司和消费者之间的商务，它涉及收集客户信息、购买实体商品（即有形产品如书籍或消费品）或信息商品（或电子材料或数字化内容，如软件或电子书）以及通过电子网络接收的信息产品。

它是电子商务的第二大和最早形式。其起源可以追溯到在线零售（或电子零售）。因此，更常见的 B2C 商业模式是在线零售公司，如 Amazon、Drugstore、Beyond、Barnes and Noble 和 ToysRus。其他涉及信息商品的 B2C 例子有 E-Trade 和 Travelocity 等。

此类电子商务更常见的应用是购买产品和信息以及个人财务管理领域，其涉及通过使用在线银行工具来管理个人投资和财务。

通过增加消费者对信息的访问，并允许消费者为产品或服务找到最具竞争力的价格，B2C 电子商务降低了交易成本（特别是搜索成本）。B2C 电子商务还减少了市场准入壁垒，因为建立和维护网站的成本比为企业建立"实体"结构便宜得多。对于信息产品而言，B2C 电子商务更具吸引力，因为企业不必考虑物理分销网络从而节省了额外成本。此外，对于互联网人口增长壮大的国家，提供信息产品变得越来越可行。

3. 什么是 B2G 电子商务？

企业对政府的电子商务或 B2G 通常被定义为公司和公共部门之间的商业。它是指使用互联网进行公共采购、许可程序和其他政府相关业务。这种电子商务有两个特点：一是公共部门在建立电子商务方面具有引领或主导作用；二是假设公共部门最需要使其采购系统更有效。

基于网络的采购政策提高了采购过程的透明度并降低了违规行为的风险。然而，到目前为止，B2G 电子商务市场的规模对于整个电子商务而言是微不足道的，因为政府电子采购系统仍然不发达。

4. 什么是 C2C 电子商务？

消费者对消费者的电子商务或 C2C 就是个人或消费者之间的商务。这种类型的电子商务的特征在于电子市场和在线拍卖的增长，特别是在垂直行业中，公司或企业可以从多个供应商竞标中选择他们想要的商品。它可能是在发展新市场方面具有最大潜力。

这种类型的电子商务至少有三种形式：

- 在诸如 eBay 之类的门户上进行拍卖，从而允许对网上销售的物品在线实时出价；
- 对等网络系统，如 Napster 模型（用于类似于 IRC 的聊天论坛的用户之间共享文件的协议）以及其他文件交换和稍后的货币兑换模型；
- 门户网站的分类广告，如 Excite Classifieds 和 eWanted，Pakwheels（一个互动的、买家和卖家可以谈判的在线市场，以及具有"买家主导和分类广告"功能）。

关于全球 C2C 电子商务相对规模的信息很少。然而，受欢迎的 C2C 网站，如 eBay 和 Napster 的 C2C 数字表明，这个市场是相当大的。这些网站每天产生数百万美元的销售。

（1）C2C 站点的优点

消费者对消费者电子商务有很多好处。对消费者来说，主要好处是可以降低成本。在其他电子商务网站上购买广告空间很贵。卖家可以在 C2C 网站免费或以最低费用张贴其商品。C2C 网站为希望购买和销售相关产品的买家和卖家提供了一个完美的平台。找到相关产品的能力导致了访问者的客户转化率的增加。企业主可以廉价维护 C2C 网站、增加利润而不需要花费额外的成本建立销售地点。C2C 电子商务网站的一个很好的例子是 Esty，它允许消费者购买和销售手工或复古的物品和用品，包括艺术、摄影、服装、首饰、食品、浴室和美容产品、棉被、小装饰品和玩具。

（2）C2C 网站的缺点

此类网站也有几个缺点。在这些类型的网站上进行交易需要买卖双方的合作。已经多次注意到，这两者在交易完成后并不相互合作。他们不分享可以通过信用卡或借记卡或网上银行进行的交易信息。因为买方和卖方互相不是很熟悉，这就可能导致在线欺诈。如果没有在条款和条件中提及免责声明，这可能导致诉讼被强加在任何一方或网站上。这也可能损害 C2C 网站的声誉。处理消费者对消费者电子商务网站的公司似乎已经变得非常谨慎，以防止在线欺诈。

5. 什么是移动电子商务？

移动电子商务是通过无线技术——如手持设备（如蜂窝电话）和个人数字助理（PDA）来购买和销售商品和服务。

由于通过无线设备递送内容变得更快、更安全和可升级，一些人认为移动电子商务将超过有线电子商务，成为数字商务交易的首选方法。对于亚太地区来说可能是真的，因为亚太地区的手机用户比互联网用户多。

受移动电子商务影响的行业包括：

1）金融服务：包括手机银行（当客户使用手持设备访问他们的账户并支付账单时），以及经纪服务（可以显示股票报价并从同一手持设备进行交易）。

2）电信：更改服务项目、支付账单和审查账户都可以从同一手持设备进行。

3）服务/零售：因为消费者能当场直接下订单和支付订单。

4）信息服务：包括向单个移动设备提供娱乐、财经新闻、体育数据和更新交通信息。

6. 电子商务与电子业务相同吗？

虽然"电子商务"和"电子业务"这两个词可以互换使用，但它们是不同的概念。在电子商务中，信息和通信技术（ICT）用于企业间或组织间交易（企业/组织之间的交易）和企业对消费者交易（企业/组织和个人之间的交易）。

另一方面，在电子业务中 ICT 用于增强自己的业务。它包括商业组织（营利性、政府或非营利实体）通过计算机网络进行的任何活动。电子业务的更全面的定义是：

"通过应用新经济的技术、哲学和计算模式，转变组织流程，提供额外的客户价值。"

电子业务增强了三个主要过程：

1）生产过程包括采购、订购和补充库存，付款，与供应商的电子链接以及生产控制过程及其他。

2）以客户为中心的流程，包括促销和营销工作、通过互联网销售、处理客户的采购订单和付款以及客户支持等。

3）内部管理流程，包括员工服务、培训、内部信息共享、视频会议和招聘。电子应用增强生产和销售部门之间的信息流以提高销售人员的生产力。工作组通信和内部业务信息的电子发布也更有效。

Unit 2

Text A

How to Choose an E-commerce Business Model

When it comes to starting an online business, you have a lot of choices to make. The biggest of the choices may be the most important as they will ultimately define your business model and much of the future of your business.

In this passage, we're going to show you at a high level each one of the major choices you need to consider when starting your online business along with the pros and cons so you can make the best decisions possible right from the beginning.

1. Who Do You Want to Sell to?

There are many types of e-commerce stores, all with subtle differences and nuances. Let's take a look at two of the major types of e-commerce businesses that you can run, and then we will drill down even further.

(1) B2B (Business-to-Business)

Business-to-Business refers to the model where one business sells to another business. There are both advantages and disadvantages of selling to other businesses versus selling to the end consumers. The pros of selling to other businesses are that order sizes and repeat orders are typically larger and more frequent, however, there are fewer businesses than consumers and sales cycles are typically longer with price being a heavy contributor to purchase decisions.

(2) B2C (Business-to-Consumer)

Business-to-Consumer means you are selling directly to the end consumer that will be using the product. This is the most common type of business model and what most people think about when discussing building e-commerce businesses.

It should be noted as well that there are other business models that are less common, including B2G (Business-to-Government).

2. What Type of Products Do You Want to Sell?

Now that we've covered the two major types of online business models, let's drill down a little deeper and look at the different type of products you can sell online:

(1) Physical Goods

Selling physical goods is what most people think of when they think of an online store, and it makes up the majority of online e-commerce businesses. Although physical goods are the most popular product type of item to sell, it also presents challenges including inventory storage, shipping, breakage, and insurance.

DodoCase sells iPad and iPhone cases using traditional bookbinding methods.

(2) Digital Goods

Digital goods are also a popular type of product to sell and has the advantage of not needing inventory storage or physical delivery like its physical product counterparts. Digital goods can be anything from music, ebooks, videos, images or software. The biggest disadvantage of selling digital products is piracy. However, because a digital product can be resold thousands of times over, their margins are considered the best and comes without the headaches associated with shipping and inventory management.

Example: Out of the Sandbox sells premium themes for Shopify and does so through their own Shopify store. These themes are digitally delivered immediately after purchase.

(3) Services

The third, slightly less common product type to sell online are services. Online services can range from consulting, web design and development, content writing/editing and a whole host of other service options. Selling services through an online store can be a great way to build credibility and gain exposure but typically comes with the limitation of scalability as services are typically delivered by a person and are therefore limited to that person's time.

Example: Shopify Experts is a directory of freelancers and agencies that offer services to Shopify store owners. From setting up your business and marketing to design and photography. Many of these freelancers and agencies in the Shopify Experts directory use Shopify to host their website and sell their services directly to entrepreneurs.

3. How Do You Want to Acquire Your Products?

The physical goods category and even digital goods to a certain extent can be broken down in a number of different ways. One of the most popular ways to break it down is by product acquisition type. There are four major types of methods for acquiring your products. Let's take a look at each one below:

(1) DIY (Do It Yourself)

Making your product is a common approach for many hobbyists. Whether it be jewelry, fashion or natural beauty products, making products yourself allows for the precise control over the quality and the brand but comes at the cost of high time commitment and scalability.

The primary costs associated with making your own products include the purchasing of raw materials, the storage of inventory and labor.

The most important thing to note here though is that not all products can be made by hand. Your product choices are limited to your skills and available resources.

Example: J. L. Lawson & Co. makes everything by hand in their studio in Joshua Tree, California. A family business that has been running three generations means every piece produced has a whole lot of pride in it.

(2) Finding a Manufacture

Another viable option for acquiring your product and inventory is to find a manufacturer to produce the product for you. When sourcing a manufacturer, you have the option of sourcing one domestically or from overseas. As you might see, an American manufacturer, in general, will cost more than a manufacturer from countries like China or India.

Example: GameKlip started out with the founder making game controller clips that attach a real game controller and a smartphone for the ultimate smartphone gaming experience. After demand soared though, the founder was forced to begin full-scale manufacturing of the GameKlip just to keep up with demand.

(3) Wholesale

Buying wholesale is a fairly simple and straightforward process. You buy your inventory (usually other brands) direct from the manufacturer or from a middleman supplier at a discounted wholesale rate, which you in turn, resell at a higher price.

Buying wholesale is a lower risk business model compared to manufacturing for a few reasons. First, you're dealing with brands that are already established and validated on the market so you don't run the risk of wasting time and money developing a product no one wants. Also, you don't have to purchase as nearly as high of a quantity compared to manufacturing your own product. Minimum orders will depend on the manufacturer and product; however, they're usually pretty reasonable and can even be as low as one unit.

Example: Lodge Goods sells a variety of well-made goods from craftsmen and manufacturers around America. By carrying other brands, they are able to offer a wide selection of products and brands.

(4) Drop Shipping

The main concept of drop shipping is selling products you don't actually own. Working with dropship partners is not only a product acquisition model, but also includes product fulfillment. The process works by taking orders from your online business and forwarding them to your supplier/dropship partner. They, in return, ship the product to your customer on behalf of your company. The key to making money with drop shipping is making a profit on the price difference between what you charge and what your drop shipping partners charge you.

The biggest benefit to drop shipping is the ability to offer a large selection of product without purchasing inventory up front and managing that inventory. Drop shipping can also be a great tool to help diversify your inventory and test products since it's just a matter of adding the new product to your store.

Example: Right Channel Radios is the number one source for CB radios for your off-road truck. By utilizing dropshipping as the product acquisition method, the founder is able to offer a very wide range of products and accessories in a very specific niche without any inventory costs or risk.

4. How Do You Want to Compete?

Deciding how to compete is an important decision and can significantly shape the future of your business and dictate key business decisions. There are several common ways in which you can compete in a crowded marketplace. Let's take a look at each of those options.

(1) Price

Competing on price is typically not the best options for smaller retailers for the very reason that everyone bigger than you typically has better margins and can always go lower than you. This also in the bigger picture leads to price wars that just eat away at everyone's margins.

Example: Walmart has always been known for their discount strategy and is big enough to make this strategy work for them. By purchasing products in massive quantities, they are able to get better pricing and pass that along to consumers.

(2) Quality

Competing on quality comes down to having a superior or better-made product. This can be a great way to compete and there are signs the market as a whole is shifting towards longer lasting, well-made products.

Example: Dbrand sells vinyl skins for smartphones, laptops and game consoles. Recognizing that the current market lacked high-quality skins, cut with laser precision, Dbrand took it upon themselves to create them and quickly soared to the dominant player in the skins game.

(3) Selection

Competing on selection is a great option for carving out your own space in the marketplace but also comes with the risk of increased inventory and storage of that inventory if you are utilizing any other method than drop shipping.

Example: Amazon is without a doubt the leader in e-commerce when it comes to selection. However, just because massive companies have large selections doesn't mean you can compete on this. It simply means you'll have to compete on the largest selection in a very niche category.

(4) Value Add

One of the best ways to differentiate yourself in the market is to provide additional value to your customers that compels them to purchase from you. Content in the form of really great product descriptions, learning centers, installation guides etc. is a great example of ways to provide additional value to your customers.

Example: Right Channel Radios dropships their CB radios and accessories which mean margins are slim. This can make it difficult to compete effectively against other competitors with better margins. To compensate for this, Right Channel Radios offers a ton of extra value in the form of an education center and video review on most of the products.

(5) Service

Competing on service can be difficult as a new small business but can be a winning strategy. Considering that word-of-mouth marketing is the most powerful form of marketing, it makes sense to compete and deliver an incredible customer experience that gets people talking.

Example: Zappos is known for their customer service with free shipping both ways, 365-day return policy, and 24/7 customer service. Zappos is also known for some interesting service records like a record setting 10-hour customer service call.

5. Conclusion

Answering the four major questions from this article will provide you with a good start to putting together some major components of your e-commerce business model. It's important to keep in mind that some business model combinations will require a lot more work than others so be cognizant of the true amount of time you have to invest in your business and the time investment required based on your particular business model. This will not only increase your chances of success but also the amount of enjoyment you get from building, launching and growing your online business.

New Words

ultimately	*adv.*	最后，终于，根本，基本上
subtle	*adj.*	敏感的，微妙的，精细的
nuance	*n.*	细微差别
discuss	*v.*	讨论，论述
drill	*v.*	钻孔，打眼
	n.	钻头，钻孔机
breakage	*n.*	破损，破损量
insurance	*n.*	保险，保险单，保险业，保险费
bookbinding	*n.*	装订
inventory	*n.*	详细目录，存货，财产清册，总量
counterpart	*n.*	副本，配对物，极相似的人或物
piracy	*n.*	盗版
resell	*v.*	再卖，转售
margin	*n.*	利润，差数
headache	*n.*	头痛，令人头痛之事
theme	*n.*	主题曲
consulting	*adj.*	咨询的，商议的，顾问资格的
credibility	*n.*	可信性
gain	*n.*	财物的增加，财富的获取，利润，收获
	v.	得到，赚到，获利，增加
scalability	*n.*	可扩展性，可升级性，可量测性
freelancer	*n.*	自由职业者
entrepreneur	*n.*	企业家，主办人
acquisition	*n.*	获得，获得物
hobbyist	*n.*	发烧友，爱好者，迷恋者
commitment	*n.*	委托事项，许诺，承担义务
resource	*n.*	资源，财力，办法
viable	*adj.*	能养活的，可行的

option	n.	选项，选择权，[经]买卖的特权
wholesale	n.	批发
	adj.	批发的
brand	n.	商标，牌子
middleman	n.	中间人
validate	v.	确认，证实，验证
craftsmen	n.	手艺人，匠人
dropship	v.	直接代发货，转运配送
fulfillment	n.	实现，完成，实施
diversify	v.	使多样化，做多样性的投资
niche	n.	商机
significantly	adv.	重要地，重大地
shape	n.	外形，形状，形态
dictate	v.	指令，指示，命令，规定
crowded	adj.	拥挤的，塞满的
strategy	n.	策略
precision	n.	精确，精密度，精度
dominate	v.	支配，占优势
utilize	v.	利用
incredible	adj.	难以置信的
combination	n.	结合，联合，合并
enjoyment	n.	快乐，享乐

Phrases

business model	商业模型，业务模式
at a high level	高级层面，高水平，高级别
pros and cons	利弊，优缺点，正反两方面
drill down	向下钻取（数据），向下挖掘
end consumer	终端客户
physical goods	实物产品
physical delivery	实物交货
a whole host of	大量，许多，一大堆；一整套
a great way	一个非常好的方式
to a certain extent	在一定程度上
at the cost of…	以……为代价
raw material	原材料
a whole lot of	一大堆，许多许多的
at a discount	打折扣

take orders	接订单
on behalf of …	代表……
make a profit on…	在……上获利
a matter of	大约，大概
be known for…	因……而众所周知
as a whole	总体上
carve out	开拓，创业
without a doubt	无疑地
word-of-mouth marketing	口碑营销
be cognizant of	认识到

Abbreviations

DIY (Do It Yourself)　　　　　　　自己动手制作

Exercises

[Ex. 1] Answer the following questions according to the text.

1. What are the two major types of e-commerce businesses discussed in the text?
2. What is the most common type of business model?
3. What are the most popular product type of item an online store sells?
4. What advantage does digital goods have? What is the biggest disadvantage of selling digital products?
5. What can online services range from according to the text?
6. How many major type of methods for acquiring your products? What are they?
7. What are the few reasons mentioned in the text that buying wholesale is a lower risk business model compared to manufacturing?
8. What is the biggest benefit to drop shipping?
9. What are the several common ways in which you can compete in a crowded marketplace?
10. Who has always been known for their discount strategy and is big enough to make this price strategy work for them?

[Ex. 2] Translate the following terms or phrases from English into Chinese and vice versa.

1. business model
2. domestic manufacture
3. physical delivery
4. raw material
5. word-of-mouth marketing
6. 可信性
7. 直接代发货，转运配送
8. 详细目录，存货，财产清册

9. 策略 _____   9. _____
10. 批发；批发的 _____ 10. _____

[Ex. 3] Translate the following passage into Chinese.

E-commerce

1. B2B (Business-to-Business)

Companies doing business with each other, such as manufacturers selling to distributors and wholesalers selling to retailers. Pricing is based on quantity of order and is often negotiable.

2. B2C (Business-to-Consumer)

Businesses selling to the general public typically through catalogs utilizing shopping cart software.

3. C2B (Consumer-to-Business)

A consumer posts his project with a set budget online and within hours companies review the consumer's requirements and bid on the project. The consumer reviews the bids and selects the company that will complete the project.

4. C2C (Consumer-to-Consumer)

There are many sites offering free classifieds, auctions, and forums where individuals can buy and sell thanks to online payment systems like PayPal where people can send and receive money online with ease.

[Ex. 4] Fill in the blanks with the words given below.

| transactions | retailer | advanced | customer | products |
| distribution | market | services | e-commerce | advantages |

What Is Electronic Commerce?

Electronic commerce (e-commerce) is a type of business model, or segment of a larger business model, that enables a firm or individual to conduct business over an electronic network, typically the Internet. Electronic commerce operates in four major ____1____ segments: Business-to-Business, Business-to-Consumer, Consumer-to-Consumer and Consumer-to-Business. It can be thought of as a more ____2____ form of mail-order purchasing through a catalog. Almost any product or service can be offered via ____3____, from books and music to financial services and plane tickets.

E-commerce has allowed firms to establish a market presence, or to enhance an existing market position, by providing a cheaper and more efficient ____4____ chain for their products or ____5____. One example of a firm that has successfully used e-commerce is Target. This mass ____6____ not only has physical stores, but also has an online store where the ____7____ can buy everything from clothes to coffee makers to action figures.

When you purchase a good or service online, you are participating in e-commerce. Some ____8____ of e-commerce for consumers are:

• Convenience. E-commerce can take place 24 hours a day, seven days a week.

• Selection. Many stores offer a wider array of ____9____ online than they do in their brick-and-mortar counterparts. And stores that exist only online may offer consumers a selection of goods that they otherwise could not access.

But e-commerce also has its disadvantages for consumers:

• Limited customer service. If you want to buy a computer and you're shopping online, there is no employee you can talk to about which computer would best meet your needs.

• No instant gratification. When you buy something online, you have to wait for it to be shipped to your home or office.

• No ability to touch and see a product. Online images don't always tell the whole story about an item. E-commerce ____10____ can be dissatisfying when the product the consumer receives is different from expected.

Text B

Business-to-Business

1. What Is B2B E-commerce?

It's companies buying from and selling to each other online. But there's more to it than purchasing. It's evolved to encompass supply chain management as more companies outsource parts of their supply chain to their trading partners.

扫一扫，听课文

2. I Use Electronic Data Interchange. Am I Already Doing It?

Yes. And if you're getting value from your EDI investments, there's no reason to abandon them now. But it's a good idea to think about whether any other data exchange methods have a role in your future B2B efforts. EDI has limitations, including an inflexible format that makes it difficult to use for any but the most straightforward transactions. Much of the newer e-commerce software uses XML—grammatical rules for describing data on the website—as its standard for data exchange. XML allows for more variety in the information companies exchange and was designed for open networks.

3. What Are the Differences between B2B and B2C E-commerce?

There's the obvious difference in who the customers are—companies or individuals. Beyond that, there are two big distinctions:

1) B2B efforts require negotiation. Selling to another business involves haggling over prices, delivery and product specifications. Not so with most consumer sales. That makes it easier for retailers to put a catalog online, and it's why the first B2B applications were for buying finished goods or commodities that are simple to describe and price.

2) B2B efforts require integration. Retailers don't have to integrate with their consumer customers' systems. Most companies selling to businesses do integrate because their systems have to be able to communicate with those of their customers without human intervention.

4. What Are the Benefits?

B2B e-commerce can save or make your company money. Some ways companies have

benefited from B2B e-commerce include:
- managing inventory more efficiently;
- adjusting more quickly to customer demand;
- getting products to market faster;
- cutting the cost of paperwork;
- reigning in rogue purchases;
- obtaining lower prices on some supplies.

5. What Is a B2B Exchange?

At its most basic, a B2B exchange (also called a marketplace or hub) is a website where many companies can buy from and sell to each other using a common technology platform. Many exchanges also offer additional services, such as payment or logistics services that help members complete a transaction. Exchanges may also support community activities, like distributing industry news, sponsoring online discussions and providing research on customer demand or industry forecasts for components and raw materials.

6. What's the Difference between a Public B2B Exchange and a Private One? Which One Should My Company Use?

Public exchanges are owned by industry consortia or independent investors and have their own boards of directors. Though each exchange sets its own rules, they are generally open, for a fee, to any company that wants to use them. Private exchanges are run by a single company for doing business exclusively with established suppliers and customers (although the systems that support it may be outsourced).

Which one your company uses depends on what you want to do. If you are buying and selling commodity products, public exchanges can be a good venue in which to find low prices or identify new customers. They're also becoming a popular way for a company to unload excess inventory.

7. What's the First Step I Should Take?

Start with buying so-called indirect supplies like pencils, chairs and copy paper. Most companies start here because it's easier to set up an online catalog of approved office supplies than it is to automate procurement of specially engineered parts and materials. Plus, you're not affecting day-to-day operations while you get your feet wet. While the payoff won't be as big as for more mission-critical purchases (so-called direct materials used to produce the goods or services you sell), it can be significant. The Burlington Northern Santa Fe railroad company lopped an estimated 3 percent to 28 percent off its indirect purchases and saved money internally by automating a manual process for approving purchase orders.

8. What's Collaborative B2B E-commerce?

It's marketing speak for integrating your supply chain, and it's a vision of e-commerce nirvana. You're not just sharing blueprints or your latest sales forecasts; you and your trading partners are giving each other real-time access to your ERP, product design, inventory and other systems. Companies that are doing it say it helps them get new products to market faster, reduce manufacturing time, keep inventory low and adjust more quickly to changes in customer demand.

To collaborate successfully, you and your partners each need up-to-date, functioning systems to serve up whatever data you plan to share, and a way to deliver that information electronically. That can be a big hurdle when many companies still do a lot of business by phone and fax. There's cultural resistance as well. Not every company sees the value of sharing what has been confidential information or trusts its partners with it. Some also fear online collaboration might result in layoffs.

9. Which Business Units Should Be Involved in a B2B Project?

Definitely the units that do purchasing. B2B e-commerce can drastically change how buyers do their jobs, especially if your company is one that still places orders the old fashioned way. Sales and customer service departments will need to be involved with projects that affect how you receive and process orders from customers. And don't forget the folks who manage your inventory. You may need to get other departments involved, too, depending on the functionality you're building. Also involve your suppliers, distributors and customers, and make sure there's something in the project for them.

10. What Kind of Software Do I Need? Is It Expensive?

Exactly what you need depends on whether you're a buyer or seller, whether you're dealing in indirect or direct materials and the extent to which you're integrating your supply chain. Elements of a B2B system may include software for generating purchase orders or Requests for Quotations (RFQs), processing invoices, building and managing catalogs, responding to RFQs and processing orders.

Cost is also relative. In general, the more elements of your business you want to integrate with trading partners, the more you have to spend. A March 2001 Forrester Research report pegged the cost for buyers to join an online marketplace at between $5.6 million and $22.9 million, including operating costs.

11. How Long Will It Take to Put B2B Systems in Place?

You can set up an online catalog for your customers in a few months. Starting from scratch to build a portal for your suppliers that integrates with your back-end systems may take you more than a year. The most time-consuming aspect of building B2B systems is mapping your business processes to those of your trading partners.

12. What If My Trading Partners Aren't Ready to do Business Online?

Build your B2B application and your partners will probably come to use it. Some companies have built Web portals that allow partners to place orders, input data and access information from their ERP or other back-end systems without any more investment than Internet access. If your partners have to do some of their own software development to use the application, be sure you offer them a big enough carrot (like the promise of additional business) to make the investment pay off for them.

New Words

evolve   v. (使)发展，(使)进展，(使)进化
outsource   v. 外包，外界供应

investment	n.	投资
inflexible	adj.	固定的，不可变更的
negotiation	n.	谈判，协商，商谈
abandon	v.	放弃，遗弃
limitation	n.	限制，局限性
grammatical	adj.	符合语法的，语法上的
haggle	v.	讨价还价，议价，争价
	n.	争价
delivery	n.	交付，交货
catalog	n.	目录，商品，价目表
	v.	编目录
price	v.	定价，标价
integration	n.	集成，综合，整合，一体化
paperwork	n.	文书工作
reign	v.	统治，支配，盛行，占优势
sponsor	v.	发起，主办，赞助
	n.	发起人，主办者，保证人
investor	n.	投资者
discussion	n.	讨论
exclusively	adv.	排外地，专有地
venue	n.	地点
unload	v.	摆脱……之负担，倾销，卸；卸货
automate	v.	使自动化，自动操作
procurement	n.	采购，供应，筹集
nirvana	n.	涅槃，天堂
significant	adj.	有意义的，重大的，重要的，效果显著的
order	n.	订单
	v.	命令，定购，定制
hurdle	n.	障碍，篱笆，栏
resistance	n.	反抗，抵抗，抵抗力，阻力
confidential	adj.	秘密的，机密的
layoff	n.	临时解雇，操作停止
drastically	adv.	激烈地，彻底地
quotation	n.	行情，时价，报价
invoice	n.	发票，发货单
	v.	开发票，记清单
peg	v.	固定，限定，稳定

Phrases

trading partner	贸易伙伴，生意伙伴
haggle over prices	讨价还价
product specification	产品规格
industry consortia	行业协会
depend on	依靠，依赖
from scratch	从零开始，从无到有，白手起家
back-end system	后台系统，后端系统
pay off	还清(债务等)，付清，盈利

Abbreviations

RFQs (Requests for Quotations)　　询价

Exercises

[Ex. 5]　Answer the following questions according to the text.

1. What is B2B e-commerce?
2. What is the obvious difference between B2B and B2C?
3. Beyond that, what are the two big distinctions between B2B and B2C?
4. Why do most companies selling to businesses integrate?
5. What are some ways companies have benefited from B2B e-commerce?
6. What is a B2B exchange?
7. What's the difference between public B2B exchanges and private ones?
8. What do you and your partners need if you want to collaborate successfully?
9. What elements may a B2B system include?
10. What if your partners have to do some of their own software development to use the application?

Reading Material

About E-commerce

1. Types of E-commerce

Generally speaking, when we think of e-commerce, we think of an online commercial transaction between a supplier and a client. Although this idea is right, we can be more specific and actually divide e-commerce into[1] six major types, all with different characteristics.

There are six basic types of e-commerce: Business-to-Business (B2B), Business-to-Consumer

---

1　divide into　　分成，分为

(B2C), Consumer-to-Consumer (C2C), Consumer-to-Business (C2B), Business-to-Administration (B2A), Consumer-to-Administration (C2A)

(1) Business-to-Business (B2B)

Business-to-Business (B2B) e-commerce encompasses all electronic transactions of goods or services conducted between companies. Producers and traditional commerce wholesalers[1] typically operate with this type of electronic commerce.

(2) Business-to-Consumer (B2C)

Business-to-Consumer e-commerce is distinguished by[2] the establishment[3] of electronic business relationships between businesses and final consumers. It corresponds to[4] the retail section of e-commerce, where traditional retail trade normally operates.

These types of relationships can be easier and more dynamic, but also more sporadic[5] or discontinued[6]. This type of commerce has developed greatly, due to the advent of the web, and there are already many virtual stores and malls on the Internet, which sell all kinds of consumer goods, such as computers, software, books, shoes, cars, food, financial products, digital publications, etc.

When compared to buying retail in traditional commerce, the consumer usually has more information available in terms of informative content and there is also a widespread idea that you'll be buying cheaper, without jeopardizing[7] an equally personalized customer service, as well as ensuring quick processing and delivery of your order.

(3) Consumer-to-Consumer (C2C)

Consumer-to-Consumer (C2C) e-commerce encompasses all electronic transactions of goods or services conducted between consumers. Generally, these transactions are conducted through a third party[8], which provides the online platform where the transactions are actually carried out.

(4) Consumer-to-Business (C2B)

In C2B, there is a complete reversal[9] of the traditional sense of exchanging goods. This type of e-commerce is very common in crowd sourcing based projects. A large number of individuals make their services or products available for purchase for companies seeking precisely these types of services or products.

Examples of such practices are the sites where designers present several proposals for a company logo and where only one of them is selected and effectively purchased. Another platform that is very common in this type of commerce are the markets that sell royalty-free[10] photographs,

---

1 wholesaler   *n.*   批发商
2 be distinguished by...   以……为特征
3 establishment   *n.*   确立，制定
4 correspond to   相应，符合
5 sporadic   *adj.*   零星的
6 discontinue   *v.*   停止，废止
7 jeopardize   *v.*   危害
8 third party   第三方
9 reversal   *n.*   颠倒，反转，反向，逆转
10 royalty-free   免版税

images, media and design elements, such as iStockphoto.

(5) Business-to-Administration (B2A)

This part of e-commerce encompasses all transactions conducted online between companies and public administration. This is an area that involves a large amount and a variety of services, particularly in areas such as fiscal[1], social security, employment, legal documents and registers, etc. These types of services have increased considerably[2] in recent years with investments made in e-government.

(6) Consumer-to-Administration (C2A)

The Consumer-to-Administration model encompasses all electronic transactions conducted between individuals and public administration.

Examples of applications include:
- Education—disseminating information, distance learning[3], etc.
- Social Security—through the distribution of information, making payments, etc.
- Taxes—filing tax returns, payments, etc.
- Health—appointments, information about illnesses, payment of health services, etc.

Both models involving Public Administration (B2A and C2A) are strongly associated to the idea of efficiency and easy usability of the services provided to citizens by the government, with the support of information and communication technologies.

2. Advantages of E-commerce

The main advantage of e-commerce is its ability to reach a global market, without necessarily implying a large financial investment. The limits of this type of commerce are not defined geographically[4], which allows consumers to make a global choice, obtain the necessary information and compare offers from all potential suppliers, regardless of their locations.

By allowing direct interaction with the final consumer, e-commerce shortens the product distribution chain, sometimes even eliminates[5] it completely. This way, a direct channel between the producer or service provider and the final user is created, enabling them to offer products and services that suit the individual preferences of the target market.

E-commerce allows suppliers to be closer to their customers, resulting in increased productivity and competitiveness for companies; as a result, the consumer is benefited with an improvement in quality service, resulting in greater proximity, as well as a more efficient pre- and post-sales support. With these new forms of electronic commerce, consumers now have virtual stores that are open 24 hours a day.

Cost reduction is another very important advantage normally associated with electronic commerce. The more trivial a particular business process is, the greater the likelihood[6] of its success,

---

1 fiscal   *adj.*   财政的, 国库的, 会计的
2 considerably   *adv.*   相当地
3 distance learning   远程教育
4 geographically   *adv.*   地理学上, 在地理上
5 eliminate   *v.*   排除, 消除
6 likelihood   *n.*   可能, 可能性

resulting in a significant reduction of transaction costs and, of course, of the prices charged to customers.

3. Disadvantages of E-commerce

The main disadvantages associated with e-commerce are the following:

- Strong dependence on information and communication technologies (ICT).
- Lack of legislation that adequately[1] regulates the new e-commerce activities, both nationally and internationally[2].
- Market culture is averse to[3] electronic commerce (customers cannot touch or try the products).
- The users' loss of privacy, the loss of regions' and countries' cultural and economic identity.
- Insecurity in the conduct of online business transactions.

4. Types of E-commerce Websites

An e-commerce website sells things online. The website could be owned by a company, a single person or by a group of people. It supervises the online purchases and transactions.

E-commerce sites have grown into multiple versions and types. Here we have listed them for the better understanding of how different types of trades and selling happens online.

(1) According to the Type of the Market

By type of market, we mean if the parties of a trade are both businesses, both customers or one customer and one business. These known types are seen in the normal, offline business world. Here, they are just taken to categorize[4] online business.

1) B2B. B2B e-commerce sites are businesses selling services and products to other businesses. For instance, a machine-maker selling a tailor-made chain-saw machine to a wood production house.

Such websites have comparatively low visitors than other popular types of e-commerce sites i.e. an online retailer, yet, generally the price of an average order is higher. Alibaba is a B2B online marketplace where many vendors and production houses sells things online to other production houses.

2) B2C. This is the regular online retailer. Businesses selling to customers. It is done by the business owning its own e-commerce site or selling its product on a marketplace or even on a normal e-commerce website where only selected premium sellers are present. The number of transactions and customers stays higher than the B2B transactions.

3) C2C. Such market type allows customers to interact with each other and sell things to each other. Type of the product isn't restricted to only manufactured or firsthand[5] products. A genuine online marketplace is the pure example of a C2C market where customers are selling their things to

---

1　adequately　　　adv.　充分地
2　internationally　　adv.　国际性地, 在国际间
3　be averse to　　　反对, 不情愿
4　categorize　　　v.　加以类别, 分类
5　firsthand　　adj.　直接的, 直接得来的, 直接采购的　　adv.　第一手地, 直接地

other customers. Such market could have variety of products ranging from new, second hand[1] products, home-made products to even things of antiquity.

(2) According to the Number of the Sellers

Here, the number of the sellers available on the site defines in which category the site falls in.

1) Vendor specific—single seller. A vendor specific e-commerce website is selling products of a single company. All the product range and services are listed on the website for sale. No product/services of other company are shown. Today, most of the big manufacturers also include this feature on their corporate sites. There could be also an artist's sites selling its art-products online or on YouTube site selling related merchandises. These are vendor specific e-commerce sites, where only a single manufacturer's products are being sold.

2) Online retailers—selected premium sellers. General people are most familiar with these sites. Known examples of such online retailers are Amazon, Flipkart, etc. These companies don't restrict the sellers to one production house, like a vendor specific e-commerce site does, but also don't open up selling feature to everyone either. The sellers here are chosen by the site to maintain the trust, product quality and control over other functions of the site. These premium sellers need to match some of the predefined[2] qualities set by the e-commerce website owner.

3) Online marketplace—everyone is a seller. These are called online marketplaces. Just like in a real life marketplace, you see international companies, to a single person selling their things; an online marketplace is the virtual version of such a marketplace, where multiple types of sellers are selling to multiple types of customers. To become a seller, you aren't required to be selected. You can visit the site, fill the form and begin selling things online through the marketplace. Such marketplace also includes all the types of e-commerce sites into it as there could be vendors selling their things on their own specific stores on the sites (vendor specific), there could be multinational companies[3] having their stores here (premium sellers) or even a person wanting to sell his old laser could become a seller. Types of things to be sold aren't also limited to produced or crafted things. It could widen to things of antiquity[4], rarity[5], art pieces, and almost everything which could be legally sold. eBay is the most known example of such an online marketplace.

(3) According to the Product Range

1) Single product. Single product store is dedicated to a single product without selling anything else. Such sites depend on tempting big number of customers to buy the single product.

2) Product, customers or industry specific. Some e-commerce sites sell a specific type of products manufactured by different manufacturers. Their attention is towards selling and serving the consumers of that specific industry. For instance, Diapers.com sells products only related to

---

1 second hand　　旧货，二手货
2 predefine　　*v.* 预先确定
3 multinational company　　跨国公司
4 antiquity　　*n.* 古代，古老，古代的遗物
5 rarity　　*n.* 稀有；珍品（复数）

toddlers[1]. Another site called Etsy.com sells only handmade things.

3) All products types. Here, everything is sold on a single website. A retail store is good example and is a place where every type of manufactured products is being sold to customers. Such stores give a wide-array of products types and options to customers—sometimes counting in millions.

Any e-commerce site is defined mainly by one of these types. Its customer demography[2], scale and other factors could be understood by understanding which category or categories it sits in.

参考译文

如何选择电子商务商业模式

当谈到开始一个在线业务时，你有很多选择。最大的选择可能也是最重要的，因为它将最终决定你的业务模式和业务的未来。

在本文中，我们将从更高层面上向你展示开始在线业务时需要考虑的每项选择及其利弊，以便你可以从一开始就做出最佳决策。

1. 你想把产品卖给谁？

有许多类型的电子商务商店，它们差别甚微。让我们来看看你可以运营电子商务企业的两种主要类型，然后我们将进一步深入探讨。

（1）B2B（企业对企业）

企业对企业模式是指一个企业向另一企业销售产品。销售给其他企业和销售给最终消费者各有优点和缺点。向其他企业销售的优点是订单和重复订单通常更大、更频繁。然而，企业客户比消费者的数量更少并且销售周期通常更长，价格是做出购买决定的关键因素。

（2）B2C（企业对消费者）

企业对消费者模式意味着直接将产品销售给使用该产品的最终消费者。这是最常见的商业模式类型，而且大多数人建设电子商务业务时首先想到这种商务模式。

还应当指出，还有其他一些不太常见的商业模式，包括B2G（企业对政府）。

2. 你想卖什么类型的产品？

既然我们已经介绍了两种主要类型的在线商业模式，让我们深入了解一下，看看可以在线销售的不同类型的产品：

（1）实物产品

大多数人想到在线商店时先想到销售实物产品，它是在线电子商务企业的主流。虽然实物产品是最受欢迎的销售产品类型，但它也面临一些挑战，包括库存存储、运输、破损和保险。

例如：DodoCase 使用传统的包装方法销售 iPad 和 iPhone 保护套。

---

1 toddler   *n.* 初学走路的孩子

2 demography   *n.* 人口统计学

（2）数字产品

数字产品也是一种受欢迎类型的销售产品，并且，与实物产品相比，它具有不需要库存存储或实体交付的优点。数字产品可以是音乐、电子书、视频、图像或软件。销售数字产品的最大缺点是盗版。然而，由于数字产品可以转售数千次，它们的利润被认为是最好的，没有与运输和库存管理相关的麻烦。

例如：Out Of The Sandbox 销售 Shopify 的高级主题，也通过自己的 Shopify 商店销售。这些主题在购买后立即以数字形式提供。

（3）服务

第三种不太常见的在线销售的产品类型是服务。在线服务包括咨询、网页设计和开发、内容编写或编辑以及许多其他服务选项。通过在线商店销售服务是建立可信度和获得曝光率的好方法，但是通常伴随着可扩展性的限制，因为服务通常由人完成并受该人时间的限制。

例如：Shopify Experts 是为 Shopify 商店业主提供服务的自由职业者和代理商的目录。范围从建立业务和营销到设计和摄影。这些在 Shopify 专家库中的众多自由职业者和机构使用 Shopify 托管他们的网站，并直接向企业家出售他们的服务。

3. 您想如何获取产品？

在一定程度上，实物产品甚至数字产品可以用多种方式分类。最流行的分类方法之一是按照获取产品的方式来分类。获取产品主要有四种方法，以下分述之：

（1）自制

自制产品是众多发烧友常见的方法。无论是珠宝、时尚品或天然美容产品，自制产品能精确控制质量和品牌，但耗费时日且规模受限。

自制产品的主要成本包括原材料的采购、库存和劳动力。

尤为重要的是，并不是所有产品都可以手工制作。所选产品受限于你的技能和可用资源。

例如：J. L. Lawson&Co.在加利福尼亚州约书亚树村的工作室手工制作所有东西。一个传承三代的家族企业意味着对自己制作的每个产品都自豪满满。

（2）厂家定制

获取产品和库存的另一个可行的选择是找到一个制造商为你生产产品。当选择制造商时，可以选择国内的，也可以选择海外的。也许如你看到的，一般来说，美国制造商的成本将高于来自中国或印度等国家的制造商。

例如：GameKlip 靠制作游戏控制器剪辑夹起家，这些剪辑夹把实际的游戏控制器连接到智能手机上，以便玩家在智能手机上获得极致游戏体验。需求飙升后，创始人开始全面制造剪辑夹以满足需求。

（3）批发

批量购买是一个相当简单和直接的过程。直接从制造商或中间供应商处以折扣批发价购货入库（通常是其他品牌），转而以更高的价格转售。

与制造业相比，批量购买是一种风险较低的商业模式，原因有几个。首先，你所购买的品牌已经在市场上建立了信用，所以你就没有浪费时间和金钱开发没有人想要的产品的风险。其次，与制造自己的产品相比，购买数量比自制数量少。最小订单将取决于制造商和产品。但是，它们通常是相当合理的，甚至可以只订购一件。

例如：Lodge Goods 出售各种来自美国的工匠和制造商精心制作的商品。通过销售其他

41

品牌，他们能够提供各种各样的产品和品牌。

（4）直接代发货

直接代发货的主要概念是销售实际上并不拥有的产品。与直接代发货伙伴合作不仅是产品采购模式，而且还包括产品实现。该过程通过从你的在线业务接收订单并将其转发给你的供应商或配送合作伙伴。反过来，他们代表你的公司将产品运送给你的客户。直接代发货赚钱的关键是利用你收取的费用和你的合作伙伴收取的费用之间的价格差异。

直接代发货的最大好处是能够提供大量产品，而不需要预先购买入库并管理库存。直接代发货也可以是一个非常好的方法——使你的库存多样化并测试产品，因为仅仅是把新产品添加到你的商店而已。

例如：Right Channel Radios 是你的越野车的 CB 收音机的头号来源。通过直接代发货的方式采购产品，创业者能够在非常特定的商机提供非常广泛的产品和配件，而没有任何库存成本或风险。

4. 你要如何竞争？

决定如何竞争是一个重要的决定，可以显著塑造业务的未来，并决定关键的业务决策。在一个拥挤的市场，竞争有几种常见的方式。下面，让我们来看看每个选项。

（1）价格

以价格竞争通常不是小型零售商的最佳选择，因为通常任何一个比你大的商家的利润都比你大，并且定价总是比你低。价格竞争也会在更大的局势中导致价格战，吃掉了每个人的利润。

例如：沃尔玛一直以折扣策略而闻名，并且足够大到可以使这一战略适合他们。通过大量购买产品，他们能够得到更好的定价，并以好的价格卖给消费者。

（2）质量

质量竞争的结果就是拥有一个优越的或更好的产品。这可能是一种了不起的竞争方式。有迹象表明，市场作为一个整体正在转向更持久、更精心制作的产品。

例如：Dbrand 为智能手机、笔记本式计算机和游戏机销售乙烯基保护壳。认识到当前市场缺乏高质量、用激光精确切割的保护壳，Dbrand 就自己生产，并迅速飙升到保护壳市场中的主导商家。

（3）精选

要在市场上开辟自己的空间，竞争精选是一个很棒的选择。但是，如果你不是使用直接代发货而是使用其他方法，也有增加库存和存储的风险。

例如：亚马逊毫无疑问是电子商务在选择领域的领导者。然而，只是因为大型公司有大量的精选产品并不意味着你可以如此竞争。它只是意味着你必须在某一小众类别实施最大的精选竞争。

（4）附加价值

区分自己在市场上最好的方法之一是为客户提供额外的价值，使他们从你那里购买。非凡的产品描述、学习中心、安装指南等形式是一个很好的为您的客户提供额外价值的例子。

例如：Right Channel Radios 用直接代发货方法来销售其 CB 收音机和附件，这意味着利润很小，可能使其难以有效地与其他具有更好利润的竞争对手竞争。为了弥补这一点，Right

Channel Radios 以教育中心和大多数产品的评价视频的形式提供了大量额外的价值。

（5）服务

一个新的小企业，通过服务竞争可能很难，但可以作为一个获胜的战略。考虑到口碑营销是最强大的营销形式，那么可以通过竞争和提供令人难以置信的客户体验，让人们的谈论是有意义的。

例如：Zappos 以他们的客户服务而闻名，提供免费送货和退货方式、365 天退货政策和 24/7 全天候客户服务。Zappos 也以一些有趣的服务记录知名，如设置 10h 客户服务电话记录。

5. 结论

回答本文中的四个主要问题将为你提供一个良好的开始，能够使你汇总设置电子商务业务模式的一些主要组成部分。重要的是要记住，一些业务模型组合要做更多的工作，建立自己特定的业务模式需要时间。这不仅会增加你的成功机会，而且会让你从建立、发布和发展在线业务中获得快乐。

Unit 3

Text A

What Is a Computer Network?

1. What Is a Network?

A network consists of two or more computers that are linked in order to share resources (such as printers and CD-ROMs), exchange files, or allow electronic communications.  The computers on a network may be linked through cables, telephone lines, radio waves, satellites, or infrared light beams.

The two basic types of networks include: Local Area Network (LAN) and Wide Area Network (WAN).

2. What Is Local Area Network?

A Local Area Network (LAN) is a network that is confined to a relatively small area. It is generally limited to a geographic area such as a lab, school, or building. Rarely are LAN computers more than a mile apart.

In a typical LAN configuration, one computer is designated as the file server. It stores all of the software that controls the network, as well as the software that can be shared by the computers attached to the network. Computers connected to the file server are called workstations. The workstations can be less powerful than the file server, and they may have additional software on their hard drives. On most LANs, cables are used to connect the network interface cards in each computer.

3. What Is Wide Area Network?

A Wide Area Network (WAN) connects larger geographic areas, such as Florida, the United States, or the world. Dedicated transoceanic cabling or satellite uplinks may be used to connect this type of network.

Using a WAN, schools in Florida can communicate with places like Tokyo in a matter of minutes, without paying enormous phone bills. A WAN is complicated. It uses multiplexers to connect local and metropolitan networks to global communications networks like the Internet. To users, however, a WAN will not appear to be much different than a LAN or a WAN.

4. Advantages of Installing a School Network

1) Speed. Networks provide a very rapid method for sharing and transferring files. Without a network, files are shared by copying them to disks, then carry or send the disks from one computer to another. This method of transferring files (referred to as sneakernet[1]) is very time-consuming.

2) Cost. Networkable versions of many popular software programs are available at considerable savings when compared to buying individually licensed copies. Besides monetary savings, sharing a program on a network allows for easier upgrading of the program. The changes have to be done only once, on the file server, instead of on all the individual workstations.

3) Security. Files and programs on a network can be designated as "copy inhibit", so that you do not have to worry about illegal copying of programs. Also, passwords can be established for specific directories to restrict access to authorized users.

4) Centralized software management. One of the greatest benefits of installing a network at a school is the fact that all of the software can be loaded on one computer (the file server). This eliminates that need to spend time and energy installing updates and tracking files on independent computers throughout the building.

5) Resource sharing. Sharing resources is another area in which a network exceeds stand-alone computers. Most schools cannot afford enough laser printers, fax machines, modems, scanners, and CD-ROM players for each computer. However, if these or similar peripherals are added to a network, they can be shared by many users.

6) Electronic mail(E-mail). The presence of a network provides the hardware necessary to install an e-mail system. E-mail aids in personal and professional communication for all school personnel, and it facilitates the dissemination of general information to the entire school staff. Electronic mail on a LAN can enable students to communicate with teachers and peers at their own school. If the LAN is connected to the Internet, students can communicate with others throughout the world.

7) Flexible access. School networks allow students to access their files from computers throughout the school. Students can begin an assignment in their classroom, save part of it on a public access area of the network, and then go to the media center after school to finish their work. Students can also work cooperatively through the network.

8) Workgroup computing. Workgroup software (such as Microsoft BackOffice) allows many users to work on a document or project concurrently. For example, educators located at various schools within a county could simultaneously contribute their ideas about new curriculum standards to the same document and spreadsheets.

5. Disadvantages of Installing a School Network

1) Expensive to install. Although a network will generally save money over time, the initial

---

1 Sneakernet is an informal term describing the transfer of electronic information, especially computer files, by physically moving removable media such as magnetic tape, compact discs, USB flash drives (thumb drives, USB stick) or external hard drives from one computer to another, usually in lieu of transmitting the information over a computer network. The term, a tongue-in-cheek play on net (work) as in Internet or Ethernet, refers to the wearing of sneakers as the transport mechanism for the data.

costs of installation can be prohibitive. Cables, network cards, and software are expensive, and the installation may require the services of a technician.

2) Requires administrative time. Proper maintenance of a network requires considerable time and expertise. Many schools have installed a network, only to find that they did not budget for the necessary administrative support.

3) File server may fail. Although a file server is no more susceptible to failure than any other computer, when the files server "goes down", the entire network may come to a halt. When this happens, the entire school may lose access to necessary programs and files.

4) Cables may break. Some of the configurations are designed to minimize the inconvenience of a broken cable; with other configurations, one broken cable can stop the entire network.

New Words

network	n.	网络
printer	n.	打印机
exchange	v.	交换，调换，兑换，交易；交流
file	n.	文件，档案
	v.	把……归档
cable	n.	电缆
satellite	n.	卫星，人造卫星
infrared	adj.	红外线的
	n.	红外线
beam	n.	光束，电波
	v.	播送
configuration	n.	配置，构造，结构，外形
designate	v.	指定，指派
control	v.	控制，支配，管理，操纵
	n.	控制，支配，管理，抑制，控制器，调节装置
attach	v.	加上，连上，附上
workstation	n.	工作站
connect	v.	连接，相连，联合
additional	adj.	另外的，附加的，额外的
card	n.	卡，插卡
uplink	n.	向上传输，上行线，卫星上行链路
multiplexer	n.	多路（复用）器
transfer	n.&v.	传输，传递，转移
copy	n.	副本，模仿
	v.	复制
available	adj.	可用到的，可利用的，有用的
program	n.	程序

inhibit	v.	禁止，阻止，抑制，约束
password	n.	密码，口令
directory	n.	[计]目录，工商名录
restrict	v.	限制，约束，限定
access	n.	访问，通路，入门
	v.	存取，接近
load	n.	负荷，装载量，工作量，负载，加载
	v.	装载，装填，使担负
track	v.	跟踪，追踪
	n.	轨迹，跟踪，路，磁轨，途径
modem	n.	调制解调器
scanner	n.	扫描仪
peripheral	adj.	外围的
	n.	外围设备
media	n.	媒体
cooperative	adj.	合作的，协作的，共同的
document	n.	公文，文件，文档，档案
locate	v.	位于，查找……的地点，使……坐落于；定位
simultaneously	adv.	同时地
susceptible	adj.	易受影响的
failure	n.	故障，失败，缺乏，失灵
inconvenience	n.	麻烦，不方便之处

Phrases

be confined to	局限于，被限制在
in order to	为了……
electronic communication	电子通信
telephone line	电话线
radio wave	无线电波
file server	文件服务器
hard drive	硬盘驱动器
laser printer	激光打印机
fax machine	传真机
electronic mail	电子邮件
network card	网卡

Abbreviations

CD-ROM (Compact Disc-Read Only Memory)　　　光盘驱动器

LAN (Local Area Network) 局域网，本地网
WAN (Wide Area Network) 广域网

Exercises

[Ex. 1] Answer the following questions according to the text.

1. What does a network consist of?
2. How many basic types of networks are there? And what are they?
3. What is Local Area Network?
4. What is Wide Area Network?
5. What does the file server do in a typical LAN configuration?
6. What are workstations?
7. What are cables used to do on most LANs?
8. Is a WAN complicated? What does it use multiplexers to do?
9. What do the advantages of installing a school network lie in?
10. Please list all the disadvantages of installing a school network.

[Ex. 2] Translate the following terms or phrases from English into Chinese and vice versa.

1. access   1. _____
2. electronic communication   2. _____
3. file server   3. _____
4. program   4. _____
5. electronic mail   5. _____
6. 网卡   6. _____
7. 配置，构造，结构，外形   7. _____
8. [计]目录   8. _____
9. 指定，指派   9. _____
10. 密码，口令   10. _____

[Ex. 3] Translate the following passage into Chinese.

Transmission Control Protocol (TCP) and Internet Protocol (IP) are two distinct network protocols, technically speaking. TCP and IP are so commonly used together, however, that TCP/IP has become standard terminology to refer to either or both of the protocols.

IP corresponds to the Network layer (Layer 3) in the OSI model, whereas TCP corresponds to the Transport layer (Layer 4) in OSI. In other words, the term TCP/IP refers to network communications where the TCP transport is used to deliver data across IP networks.

The average person on the Internet works in a predominately TCP/IP environment. Web browsers, for example, use TCP/IP to communicate with Web servers.

[Ex. 4] Fill in the blanks with the words given below.

| business | meet | resource | stage | responsible |
| security | data | network | retailers | requirements |

How to Handle Customer Financial Data

PCI compliance is a term familiar to many people researching e-commerce regulations. As an e-commerce site owner, one of the standards you will need to know about is the PCI DSS standard, which is short for Payment Card Industry (PCI) Data Security Standard (DSS). All organizations, including online ___1___, must follow this standard when storing, processing and transmitting credit card data.

The PCI Security Standards Council is the organization—founded by a number of financial institutions including JCB International, MasterCard and Visa—that is ___2___ for the development and implementation of ___3___ standards for account data protection. Through its PCI Security Standards, the organization seeks to enhance payment account ___4___ security.

There are a number of security initiatives in this standard, such as using a firewall between a wireless ___5___ and the cardholder data environment, making use the latest security and authentication, and using a network intrusion detection system. The PCI DSS standard, as of September 2009 (DSS v 1.2), includes the following 12 ___6___ for best security practices:

To achieve PCI compliance, an online retailer must ___7___ all PCI DSS requirements. The PCI DSS standard is broken down into six milestones with a number of requirements to be fulfilled at each ___8___. The PCI Security Standards Council website offers this PDF, which is designed to help merchants to better understand the requirements. It is probably the best ___9___ online to begin to understand what compliance entails.

There's no question that meeting PCI compliance is a challenge for small business e-commerce site owners—and being certified as PCI-compliant is a time-consuming process. One way that a small ___10___ can meet standards is to outsource PCI to a third party that has the experience and payment system to ensure your business meets PCI regulations.

Text B

A Basic Guide to the Internet

The Internet is a computer network made up of thousands of networks worldwide. No one knows exactly how many computers are connected to the Internet. It is certain, however, that these number in the millions and are growing.

扫一扫，听课文

No one is in charge of the Internet. There are organizations which develop technical aspects of this network and set standards for creating applications on it, but no governing body is in control. The Internet backbone, through which Internet traffic flows, is owned by private companies.

All computers on the Internet communicate with one another using the Transmission Control Protocol/Internet Protocol suite, abbreviated to TCP/IP. Computers on the Internet use a client/server architecture. This means that the remote server machine provides files and services to the user's local client machine. Software can be installed on a client computer to take advantage of the latest access technology.

An Internet user has access to a wide variety of services: electronic mail, file transfer, vast information resources, interest group membership, interactive collaboration, multimedia displays, real-time broadcasting, breaking news, shopping opportunities, and much more.

The Internet consists primarily of a variety of access protocols. Many of these protocols feature programs that allow users to search for and retrieve material made available by the protocol.

The following are the components of the Internet.

1. World Wide Web

The World Wide Web (abbreviated as the Web or WWW) is a system of Internet servers that supports hypertext to access several Internet protocols on a single interface. Almost every protocol type available on the Internet is accessible on the Web. This includes e-mail, FTP, Telnet, and Usenet News. In addition to these, the World Wide Web has its own protocol: HyperText Transfer Protocol[1], or HTTP. These protocols will be explained below.

The World Wide Web provides a single interface for accessing all these protocols. This creates a convenient and user-friendly environment. It is not necessary to be conversant in these protocols within separate, command-level environments, as was typical in the early days of the Internet. The Web gathers together these protocols into a single system. Because of this feature, and because of the Web's ability to work with multimedia and advanced programming languages, the Web is the most popular component of the Internet.

The operation of the Web relies primarily on hypertext as its means of information retrieval. HyperText is a document containing words that connect to other documents. These words are called links and are selectable by the user. A single hypertext document can contain links to many documents. In the context of the Web, words or graphics may serve as links to other documents, images, video, and sound. Links may or may not follow a logical path, as each connection is programmed by the creator of the source document. Overall, the Web contains a complex virtual web of connections among a vast number of documents, graphics, videos, and sounds.

Producing hypertext for the Web is accomplished by creating documents with a language called HyperText Markup Language, or HTML. With HTML, tags are placed within the text to accomplish document formatting, visual features such as font size, italics and bold, and the creation of hypertext links. Graphics and multimedia may also be incorporated into an HTML document.

HTML is an evolving language, with new tags being added as each upgrade of the language is developed and released. For example, visual formatting features are now often separated from the

---

1 The HyperText Transfer Protocol (HTTP) is an application protocol for distributed, collaborative, hypermedia information systems. HTTP is the foundation of data communication for the World Wide Web. Hypertext is structured text that uses logical links (hyperlinks) between nodes containing text. HTTP is the protocol to exchange or transfer hypertext.

HTML document and placed into Cascading Style Sheets(CSS).[1] This has several advantages, including the fact that an external style sheet can centrally control the formatting of multiple documents. The World Wide Web Consortium (W3C), led by Web founder Tim Berners-Lee, coordinates the efforts of standardizing HTML. The W3C now calls the language XHTML and considers it to be an application of the XML language standard.

The World Wide Web consists of files, called pages or home pages, containing links to documents and resources throughout the Internet.

The Web provides a vast array of experiences including multimedia presentations, real-time collaboration, interactive pages, radio and television broadcasts, and the automatic "push" of information to a client computer. Programming languages such as Java, JavaScript, Visual Basic, Cold Fusion and XML extend the capabilities of the Web. Much information on the Web is served dynamically from content stored in databases. The Web is therefore not a fixed entity, but one that is in a constant state of development and flux.

2. E-mail

Electronic mail, or e-mail, allows computer users locally and worldwide to exchange messages. Each user of e-mail has a mailbox address to which messages are sent. Messages sent through e-mail can arrive within a matter of seconds.

A powerful aspect of e-mail is the option to send electronic files to a person's e-mail address. Non-ASCII files, known as binary files, may be attached to e-mail messages. These files are referred to as MIME attachments. MIME stands for Multimedia Internet Mail Extension, and was developed to help e-mail software handle a variety of file types. For example, a document created in Microsoft Word can be attached to an e-mail message and retrieved by the recipient with the appropriate e-mail program. Many e-mail programs offer the ability to read files written in HTML, which is itself a MIME type.

3. Telnet

Telnet is a program that allows you to log into computers on the Internet and use online databases, library catalogs, chat services, and more. There are no graphics in Telnet sessions, just text. To Telnet to a computer, you must know its address. This can consist of words (locis.loc.gov) or numbers (140.147.254.3). Some services require you to connect to a specific port on the remote computer. In this case, type the port number after the Internet address. Example: telnet nri.reston.va.us 185.

Telnet is available on the World Wide Web. Probably the most common Web-based resources available through Telnet have been library catalogs, though most catalogs have since migrated to the

---

1 Cascading Style Sheets (CSS) is a style sheet language used for describing the presentation of a document written in a markup language. Although most often used to set the visual style of web pages and user interfaces written in HTML and XHTML, the language can be applied to any XML document, including plain XML, SVG and XUL, and is applicable to rendering in speech, or on other media. Along with HTML and JavaScript, CSS is a cornerstone technology used by most websites to create visually engaging webpages, user interfaces for web applications, and user interfaces for many mobile applications.

Web. A link to a Telnet resource may look like any other link, but it will launch a Telnet session to make the connection. A Telnet program must be installed on your local computer and configured to your Web browser in order to work.

With the popularity of the Web, Telnet is less frequently used as a means of access to information on the Internet.

4. File Transfer Protocol

File Transfer Protocol (FTP) is both a program and the method used to transfer files between computers. Anonymous FTP is an option that allows users to transfer files from thousands of host computers on the Internet to their personal computer account. FTP sites contain books, articles, software, games, images, sounds, multimedia, course work, data sets, and more.

If your computer is directly connected to the Internet via an Ethernet cable, you can use one of several PC software programs, such as WS_FTP for Windows, to conduct a file transfer.

FTP transfers can be performed on the World Wide Web without the need for special software. In this case, the Web browser will suffice. Whenever you download software from a website to your local machine, you are using FTP. You can also retrieve FTP files via search engines such as FtpFind, located at http://www.ftpfind.com/. This option is easiest because you do not need to know FTP program commands.

5. E-mail Discussion Groups

One of the benefits of the Internet is the opportunity it offers to people worldwide to communicate via e-mail. The Internet is home to a large community of individuals who carry out active discussions organized around topic-oriented forums distributed by e-mail. These are administered by various types of software programs.

A great variety of topics are covered by discussion groups. When you subscribe to a group, messages from other subscribers are automatically sent to your electronic mailbox. You subscribe by sending an e-mail message to the address of the group. You must have an e-mail account to participate in a listserv discussion group. Visit Tile.net at http://tile.net/ to see an example of a site that offers a searchable collection of e-mail discussion groups.

Listserv, majordomo and Listproc are among the programs that administer e-mail discussion groups. The commands for subscribing to and managing your list memberships are similar to those of listserv.

6. Usenet News

Usenet News is a global electronic bulletin board system in which millions of computer users exchange information on a vast range of topics. The major difference between Usenet News and e-mail discussion groups is the fact that Usenet messages are stored on central computers, and users must connect to these computers to read or download the messages posted to these groups. This is distinct from e-mail distribution, in which messages arrive in the electronic mailboxes of each list member.

Usenet itself is a set of machines that exchanges messages, or articles, from Usenet discussion forums, called newsgroups. Usenet administrators control their own sites, and decide which (if any) newsgroups to sponsor and which remote newsgroups to allow into the system.

There are thousands of Usenet newsgroups. These range from academic to recreational topics. Serious computer-related work takes place in Usenet discussions. A small number of e-mail discussion groups also exist as Usenet newsgroups.

The Usenet newsfeed can be read by a variety of newsreader software programs. For example, the Netscape suite comes with a newsreader program called Messenger. Newsreaders are also available as standalone products.

Usenet is not as popular nowadays as it once was. Blogs and RSS feeds are newer modes of communication that have caught the interest of Internet users.

7. Chat & Instant Messaging

Chat programs allow users on the Internet to communicate with each other by typing in real time. They are sometimes included as a feature of a website, where users can log into the "chat room" to exchange comments and information about the topics addressed on the site. Chat may take other, more wide-ranging forms. For example, America Online is well known for sponsoring a number of topical chat rooms.

Internet Relay Chat (IRC) is a service through which participants can communicate to each other on hundreds of channels. These channels are usually based on specific topics. While many topics are frivolous, substantive conversations are also taking place. To access IRC, you must use an IRC software program.

A variation of chat is the phenomenon of instant messaging. With instant messaging, a user on the Web can contact another user currently logged in and type a conversation. Most famous is America Online's Instant Messenger. ICQ, MSN and Yahoo also offer chat programs. Open source chat programs include GAIM and Jabber.

New Words

number	*v.*	总计，计有
backbone	*n.*	脊椎，中枢，骨干，支柱
suite	*n.*	套，组
client	*n.*	客户机，顾客，委托人
remote	*adj.*	远程的，遥远的
local	*adj.*	当地的，局部的
install	*v.*	安装
multimedia	*n.*	多媒体
	adj.	多媒体的
retrieve	*v.*	检索，重新得到
	n.	找回
hypertext	*n.*	超文本
environment	*n.*	环境

separate	*adj.*	分开的，分离的，个别的，单独的
	v.	分开，隔离，分散，分别
video	*n.*	电视，录像，视频
	adj.	电视的，视频的，录像的
tag	*n.*	标识，标签，标记符
font	*n.*	字体，字形
italic	*adj.*	斜体的
	n.	斜体字，斜体
bold	*n.*	粗体
founder	*n.*	创始人，奠基人
array	*n.*	排列，大批，数组
dynamical	*adj.*	动态的
flux	*n.*	不断变动，流动
message	*n.*	消息，通信，信息
recipient	*n.*	接受者
chat	*v.*	聊天，闲谈，非正式的谈话
	n.	聊天
session	*n.*	对话期，一段时间
port	*n.*	端口
migrate	*v.*	移动，移往，使移居，使移植
anonymous	*adj.*	匿名的
site	*n.*	站点，网站
suffice	*v.*	足够，有能力，使满足
participate	*v.*	参与，参加，分享，分担
command	*n.*	命令，掌握
	v.	命令，支配
download	*v.*	下载
newsgroups	*n.*	新闻组
recreational	*adj.*	休养的，娱乐的
channel	*n.*	通道，信道，频道

Phrases

in charge of	负责
set standards	制定标准
in control	控制
governing body	管理机构
communicate with	与……沟通，交流
take advantage of	利用
access to	有权使用，有权访问

file transfer	文件传输
interest group membership	兴趣小组成员
interactive collaboration	交互协作
multimedia display	多媒体播放
real-time broadcasting	实时播放；即时群播
breaking news	突发新闻
advanced programming languages	高级程序语言
mailbox address	邮箱地址
electronic bulletin board system	电子布告栏系统

Abbreviations

TCP (Transmission Control Protocol)	传输控制协议
IP (Internet Protocol)	网际协议
WWW (World Wide Web)	万维网
FTP (File Transfer Protocol)	文件传输协议
HTTP (HyperText Transfer Protocol)	超文本传输协议
CSS (Cascading Style Sheets)	层叠样式表
XHTML (eXpand HyperText Markup Language)	扩展超文本标识语言
ASCII (American Standard Code for Information Interchange)	美国信息交换标准码
MIME (Multimedia Internet Mail Extension)	多用途的网际邮件扩充协议
PC (Personal Computer)	个人计算机

Exercises

[Ex. 5] **Fill in the following blanks according to the text.**

1. All computers on the Internet communicate with one another using _____, abbreviated to _____.

2. An Internet user has access to a wide variety of services: _____, _____, vast information resources, interest group membership, interactive collaboration, _____, _____, breaking news, shopping opportunities, and much more.

3. The World Wide Web is a system of Internet servers _____.

4. HyperText is a document _____.

5. E-mail allows computer users _____.

6. Telnet is a program _____ on the Internet and use _____, _____, _____, and more. There are no _____ in Telnet sessions, just _____.

7. Whenever you download software from a website to your local machine, you are using _____.

8. Listserv, majordomo and Listproc are among the programs that administer _____.

55

9. Usenet News is a _____ in which millions of computer users _____.

10. Chat programs allow users on the Internet to communicate with each other by _____.

Reading Material

Network Security

Relentless cyber[1] criminals, disgruntled[2] current and former employees and careless[3] users can bring down your computer networks and compromise[4] data. Network security is made up of the hardware, software, policies and procedures designed to defend against both internal and external threats[5] to your company's computer systems. Multiple layers of hardware and software can prevent threats from damaging computer networks, and stop them from spreading if they slip past your defenses.

The most common threats to your systems:

- Malicious[6] programs like viruses, worms[7], Trojan horses, spyware[8], malware[9], adware[10] and botnets[11];
- Zero-day and zero-hour attacks[12];
- Hacker attacks;
- Denial of Service (DoS)[13] and Distributed Denial of Service Attacks (DDoS); and
- Data theft.

These threats look to exploit:

- Unsecured wireless networks;
- Unpatched software and hardware;
- Unsecured websites;
- Potentially unwanted applications (PUAs);
- Weak passwords;

---

1 cyber   n.   计算机（网络）的，信息技术的
2 disgruntled   adj. 不满的，不高兴的
3 careless   adj. 粗心的，疏忽的
4 compromise   v.   危及……的安全，妥协，退让
5 threat   n.   威胁
6 malicious   adj. 怀恶意的
7 worm   n.   蠕虫
8 spyware   n.   间谍软件
9 malware   n.   恶意软件
10 adware   n.   广告软件
11 botnet   n.   僵尸网络
12 zero-hour attack   零时漏洞攻击
13 Denial of Service (DoS)   拒绝服务

- Lost devices; and
- Unwitting users or users with malicious intent[1].

1. Top 5 Fundamentals of Network Security

These network security fundamentals are vital to downtime[2] prevention, government regulation compliance, reduced liability and reputation protection.

(1) Keep Patches[3] and Updates Current

Cyber criminals exploit vulnerabilities[4] in operating systems, software applications, web browsers and browser plug-ins[5] when administrators are lax[6] about applying patches and updates. In particular, verify that office computers are running current versions of these much used programs:

- Adobe Acrobat and Reader;
- Adobe Flash;
- Oracle Java;
- Microsoft Internet Explorer;
- Microsoft Office Suite.

Keep an inventory to make sure each device is updated regularly, including mobile devices and network hardware. And make sure Windows and Apple computers have automatic updating enabled.

(2) Use Strong Passwords

By now, most users know not to write their passwords on Post-It Notes[7] that are plastered[8] to their monitors. But there's more to keeping passwords secure than keeping them out of plain sight.

The definition of a strong password is one that's difficult to detect by humans and computers, is at least 6 characters, preferably more, and uses a combination of upper- and lower-case letters[9], numbers and symbols.

Symantec gives additional suggestions:

- Don't use any words from the dictionary. Also avoid proper nouns[10] or foreign words.
- Don't use anything remotely related to your name, nickname[11], family members or pets.
- Don't use any numbers someone could guess by looking at your mail like phone numbers and street numbers.

---

1 with malicious intent   怀有恶意的
2 downtime   *n.* 停工期
3 patch   *n.* 补丁
4 vulnerability   *n.* 弱点，攻击
5 plug-in   插件程序
6 lax   *adj.* 松懈的，不严格的
7 Post-It Notes   便利贴
8 plaster   *v.* 粘贴
9 lower-case letter   小写字母
10 proper noun   专有名词
11 nickname   *n.* 诨名，绰号，昵称

- Choose a phrase that means something to you, take the first letter of each word and convert some into characters.

The SANS Institute recommends passwords be changed at least every 90 days, and that users not be allowed to reuse their last 15 passwords. They also suggest that users be locked out of their accounts for an hour and a half after eight failed log-on attempts within a 45-minute period.

Train users to recognize social engineering techniques used to trick[1] them into divulging[2] their passwords. Hackers are known to impersonate tech support to get people to give out their passwords or simply look over users' shoulders while they type in their passwords.

(3) Secure Your VPN[3]

Data encryption and identity authentication are especially important to securing a VPN. Any open network connection is a vulnerability hackers can exploit to sneak onto your network. Moreover, data is particularly vulnerable while it is traveling over the Internet. Review the documentation for your server and VPN software to make sure that the strongest possible protocols for encryption and authentication are in use.

Multi-factor authentication is the most secure identity authentication method. The more steps your users must take to prove their identity[4], the better. For example, in addition to a password, users could be required to enter a PIN[5]. Or, a random[6] numerical code generated by a key-fob authenticator every 60 seconds could be used in conjunction with[7] a PIN or password.

It is also a good idea to use a firewall to separate the VPN network from the rest of the network. Other tips include:

- Use cloud-based e-mail and file sharing instead of a VPN.
- Create and enforce user-access policies. Be stingy[8] when granting access to employees, contractors and business partners.
- Make sure employees know how to secure their home wireless networks. Malicious software that infects[9] their devices at home can infect the company network via an open VPN connection.
- Before granting mobile devices full access to the network, check them for up-to-date anti-virus software[10], firewalls and spam filters[11].

---

1 trick   *n.* 诡计，骗局，恶作剧，窍门，诀窍   *vt.* 欺骗，哄骗
2 divulge   *v.* 泄露，暴露
3 VPN (Virtual Private Network)   虚拟专网络
4 Identity   *n.* 身份
5 PIN (Personal Identification Number)   个人身份号码
6 random   *n.* 随意，任意   *adj.* 随机的，任意的，随便的
7 in conjunction with   与……协力
8 stingy   *adj.* 吝啬的，小气的
9 infect   *v.* 传染，感染
10 anti-virus software   防病毒软件
11 spam filter   垃圾邮件过滤器

(4) Actively Manage User Access Privileges[1]

Inappropriate[2] user-access privileges pose a significant security threat. Managing employee access to critical data on an ongoing basis should not be overlooked. More than half of 5,500 companies recently surveyed by HP and the Ponemon Institute said that their employees had access to "sensitive[3], confidential[4] data outside the scope of their job requirements". In reporting on the study's findings, eWeek said "general business data such as documents, spreadsheets, e-mails and other sources of unstructured[5] data were most at risk for snooping[6], followed by customer data". When an employee's job changes, make sure the IT department is notified so their access privileges can be modified to fit the duties of the new position.

(5) Clean Up Inactive[7] Accounts

Hackers use inactive accounts once assigned to contractors and former[8] employees to gain access and disguise[9] their activity. The HP/Ponemon Institute report did find that the companies in the survey were doing a good job deleting accounts once an employee quit or was laid off. Software is available for cleaning up inactive accounts on large networks with many users.

2. Five Bonus Network Security Tips

Besides the above five network security fundamentals, it's also a good idea to:

1) Maintain a list of authorized software and prevent users from downloading applications that aren't on the list. Software inventory applications can track type, version and patch level.

2) Update the company's written security policies. For example, spell out[10] which, if any, personal devices are allowed to access the company network and state explicitly how much time users have to report lost or stolen devices. Look into Mobile Device Management (MDM) software that can remotely wipe[11] devices.

3) Segregate[12] critical data from the rest of the network and require users to authenticate themselves before accessing it.

4) Run vulnerability scanning tools at least once a week and conduct penetration testing[13].

5) Continuously monitor network traffic to detect unusual[14] patterns of activity and possible threats.

1　privilege　　　*n.* 特权, 特别待遇　　*v.* 给与……特权, 特免
2　inappropriate　*adj.* 不适当的
3　sensitive　　　*adj.* 敏感的
4　confidential　 *adj.* 秘密的, 机密的
5　unstructured　 *adj.* 非结构化的, 未组织的
6　snoop　　　　　*v.* 探听, 调查, 偷窃　*n.* 到处窥视, 爱管闲事的人
7　inactive　　　 *adj.* 不活动的, 停止的
8　former　　　　 *adj.* 从前的, 以前的
9　disguise　　　 *v.* 假装, 伪装, 掩饰　*n.* 伪装
10　spell out　　 讲清楚, 清楚地说明
11　wipe　　　　　*v.* 消除, 擦去
12　segregate　　 *v.* 隔离
13　penetration testing　　渗透测试
14　unusual　　　 *adj.* 不寻常的, 与众不同的

参 考 译 文

什么是计算机网络？

1．什么是网络？

网络由两个或多个连接在一起的计算机组成，以便共享资源（如打印机和光盘驱动器）、交换文件或进行电子通信。网络上的计算机可以用电缆、电话线、无线电波、卫星或红外线光束连接。

网络的两种基本类型包括：局域网（LAN）和广域网（WAN）。

2．什么是局域网？

局域网是局限于一个较小范围的网络。它通常局限于一个地理区域，如实验室、学校或一个建筑物内。局域网上的计算机之间的距离很少超过 1mile[1]。

局域网的典型配置是指定一台计算机为文件服务器。文件服务器存储控制网络的所有软件以及能够被连接到网络上的计算机所共享的软件。连接到服务器上的计算机称为工作站。工作站的功能可以小于文件服务器，在它们的硬盘驱动器上可以有附加软件。在大部分的局域网中，人们用电缆来连接每个计算机的网卡。

3．什么是广域网？

广域网连接更大的地理区域，如佛罗里达州、美国或全世界。可以使用专用的横越大洋的电缆或卫星系统来连接这类网络。

通过使用广域网，佛罗里达州的学校可以与东京等地进行快速交流，而无须支付巨额电话费。广域网很复杂，它用多路转换器把局域网和城域网连接到全球通信网络上，如互联网。然而，对用户来说，局域网和广域网看上去区别不大。

4．安装校园网的优势

1）速度快。校园网提供了一种非常快的共享和传输文件的方法。没有网络，就只能通过把文件复制到软盘上来共享，然后再把软盘从一台计算机带到或送到另一台计算机上。这种传输文件的方法（被称为 sneaker-net "潜网"）非常耗时。

2）成本低。与购买单个的得到许可的程序相比，许多软件程序的网络版非常节约资金。除此之外，在网络上共享程序可以更容易地升级程序，只需在文件服务器上进行一次修改而无须修改所有单个的工作站。

3）安全。可以指定网络上的文件和程序为"严禁复制"，这样就不必担心程序的非法复制了。也可以通过给一些特殊目录设置密码来限定只能被授权用户访问。

4）软件管理集中化。在校园安装网络的最大好处之一是所有软件都可以装到一个计算机（服务器）上。这样就不需要花费时间和精力给整个大楼里独立的计算机安装升级软件和跟踪文件。

5）资源共享。资源共享是网络优于单独计算机的另一个方面。大部分学校都不能给每台计算机配备足够的激光打印机、传真机、调制解调器、扫描仪和 CD-ROM 播放器。但

---

1   1 mile=1609.344m。

是，如果把这些或类似的外部设备添加到校园网上，许多用户就可以共享。

6）电子邮件。校园网的出现为安装电子邮件系统提供了必备的硬件。电子邮件有助于学校全体人员个人与专家进行交流，它促进了通用信息在全体员工中的传达。学生可以在局域网上通过电子邮件与他们学校的老师和同学交流。如果该局域网与互联网连接，学生就可以与世界各地的人交流了。

7）灵活访问。校园网可以使学生在整个校园内的计算机上访问自己的文件。学生可以开始在教室做作业，然后把一部分保存到校园网的公共访问区域，放学后再到媒体中心去完成剩余的作业。

8）工作组计算。工作组软件（如 Microsoft BackOffice）允许许多用户同时处理一个文件或做一个项目。例如，一县之内的不同学校的教学管理者可以同时把自己对新课程目标的观点发送到同一文档和电子表格中。

5. 安装校园网的劣势

1）安装费用昂贵。从长远来看，尽管网络通常会节约资金，但最初的安装费高得惊人。电缆、网卡和软件很昂贵，而且安装需要技术人员服务。

2）需要时间来管理。正常的网络维护需要大量的时间和专门技能。许多学校已经安装了网络，结果发现它们没有足够的预算进行必要的管理支持。

3）文件服务器可能会发生故障。尽管文件服务器没有其他计算机那么容易发生故障，但文件服务器"倒下"时，整个网络可能就中断了。一旦发生这种情况，整个学校就不能访问必要的程序和文件。

4）电缆可能断裂。一些结构的设计尽量减小电缆断裂带来的不便，而在另一些结构中，一根电缆断了就会导致整个网络中断。

Unit 4

Text A

How to Build an E-commerce Website

In the age of the Internet, e-commerce is attracting more and more customers. An online store is becoming a crucial element to any business plan, but starting one can be a monumental task. This article will give you some simple steps to get your store up and running in no time.

Step 1

Decide what you're selling. You should consider narrowing your scope to capture a niche market, however, not so narrow that it's hard to find customers. For example, if you are thinking of selling books, selling vintage books might be a better option. On the other hand, only selling 17th century ghost stories probably won't take you very far. If you are serious about your online store, you will probably spend a lot of time constructing and tweaking your website and especially marketing it, so choose something you have some interest in.

Step 2

Select a shopping cart. The shopping cart software allows you to set up your products and services for sale on the Internet. There are many commercially available shopping carts available to choose from. You will want to select the cart that offers the functionality you are looking for.

You will want to look for a cart that offers merchant tools, supports many payment options, offers configuration for shipping and taxes, offers real-time statistics and reporting, and has the appropriate security.

You will also want to select a shopping cart that is compatible with your payment gateway. This will illuminate the cost associated with integrating your shopping cart and merchant account.

Step 3

Choose your e-commerce platform. There are a ton of options out there, so before you choose you should sit down and decide exactly what features you do and do not want in an online store. There are some main types of sites you can choose from:

- If you're looking for something which requires low maintenance and don't want to deal with the hassle of supplying and shipping your own inventory there are numerous large websites (such as Amazon) that will let you set up a more specialized store selling their products for a

commission.
- If you want to supply your own inventory and you're willing to pay a monthly fee, Yahoo! Merchant Solutions is the most popular route. It has a ton of features and starts at about $40 a month plus a set up fee of $50 and transaction fees at around 1.5%.
- If you are going to pay a monthly fee, make sure to do a lot of research first. Make sure the site is easy to use and organize, because if you decide you want to switch sites later, you'll have wasted that money. Also, when choosing a site with a transaction fee, consider your profit margins, as they are based on total price of the item, not your net profit.
- If you want to supply your own inventory and don't want to pay a monthly fee, or you want to get your feet wet before committing a monthly program, you should look for a site that 100% free (no monthly fees, transactions fees or hidden charges), and has an upgrade option.

This way, you can get your store up and running, earn some profits, and get used to the site before deciding if you want to pay for extra features. It's win-win because if you decide you never want to pay for it, you don't have to, and if you decide you need the extra features you don't have to go through the giant headache of moving stores.

An example of this kind of site is MiiDuu.com, which is completely free for a standard store and about $30 a month for a pro store. The standard store is already feature rich and very user friendly, so it's a great entryway into e-commerce.

Step 4

Set up your store. This is where the work comes in. You'll need to get all of your details together and sit down and fill out all of the necessary information. All of the above mentioned sites are easy to use and don't require much tech savvy.

Enter all your products, payment options, shipping options, applicable taxes, etc. first. Check and double check them; it doesn't matter how good your site looks if the customers can't use it. That being said, it is extremely important how your site looks. Obviously, you need to make sure it is professional and aesthetically pleasing, however, you also want to make sure it is easy to navigate and find products.

You should organize all of your products into intuitive categories and sub categories. If your hosting site has "featured products" or "best selling products" options, you should set those up as well. You should visit your store front often and try to navigate yourself frequently during the set up process.

Having friends and family test it out can also be quite helpful in figuring out any problems with your layout or checkout process.

Step 5

Set up your payment gateway. The payment gateway is the application that connects your website shopping cart to your merchant account. The job of the payment gateway is to collect the credit card information from the customer, encrypt it and sent it to the merchant account for processing.

When selecting a payment gateway you should select one that is compatible with your shopping cart, offers good pricing and has the ability to facilitates all payment functions (payments, voids, refunds, etc.). It should offer robust fraud protection, be PCI compliant and have an interface for you to run reports on your sales.

Step 6

Select a merchant account. The merchant account's job is to authorize the card that is being used for payment and then deposit those authorized transactions into your bank account. It's important to choose a merchant account that offers good rates on processing, has 24 hours turn around on settled transactions, offers live customer support, has high approval rates and low merchant attrition. You want a processor that stands behind your account and consults you as to the very best way to set up your e-commerce website.

Step 7

Market your store. There are a lot of stores out there, so make sure to market, market, and market. An online store is not like a physical store where people will just pass by on their way to other things even if you aren't advertising.

You will need to make sure to use a lot of keywords in your store text and create many back links (links to your store from other sites) in order to drum up traffic and move your way up the search engine results.

First you should research keywords by searching for them in Google or Yahoo! or your search engine of choice and gauging the popularity of the keyword. If it gets millions of hits in 0.25 seconds, it's going to be very hard to climb up the results and get your store seen. At the same time, if it gets 4 hits, odds are you aren't going to drum up much business that way either, so be sure to choose a happy medium.

Once you choose your keywords, be sure to use them! Blogging is a great way to do this, especially if you are posting relevant, interesting posts and not just advertisements. For example, if you have a vintage book store, you might have a blog where you discuss interesting passages or tidbits or articles about vintage books with links back to your store.

Make sure to use your target keywords in your blog frequently. You'll also want to get as many subscribers as possible and try to get as many people as possible to link back to you.

Step 8

Maintain your site. Now that you have your store all set up and have a steady stream of customers, make sure to keep it maintained! You want your customers to keep coming back, so update your inventory and featured products regularly. You'll also want to update your keywords to make them more effective.

To do this, sign up for a service such as Google Analytics so you can see what people searched to get to your site. From there you can see which keywords are working and which ones aren't and tweak your keywords accordingly!

New Words

crucial	*adj.*	决定性的，关键性的，极其显要的
element	*n.*	元素
monumental	*adj.*	纪念碑的，纪念物的，不朽的，非常的
narrow	*v.*	收缩，缩小，窄化，变窄
	adj.	狭小的，窄的
vintage	*adj.*	古老的，最佳的，过时的
ghost	*n.*	鬼，幽灵
serious	*adj.*	严肃的，认真的，严重的
construct	*v.*	构成，修建，建造，创立
tweak	*v.*	编织
market	*v.*	推销
	n.	市场
commercially	*adv.*	商业地，贸易地
available	*adj.*	可获得的，有空的，可购得的，能找到的
offer	*v.*	提供
functionality	*n.*	功能性
statistic	*adj.*	统计的，统计学的
	n.	统计量
appropriate	*adj.*	适当的
gateway	*n.*	门，通路，网关
illuminate	*v.*	阐明，说明
platform	*n.*	平台
hassle	*n.*	激战
	v.	争论；与……争辩
numerous	*adj.*	数不清的，很多的，许多的
commission	*n.*	委托，代办(权)，代理(权)
route	*n.*	途径，路线，路程，通道
organize	*v.*	组织
switch	*v.*	转换，转变
commit	*v.*	犯罪，做错事，把……托付给；保证
earn	*v.*	赚得，获得
giant	*adj.*	巨大的，特大的，伟大的
	n.	伟人，巨人
entryway	*n.*	入口通道
aesthetically	*adv.*	审美地，美学观点上地
intuitive	*adj.*	直觉的，直观的
sub	*n.*	子

layout	*n.*	规划，设计，布局
checkout	*v.*	检查，检验，校验
encrypt	*v.*	加密，将……译成密码
refund	*v.*	退款，退还，偿还
	n.	退款，偿还额
interface	*n.*	界面，接口
compliant	*adj.*	兼容的，适应的
authorize	*v.*	审定，授权，批准，委托
deposit	*v.*	存放
	n.	存款，押金，保证金
settled	*adj.*	结算的
keyword	*n.*	关键字
gauge	*v.*	测量，测定
hit	*n.*	点击
tidbit	*n.*	(=titbit)珍闻，小栏报道
blog	*n.*	博客，网志
	v.	维护网志
steady	*adj.*	稳固的，稳定的
	v.	（使）稳定，（使）稳固

Phrases

in the age of	在……时代
crucial element	关键元素
in no time	立刻，马上，很快
shopping cart	购物车
look for	寻找，期待
merchant tool	商家获取利益的工具
payment option	支付选项
be compatible with	适合，一致
payment gateway	支付网关
associated with	与……有关
specialized store	专卖店
a ton of	许多，大量
set up fee	开设费，设立费，设置费
transaction fee	交易费
make sure	确保，务必，务请
profit margin	利润空间，利润率
be based on	基于

net profit	净利，纯利
get one's feet wet	着手，动手，亲自参加
hidden charge	隐藏的费用
upgrade option	升级选项
get used to	习惯
pay for	支付
extra feature	额外功能
go through	遭受，经历
pro store	专业店
standard store	标准店
fill out	填写
store front	店面；门店销售系统
figure out	解决，断定，领会到
approval rate	支持率
stand behind	后援，做后盾
drum up	招徕，竭力争取，兜揽(生意)
back link	反向链接
search engine	搜索引擎
climb up	向上爬，攀登
happy medium	折中办法

Abbreviations

PCI (Peripheral Component Interconnect)　　外部设备互连

Exercises

[Ex. 1]　Answer the following questions according to the text.

1. What should you do when you decide what you are selling?
2. What does the shopping cart software do?
3. What should you do before you choose your e-commerce platform?
4. What should you do when choosing a site with a transaction fee? Why?
5. If you want to supply your own inventory and don't want to pay a monthly fee, what should you do?
6. What should your site be?
7. What is the payment gateway? What is its job?
8. What is the merchant account's job?
9. What will you need to do in order to drum up traffic and move your way up the search engine results?
10. What is the last step to get your store up and running in no time?

[Ex. 2]   Translate the following terms or phrases from English into Chinese and vice versa.

1. back link
2. net profit
3. payment gateway
4. pro store
5. search engine
6. 专卖店
7. 交易费
8. 购物车
9. 加密，将……译成密码
10. 兼容的，适应的

[Ex. 3]   Translate the following passage into Chinese.

The 7 E-commerce Business Structures

Not all e-commerce businesses are the same, and not all successful e-commerce businesses are the same. However, all the successful ones do fit into similar moulds.

By consciously building your business based on one of these structures, you will build a better business faster.

The 7 e-commerce business structures were created based on wide experience of e-commerce businesses. Whichever one you have fundamentally influences every facet of your business, so if you want to succeed fast you need to pick one and stick to it.

1) Online Only—the only way to see the products is online.

2) Mail Order—a transactional website plus a printed catalogue, and possibly one or two physical stores.

3) Big Bricks and Clicks—lots of physical stores and an e-commerce website.

4) Boutique Bricks and Clicks—just one or two physical locations plus the e-commerce website.

5) Mainstream PiggyBack—using the likes of Amazon or eBay to market the products, with no website of their own.

6) Niche PiggyBack—where sellers of similar products come together to market more easily, usually retaining their own blog or e-commerce site elsewhere, too. The craft world (Etsy, Folksy), hotels (hotels.com, laterooms.com), jewellery (Boticca), and books (abebooks.co.uk) are just a handful of examples.

7) Full Multichannel—Using multiple shops, catalogues, and e-commerce—by far the most complex and most difficult to achieve and run (e.g. Bravissimo, Crew Clothing, Next).

If your e-commerce business is to be successful it needs to fit into one of these seven structures. Over the years it may progress between them—so you may start on a Niche PiggyBack structure, move to an Online Only, and finally a Boutique Bricks and Clicks.

[Ex. 4]   Fill in the blanks with the words given below.

| related | rely | engine | displayed | layout |
| present | helps | buying | separate | spread |

A Beginner's Guide to Creating an E-commerce Site Structure

Ensuring a site is structured correctly is paramount to the performance of all good e-commerce campaigns. While the structure of a website is critical to aiding and influencing a customer's ___1___ behaviour, it is also integral to achieving greater levels of traffic and exposure through SEO efforts.

A well-structured website enables search ___2___ spiders to crawl it more efficiently and understand its content more thoroughly, consequently ranking your site as accurately as possible. There are three areas which are key to creating the optimal site structure: category/sub-categories, products and URLs.

1. Category/Sub-Category

For any e-commerce website, it is essential to organise the category structure in a way that is clear, concise and ultimately makes sense. An ideal e-commerce URL structure should look something like this:

Domain.com/category/

Domain.com/category/sub-category/

The above ___3___ reflects and adheres to the consumer journey, while also making sure that search engines can appreciate this narrowing of product selections. Combined with an intuitive navigation that lends itself to good internal linking, this URL structure can help search engines to accurately ___4___ the domain authority throughout the site.

2. Products

Of course, it follows suit that all individual products live within the sub-categories of the store. If we continue the logic above, it would make perfect sense for the URL structure for products to look like this:

Domain.com/category/sub-category/product

However, a difficulty arises when a product exists in more than one category. If it does, there is the potential for two ___5___ URLs that contain the exact same content and this ultimately leads to duplicate content problems, so it is best to be avoided.

If this is the case, the best solution is to house the products on the top level, like this:

Domain.com/product.html

This ensures search engines will only index one URL with this content. However, this really is dependent upon the e-commerce CMS system you're using, and whether or not products can or will be ___6___ in multiple categories, so keep this in mind.

3. URLs

The above shows the correct way in which URLs should be formatted with regards to category/sub-categories and products.

Please note that for category/sub-category URLs the .html suffix has been removed from the end of the URL. This can help to further cement the silo structuring of the ___7___ categories, and help search engines in understanding the relationship between the parent and child categories, as below:

Domain.com/category/ is the parent URL structure for these child URLs: Domain.com/category/sub-category/.

Removal of the .html suffix ___8___ this silo structure and the distribution of authority/equity.

It is also key that URLs could not be seen by search engines as spammy, and that keywords are not ___9___ just for the sake of SEO. This means that repeated and unnecessary keywords should be removed.

Domain.com/shoes/red-shoes/ should be renamed Domain.com/shoes/red/ so that search engines do not see the site as over-optimised.

Increase Your Organic Visibility

Not all of us are lucky enough to have a domain authority big enough to drive traffic despite poor site structure (you know who you are…), and for those smaller brands that ___10___ on great content the correct implementation is imperative for the search engine bots and users to effectively see your hard work.

Whether you can implement the correct structure before the site goes live or make the changes retrospectively, working to the above is sure to improve your visibility in the major search engines.

Text B

Website Navigation and Its Impact on E-commerce

Quality website navigation is the skeletal structure of any website. In many ways, it's the most important part of a site's design. Generally, navigation consists of links that lead users to various website sections. Most commonly placed across the page header or along a side head, site navigation shows users how to use the site, what it does and where they can find what they're looking for.

扫一扫，听课文

Website navigation describes both the structure of a website and the act of navigating by the user. The cleaner and clearer the structure, the better the user's experience. Quality user experience without confusion or frustration keeps users on a website longer, which in turn helps conversion rates and improves search engine optimization (SEO).

1. Navigation Best Practices

There have been many different ways to present the user with a website's navigation, though not all of them are optimal for user experience or SEO. What they all share in common is placement:

As a rule, the site navigation (also known as the main navigation) appears on (nearly) every page of the site, unchanged and constant. It is both the anchor and the map for the user.

2. Text Links

Use descriptive words or phrases in your website's main navigation. This has been the standard way to present site navigation since the first commercial Web browsers were released, and even with all the design tricks that have been invented since, it is still the best. Text is easy for Web designers to update, comprehensible to users and visible to search engines.

Many sites still use dropdown menus (users place their mouse over a menu item and another menu is exposed) in their main navigation, although the practice has tailed off in recent years as developers understand the relationship between internal linking and SEO.

Dropdown menus are invisible to search engines. Similar to the way a user reads, comprehends and follows a text link, search engines "crawl" a website. The more links that lead to and out of a given page, the more importance and higher ranking the engine gives to that page. By using dropdown menus, all that potential SEO is lost.

3. Descriptive Titles

Closely related to simple text navigation is giving those navigational links strong descriptive names. Strong names tell users exactly what they'll find when they click a link, set the tone of a website and produce good keyword associations for search engines.

For example, many websites have "About" or "What we do" pages. Those labels mean nothing to either the audience or a search engine. Instead, they come up with a descriptive keyword for the navigational link. Instead of "About us", a clothing store might say "Our fashion philosophy", or a gardening supply store might say "Dig all the dirt on us".

4. Good Structure

Keep the main navigation as simple as possible. Human mind is not capable of holding so many items at once. It's best to have only a few top-level menu items. The optimal number of main menu items is three to seven. If too many, the users' eyes will glaze over, and they'll find some other place to shop.

Take a clothing store for example. The cleanest main navigation would simply be "Men" "Women" and "Children". Each of these big categories will have their own sub-categories, branching out like a tree, but no matter how complicated the branching becomes, users will always have an easy way back to the main trunk.

There are SEO benefits to having fewer navigation items, as well. A page's rank depends on many factors, but two of the most important are the number of links to and from a page and the number of visits a page gets. The less scattered your navigation, the more hits your main category pages will receive, the better their search engine visibility.

Good structure begins early in the website's design stage well before colors, fonts and layout are decided. Mapping out every possible page on a website and placing them in a logical order does more to help users navigate your site than anything else you can do.

5. Breadcrumbs[1]

Letting a website's branches get too complicated is its own pitfall, however. Website navigation should be shallow, meaning that users don't have to make too many clicks in order to find what they want. Too many clicks can become frustrating and confusing.

Using navigational breadcrumbs is one way to keep users from getting lost. Breadcrumbs are automatically generated series of links, usually at the top of the page beneath the main navigation, which shows the users a list of the links that they took in order to get to the present page. The user can click on any of the breadcrumb links to return to a higher-level page.

Breadcrumbs serve several purposes. They show the user that they are still in the correct section. They give the user an easy way to get back to higher level categories if they wish to look at different items. They create more links between pages for improved SEO.

Breadcrumbs are especially useful for e-commerce sites, which typically have a few clicks to get from general categories to product pages.

6. Sitemaps

Sitemaps aren't really for users anymore. It is a dedicated page that lists every page on a website, usually in hierarchical order. Most content management systems now have applications that automatically generate and update sitemap pages, and although most users will never see it, there is usually an unobtrusive link to it somewhere in a website's footer.

The reason that sites still have sitemaps has everything to do with SEO. Search engines actively look for sitemaps so they can crawl the rest of the site more efficiently. No matter what way is used, to get the search engine's attention is the ultimate goal.

Website navigation can't be done haphazardly. It is how the public and search engines interact with your site. From clear, top-level navigation to ample linking between pages, users must know where they are at all times. It takes a great deal of up front planning to do it right. And as your website grows, you need to revisit your navigation and site structure periodically to keep it from becoming a tangle. Users come and go pretty quickly on the Internet. Keeping things simple and clear will keep them on your site longer and boost your site's visibility in the future.

✍ New Words

skeletal	*adj.*	骨骼的
confusion	*n.*	混乱，混淆
frustration	*n.*	挫败，挫折，受挫
unchanged	*adj.*	无变化的，未改变的
anchor	*n.*	锚
	v.	抛锚，锚定
trick	*n.*	窍门，诀窍

---

1 面包屑导航(Breadcrumb Navigation)这个概念来自童话故事"汉泽尔和格雷特尔"。当汉泽尔和格雷特尔穿过森林时，在沿途走过的地方都撒下了面包屑，让这些面包屑来帮助他们找到回家的路。所以，面包屑导航的作用是告诉访问者他们目前在网站中的位置以及如何返回。

comprehensible	adj.	可理解的，易于了解的
visible	adj.	看得见的，明显的，显著的
	n.	可见物
mouse	n.	鼠标器
menu	n.	菜单
invisible	adj.	看不见的，无形的
comprehend	v.	领会，理解，包括(包含)，由……组成
crawl	v.	爬行，蠕动，缓慢地行进
	n.	爬行
click	v.	点击
	n.	滴答声
label	n.	标签，签条，商标，标志
	v.	贴标签于，指……为，分类，标注
gardening	n.	园艺，造园
rank	n.	排名，等级
scattered	adj.	离散的，分散的
visibility	n.	可见度，可见性，明显度
pitfall	n.	缺陷
shallow	adj.	浅的，浅薄的，表面的，皮毛的
sitemap	n.	网站地图
hierarchical	adj.	分等级的
unobtrusive	adj.	不突出的，不引人注目的
footer	n.	页脚
haphazard	n.	偶然，偶然事件
	adj.	偶然的，随便的
	adv.	偶然地
periodically	adv.	周期性地，定时性地
tangle	n.	混乱状态
	v.	处于混乱状态

Phrases

in many ways	在许多方面
dropdown menu	下拉式菜单
menu item	菜单项
tail off	缩小，变少
internal linking	内部链接
be capable of	能够
top-level menu	顶层菜单
glaze over	呆滞

branch out	长出枝条，扩展范围
map out	筹划，安排，制订
keep from	阻止，抑制
get lost	迷路
content management system	内容管理系统

Exercises

[Ex. 5]   Fill in the following blanks according to the text.

1. Generally, navigation consists of links that lead users to _____.

2. Site navigation is most commonly placed _____ or _____. It shows users how to _____, what it does and _____.

3. As a rule, the site navigation, which is also known as _____, appears on (nearly) every page of the site, _____. It is _____.

4. Many sites still use _____ in their main navigation, although the practice has tailed off in recent years as developers understand the relationship _____.

5. Strong names tell users _____ when they click a link, _____ and _____ for search engines.

6. The optimal number of main menu items is _____. If too many, the users' eyes _____, and they'll _____.

7. A page's rank depends on many factors, but two of the most important are _____ and _____.

8. _____ and _____ does more to help users navigate your site than anything else you can do.

9. Breadcrumbs are_____, usually at the top of the page beneath the main navigation, which shows the users a list of the links that they take in order to _____.

10. Most content management systems now have applications that automatically generate and update _____. The reason that sites still have sitemaps has everything to do with _____. Search engines actively look for sitemaps so they can _____.

Reading Material

Shopping Cart Software

In online marketing, a shopping cart is a piece of e-commerce software on a web server that allows visitors to an Internet site to select items for eventual[1] purchase, analogous to the American English term "shopping cart". In British English, it is generally known as[2] a shopping basket[3],

---

1 eventual   *adj*.   最后的，结局的
2 be known as   被认为是
3 shopping basket   购物篮

almost exclusively shortened on websites to "basket".

The software allows online shopping customers to accumulate[1] a list of items for purchase, described metaphorically[2] as "placing items in the shopping cart" or "add to cart". Upon checkout, the software typically calculates a total for the order, including shipping and handling (i.e., postage and packing[3]) charges and the associated taxes, as applicable.

1. History

The development of web shop systems took place right after the Internet became a mass medium. This was a result of the launch of the browser Mosaic in 1993 and Netscape in 1994. It created an environment in which web shops were possible. The Internet, therefore, acted as the key infrastructure developments that contributed to the rapid diffusion of the e-commerce, which is a subset[4] of e-business that describes all computer-aided business transactions. In 1998 a total of 11 e-business models were observed, one of which was the e-shop business model for a B2C business—also called the "online shop". The two terms "online shop" and "electronic shop or e-shop" are used interchangeably[5]. The term "online shopping" was invented much earlier in 1984. For example, TV shopping often used the term before the popularity[6] of the online method. Today the term primarily refers to the B2C transactional business model. In order to enable online shopping a software system is needed. Since online shopping in the context of the B2C business model became broadly available to the end consumer, internet-based online shops evolved.

For online shopping systems in this context, the narrower term "web shop" is used. No term has become solidly established for a B2C e-commerce software system. Whereas in the German-speaking region terms such as "web shop software" or "online shop software" are used, the term "shopping cart software" has become established in the United States.

2. Technical Definition

These applications typically provide a means of capturing a client's payment information, but in the case of a credit card they rely on the software module of the secure gateway provider, in conjunction with the secure payment gateway, in order to conduct secure credit card transactions online.

Some setup must be done in the HTML code of the website, and the shopping cart software must be installed on the server which hosts the site, or on the secure server which accepts sensitive ordering information. E-shopping carts are usually implemented using HTTP cookies[7] or query strings[8]. In most server-based implementations, however, data related to the shopping cart is kept in the session[9] object and is accessed and manipulated on the fly, as the user selects different items

---

1 accumulate   v. 积聚,堆积

2 metaphorically   adv. 隐喻性地,比喻性地

3 packing   v. 包装 n. 包装

4 subset   n. 子集

5 interchangeably   adv. 可交替地

6 popularity   n. 普及,流行

7 cookie   cookie 是当你访问某个站点时,随某个 HTML 网页发送到你的浏览器中的一小段信息。

8 string   n. 串

9 session   n. 对话

from the cart. Later at the process of finalizing[1] the transaction, the information is accessed and an order is generated against the selected item thus clearing the shopping cart.

Although the most simple shopping carts strictly allow for an item to be added to a basket to start a checkout process (e.g., the free PayPal shopping cart), most shopping cart software provides additional features that an Internet merchant uses to fully manage an online store. Data (products, categories, discounts, orders, customers, etc.) is normally stored in a database and accessed in real time by the software.

Shopping cart software is also known as e-commerce software, e-store software, online store software or storefront software and online shop.

3. Components[2]

Storefront: the area of the Web store that is accessed by visitors to the online shop. Category, product, and other pages (e.g., search, bestsellers, etc.) are dynamically generated by the software based on the information saved in the store database. The look of the storefront can normally be changed by the store owner so that it merges with the rest of the web site (i.e., with the pages not controlled by the shopping cart software in use on the store).

Administration: the area of the Web store that is accessed by the merchant to manage the online shop. The amount of store management features changes depending on the sophistication of the shopping cart software chosen by the merchant, but in general a store manager is able to add and edit products, categories, discounts, shipping and payment settings, etc. Order management features are also included in many shopping cart programs. The administration area can be:

- Web-based (accessed through a web browser);
- Desktop-based (a desktop application that runs on the user's computer and then transfers changes to the storefront component).

4. Types

Shopping cart software can be generally categorized into three types of e-commerce software:

1) Open source software. The software is released under an open source licence[3] and is very often free of charge[4]. The merchant has to host the software with a Web hosting service. It allows users to access and modify the source code of the entire online store.

2) Licensed software. The software is downloaded and then installed on a Web server. This is most often associated with a one-time fee[5]. The main advantages of this option are that the merchant owns a license and therefore can host it on any web server that meets the server requirements.

3) Hosted service. The software is never downloaded, but rather is provided by a hosted service provider and is generally paid for on a monthly or annual basis. It is also known as the Application

---

1 finalize   v.   完成，把……最后定下来，定案
2 component   n.   成分，部件   adj.   组成的，构成的
3 licence   n.   执照，许可证，特许   v.   许可，特许，认可，发给执照
4 free of charge   免费
5 one-time fee   一次性收费

Service Provider (ASP)[1] software model. Some of these services also charge a percentage of sales in addition to the monthly fee. This model often has predefined templates that a user can choose from to customize[2] their look and feel. Predefined[3] templates limit how much users can modify or customize the software with the advantage of having the vendor continuously keep the software up to date for security patches as well as adding new features.

5. PCI Compliance

The PCI security standards are a blanket of regulations set in place to safeguard payment account data security. The council that develops and monitors these regulations is composed of[4] the leading providers in the payment industry: American Express, Discover Financial Services, JCB International, MasterCard Worldwide, and Visa Inc. Essentially, they define the best practices for storing, transmitting, and handling of sensitive information over the Internet.

Visa Inc. can hold shopping cart software providers responsible for liability that may occur as a result of non-compliance to Visa's regulations[5]. For this reason, Visa Inc. may require that online merchants use shopping cart software providers from their list of PCI DSS[6]—validated service providers.

参考译文

如何建立电子商务网站

在互联网时代，电子商务吸引着越来越多的客户。网上商店正在成为所有商业计划的关键因素，但建立一个网上商店可能是一个巨大的任务。本文将提供一些简单的步骤，让你建立商店并立即运行。

步骤1

决定你要卖什么。你应该考虑缩小你的范围，以捕捉一个缝隙市场，但不要狭窄到很难找到客户。例如，如果你想卖书，卖古旧书可能是一个更好的选择。另一方面，只卖17世纪的鬼故事书可能不会有前途。如果你认真对待你的网上商店，就可能要花很多时间来构建和调整网站，尤其是推销网站，所以要选择你有兴趣的东西去卖。

步骤2

选择购物车。购物车软件让你能在互联网上销售产品和服务。有许多商业购物车可供选择。你需要选择能够提供你所需的功能的购物车。

你需要寻找一个这样的购物车：可以提供商家工具，支持多种付款选项，能够处理运费和税收、提供实时统计和报告并具有适当的安全性。

---

1 application service provider (ASP)　应用服务提供者
2 customize　*v.* 定制，用户化
3 predefine　*adj.* 预定义的
4 be composed of　由……组成
5 regulation　*n.* 规则，规章；调节，校准
6 PCI DSS (Payment Card Industry Data Security Standard)　付费卡行业数据安全标准

你还需要选择与你的付款网关兼容的购物车。这将显示与购物车和商家账户相关的费用。

步骤 3

选择你的电子商务平台。现在有很多选项，所以在你选择之前，你应该坐下来，决定你的网上商店确实需要和不需要的功能。可以选择的网站主要有以下几类：

- 如果你正在寻找需要低维护的东西，并且不想处理供货和运送自己库存的麻烦，有许多大型网站（如亚马逊）允许你建立更专业的商店出售他们的产品，但他们收取佣金。
- 如果你想卖自己的库存，并愿意按月付费，那么雅虎商人的解决方案是最流行的办法。它有很多功能，约每月 40 美元的基本费加 50 美元的设置费，以及约 1.5％的交易费。
- 如果你要支付月费，请务必提前做大量的研究。确保网站易于使用和组织，因为如果决定后又要换网站，就会浪费这笔钱。此外，在选择具有交易费用的网站时，请考虑你的利润率，因为它们是基于项目的总价格而不是净利润。
- 如果你想提供自己的库存，不想支付每月费用，或者你想在进行每月计划之前先探探路，你应该寻找一个 100％免费的网站（没有月费、交易费或隐藏费用），并可以选择升级。

这样，可以开始运行你的商店，赚取利润，并逐渐习惯该网站，然后再决定是否要购买额外的功能。它是双赢的，因为如果你不想买就不必买。如果你决定需要额外的功能，迁移商店就很容易。

MiiDuu.com 是此类网站的一个范例，它是完全免费的标准商店和约 30 美元一个月的专卖店。标准商店已经具备丰富的功能，也颇为用户友好，所以它是进入电子商务的一个很好的入口。

步骤 4

设置你的商店。这是工作的地方。你需要聚拢所有的细节，坐下来认真填写所有必要的信息。所有上述网站都易于使用，并且不需要太精通技术。

首先输入所有产品、付款选项、运费选项及适用税金等。检查再检查。如果客户不能使用你的网站，那么它看起来多好也没用。话虽如此，网站展现还是非常重要的。显然，需要确保其专业和美观，但是，也要确保易于浏览和查找产品。

应该将所有产品组织成直观的类别和子类别。如果你的托管网站有"特色产品"或"最畅销产品"选项，应该设置它们。你应该经常访问你的店面，并在设置过程中经常导航到你的商店。

让朋友和家人测试它可以非常有助于弄清楚布局或检查过程中遇到的任何问题。

步骤 5

设置你的支付网关。支付网关是把网站购物车连接到商家账户的应用程序。支付网关的工作是从客户处收集信用卡信息，对其加密并发送到商家账户进行处理。

选择支付网关时，应选择与购物车兼容、提供良好的价格并且提供各种付款功能（付款、空缺、退款等）的付款网关。它应该提供强大的欺诈保护、与 PCI 兼容并有提供销售报告的接口。

步骤 6

选择商家账户。商家账户的工作是批准付款卡，然后将这些批准的交易存入你的银行账户。重要的是选择一个商业账户：提供好的处理费率、进行 24h 结算交易、提供实时客户支持、认可度高和商业损耗低。需要一个处理机支持你的账户，并为你提供咨询，以最佳方式设置你的电子商务网站。

步骤 7

推销你的商店。商店很多，所以必须推销、推销、推销。网上商店与实体店不一样，人们只要路过就能看到实体店，而你不做广告就没人知道你的网上商店。

需要确保在网上商店文字中使用大量关键字，并创建许多反向链接（从其他网站到你的商店的链接），以增加流量并提高在搜索引擎结果上的排名。

首先，应该通过在谷歌或雅虎或你选择的搜索引擎中搜索关键字，并衡量关键字的受欢迎程度来研究关键字。如果它在 0.25s 内获得数百万的受欢迎的关键词，那么要提升结果并让人们看到你的商店是很难的。同时，如果它搜索到 4 个关键词，你也不会有很多的业务。所以一定要选择一个折中方法。

一旦选择了关键字，请务必使用它们！发表博客文章是一个很好的方式，特别是当你发布相关的、有趣的帖子，而不只是广告时。例如，如果你有一个古旧书店，你可能同时有一个博客，你可以在那里讨论古旧书籍中有趣的段落或一些花边新闻或与其相关的文章，并链接到你的网上商店中。

务必经常在你的博客中使用目标关键字。还要力求获得尽可能多的订阅者，并尝试尽可能多的人来链接到你的网站。

步骤 8

维护你的网站。现在你已经建好了你的网上商店并有了稳定的客户流，一定要维护好它！如果你希望客户不断回访，就请定期更新存货和特色产品。你还需要更新关键字，使其更有效。

为此，请注册 Google Analytics 等服务，以便查看哪些客户搜索过你的网站。从那里，你可以看出哪些关键字有用、哪些没用，并相应地调整你的关键字！

Unit 5

Text A

Five Ways to Market Your E-commerce Site

We're starting to hear more and more terms like "growth hacking"[1] in the e-commerce industry, and I for one don't really care for it. As any seasoned veteran of e-commerce will tell you, you need sustainable, long term marketing plans in place—not short term "growth hacks". There's the old analogy of the tortoise and the hare—that "slow and steady wins the race", and the same is true in business, particularly e-commerce.

This article is aimed at any small business owner in the e-commerce sector—whether you're just starting out, or you're looking for more effective ways to market your e-commerce site. The marketing techniques I'll discuss in this article can all be done yourself.

1. Social Media

Most big brands and companies out there appear to have a great deal of "love" for social media. In private, however, a lot of these companies will complain there's very little ROI from social media. I tend to disagree—there's no foolproof way of calculating overall ROI from social media. To that end, it's impossible to say how good or bad the ROI actually is. If it was that bad and social media marketing campaigns were akin to throwing money down the drain, I doubt you'd see quite as many companies (big and small) taking it so seriously.

You don't have to spend hours on end each day in order to promote your business via social media; some of the best campaigns are executed in a little under an hour each day. You must first select the platforms you'll use—the best platforms for e-commerce businesses tend to be Facebook, Google+, Pinterest and Twitter.

It's then just a case of finding interesting, industry-related news and trends to share and building a following. Of course you should definitely share links to your website and feature specific

---

1 Growth hacking is a process of rapid experimentation across marketing channels and product development to identify the most effective, efficient ways to grow a business. Growth hacking refers to a set of both conventional and unconventional marketing experiments that lead to growth of a business. Growth hackers are marketers, engineers and product managers that specifically focus on building and engaging the user base of a business. Growth hackers often focus on low-cost alternatives to traditional marketing, e.g. using social media, viral marketing or targeted advertising instead of buying advertising through more traditional media such as radio, newspaper, and television.

products, but just remember to keep these few and far between. On my own social media campaigns I work to a ratio of 80/20—that's 80% topical industry news, and 20% plugging my site or products. If you just plug your site or products in every status update or tweet, you'll find it very hard to engage fans and stoke interaction, which is the ultimate goal on social media.

2. PPC

PPC is a very general term—it stands for pay per click. There are lots of different components involved in PPC, from search network advertising to retargeting, through to Google Product Listing Ads[1] (PLAs). PPC has come a long way over the last few years, and it's a really good way to advertise an e-commerce website in a sustainable, profitable manner. You'll hear plenty of naysayers exclaiming that "PPC isn't profitable"— but it can be for most people. You can't simply throw a campaign online and hope for it to make lots of money from day one. If you could do that then everyone would be at it. With PPC you have to make a commitment to testing and bettering your campaigns on an on-going basis. Only when you make this commitment will you really start to reap the rewards that PPC has to offer.

At the present time, the best PPC options out there are Google PLAs and retargeting. Although traditional text ads definitely still work well both on the search and display networks, PLAs and retargeting are yielding by far the best (and most profitable) results for my e-commerce websites at the present time. PLAs are specifically for e-commerce websites—they present searchers with a picture of the item they're looking for in the SERPS[2]. The CPC tends to be lower than search text ads, whilst the conversion rate is higher. There are various reasons for this, including the fact that buyers are "qualified" before clicking on PLAs—hey can see a picture of the item, they can see the name of the merchant and they can also see the price. If they know all of that information and they proceed to click through, there's a high chance they'll convert.

Retargeting is becoming increasingly popular—but it's nothing new. If you've ever wondered why you're bombarded with display network ads for websites you've previously visited, retargeting is the answer! If ad networks see a cookie from a specific website, they can target ads from that website to you. Retargeted traffic tends to be fairly cheap but the conversion rates are exponentially higher than other, standard traffic garnered from the display network. Traditionally it was difficult to set up retargeting campaigns, but now there are neat tools like AdRoll that make it really easy to get started.

Good old search text ads and image display ads still work, but if you want a sustainable,

---

1 Product Listing Ads, or PLAs, are a form of paid advertising using Google AdWords and the Google Merchant Center. The ads appear with a product image, the name of the product, the price of the product, and the retailer offering the product.

2 A search engine results page (SERP) is the page displayed by a search engine in response to a query by a searcher. The main component of the SERP is the listing of results that are returned by the search engine in response to a keyword query, although the page may also contain other results such as advertisements.

The results are of two general types, organic (i.e., retrieved by the search engine's algorithm) and sponsored (i.e., advertisements). The results are normally ranked by relevance to the query. Each result displayed on the SERP normally includes a title, a link that points to the actual page on the Web and a short description showing where the keywords have matched content within the page for organic results. For sponsored results, the advertiser chooses what to display.

81

profitable e-commerce website you can't simply work with these two "easy options". You've really got to push the boat out and work with PLAs and retargeting too. You've also got to go beyond just Google AdWords—look at other PPC networks to market on (Bing Ads, Facebook Ads and Twitter are just a few you should consider).

3. PR

I've heard people reciting ridiculous claims including "PR is the new SEO". PR basically involves generating a buzz around your brand or website; this is typically done via getting your website in newspapers, on the TV, on popular niche blogs and so on. In some niches PR is a great way of building a reputation—it's a great way to market to your target audience.

Next time you open the newspaper and see a review of a product, chances are that product has been gifted to the newspaper by the brand. In return they get exposure for their product off the back of the review (good or bad). PR is deadly simple but majorly effective—the problem with PR is working out exactly where to start. It can seem daunting and pointless trying to contact random people from the TV or newspapers to see if they want to review your products.

If you're completely new to the world of PR, take my advice and try contacting a few blog owners in your industry to see if they'd be happy to review your products or website in a post. Some may say no, some won't reply to your e-mail, but almost certainly some will respond to you. Simply by having your website featured in a post on a popular blog, you can drive thousands of targeted visitors to your e-commerce site. Once you've mastered the art of contacting bloggers for PR purposes, you can set your sights on journalists and other outlets like newspapers and TV. Although PR is essentially free, it's a time consuming exercise. It takes time to nurture relationships in the PR industry. You won't have an awesome PR campaign overnight.

It's impossible to discuss the ins and outs of television and print media PR in this article, but by releasing topical, factual press releases when there has been a development with your company, you'll almost certainly get requests from journalists looking for further information, and possibly even review products for them to feature.

4. Radio Advertising

I could quite easily have titled this section "offline advertising", but I decided that would have been a bit too vague. Instead I've decided to home in on radio advertising. It's very effective indeed, especially on smaller, local radio stations. Sometimes a short ad slot can cost sub $200, whilst your ad will reach thousands of listeners.

Although not in the e-commerce industry, I know of individuals in the insurance niche having major success with radio advertising. The cost per lead in some insurance niches can be upwards of $200 via marketing methods like PPC. So if these people can pay $200 for an ad slot on the radio and pull in just one or two leads, they're able to see better results via offline marketing than they can via PPC.

Radio advertising is overlooked by lots of e-commerce businesses out there. Of course there are rules and best practices you should follow. Radio advertising isn't profitable all year round, and if you pay for advertising late night, not many people will be exposed to your ad. It's important to get your timing right and of course the advert itself, but with a little trial and error radio advertising can be hugely effective for websites, including e-commerce websites.

5. Multichannel Selling

A really easy way to market your e-commerce website without spending a lot of money is to sell on multiple channels. Take advantage of platforms like the Amazon marketplace and eBay—include a business card or promotional flyer with the items you dispatch. Include a discount code on that flyer and watch in amazement as buyers buy directly from you in the future. There are hundreds of reasons why multichannel selling is absolutely essential for e-commerce businesses. The fact you can poach customers from these big marketplaces has to be one of the main reasons.

I looked at big brands that sell via marketplaces like eBay in one of my previous posts—and I said then that their reasons for doing so are to further the reach of their brand. So if the big guys are doing it, you should be too! Never underestimate the importance of multichannel selling as a part of your marketing strategy. It's sustainable, profitable and a great way to pull in new customers with minimal effort.

You're probably wondering why I've omitted SEO traffic from my list of marketing methods, right? The way I see it, organic traffic has become way too unpredictable to be called "sustainable". I've seen websites fall out of the SERPS overnight for a variety of reasons. Sometimes it's clear that a webmaster has broken Google's guidelines, other times it's a little more murky. Nowadays I don't work on driving organic traffic at all. Any organic traffic my website does receive is a bonus.

There are countless companies out there trying to sell marketing services to e-commerce website owners. There are countless "gurus" and companies trying to sell courses and material designed to turn you into a marketing genius overnight (or so they say). The simple fact is that in order to succeed you don't need to buy any of these things. All the information you need in order to market your website sustainably and successfully is out there on the Internet. If you're starting an e-commerce business on a shoe string budget then you'll have to bite the bullet and learn about marketing, but there's no reason why you can't make a real success of your e-commerce website's marketing campaign if you invest lots of time and effort. If marketing an e-commerce business was easy, everyone would be doing it. Without a little effort on your part, you won't be successful in e-commerce.

New Words

seasoned	*adj.*	经验丰富的，老练的
veteran	*n.*	老手，富有经验的人
	adj.	经验丰富的
sustainable	*adj.*	足可支撑的，养得起的
complain	*v.*	抱怨，悲叹，控诉
foolproof	*adj.*	十分简单的，十分安全的，极坚固的
campaign	*n.*	(商业性)活动
	v.	参加活动，从事活动

akin	adj.	同族的，类似的
seriously	adv.	认真地，真诚地
following	adj.	下面的，其次的，接着的
	n.	下列事物，跟随者，粉丝
definitely	adv.	明确地，干脆地
interaction	n.	交互
retargeting	n.	重新定位目标，访客挽回，再营销
profitable	adj.	有利可图的
manner	n.	风格，方式，样式
naysayer	n.	反对者，否认者
exclaim	v.	呼喊，惊叫，大声叫
reap	v.	收割，收获
searcher	n.	搜索者
qualified	adj.	有资格的
bombard	v.	炮轰，轰击
fairly	adv.	相当地，还算，清楚地
exponential	n.	指数
	adj.	指数的，幂数的
neat	adj.	灵巧的，灵活的，整洁的，有用的
ridiculous	adj.	荒谬的，可笑的
daunting	adj.	使人畏缩的，使人沮丧的
pointless	adj.	无意义的
journalist	n.	新闻记者，从事新闻杂志业的人
awesome	adj.	引起敬畏的，可怕的
vague	adj.	含糊的，不清楚的，茫然的
overlook	v.	俯瞰，远眺，没注意到
multichannel	adj.	多渠道的
promotional	adj.	促销的，宣传的，奖励的
flyer	n.	(广告)传单
dispatch	v.	分派，派遣
poach	v.	偷猎，窃取，水煮
underestimate	v.	低估，看轻
unpredictable	adj.	不可预知的
overnight	adv.	一夜之间，突然，很快
	adj.	一整夜的，晚上的，突然的，很快的
webmaster	n.	网站管理员
murky	adj.	含糊的，黑暗的
bonus	n.	奖金，红利
guru	n.	(受下属崇敬的)领袖，头头

successfully		*adv.*	顺利地,成功地

✎ Phrases

growth hacker	增长黑客,成长黑客,既懂技术又懂营销的高端人才
slow and steady	稳扎稳打地
start out	出发,动身
social media	社交媒体
a great deal	大量
stand for	代表,代替,象征
Google Product Listing Ads (PLAs)	谷歌产品列表广告
plenty of	许多
at the present time	目前
text ads	文本广告
conversion rate	转化率
target audience	目标受众
in return	作为报答
work out	设计出,做出,计算出,消耗完
reply to	回答,回复
ins and outs	特色,细节,前前后后,来龙去脉,里里外外
offline advertising	离线广告,线下广告
home in on	瞄准,对准,锁定;回到
upward of	超过,多于
ad slot	广告位,广告时段
best practice	最优方法
be exposed to	遭受,暴露于……
trial and error	反复试验
business card	名片
fall out of	放弃(习惯等)
marketing strategy	市场战略
organic traffic	有机流量
on a shoe string budget	经济拮据,有限的预算,紧缩的预算
bite the bullet	咬紧牙关,忍受困难

✎ Abbreviations

ROI (Return On Investment)	投资回报率
PPC (Pay Per Click)	点击付费广告
SERPs (Search Engine Result Pages)	搜索引擎结果页面
PR (Public Relationship)	公共关系
SEO (Search Engine Optimization)	搜索引擎优化

Exercises

[Ex. 1] Answer the following questions according to the text.

1. What do most big brands and companies out there appear to do?
2. What will a lot of these companies do in private?
3. What is the ultimate goal on social media?
4. What is PPC?
5. What are the best PPC options out there at the present time?
6. What does PR basically involve?
7. What can you do once you've mastered the art of contacting bloggers for PR purposes?
8. How much can the cost per lead in some insurance niches be?
9. What is a really easy way to market your e-commerce website without spending a lot of money?
10. What does the author tell us never to underestimate?

[Ex. 2] Translate the following terms or phrases from English into Chinese and vice versa.

1. ad slot
2. conversion rate
3. growth hacker
4. offline advertising
5. organic traffic
6. 社交媒体
7. 奖金，红利
8. 指数；指数的，幂数的
9. 交互
10. 多渠道的

[Ex. 3] Translate the following passage into Chinese.

During the sales process there may be interim steps that occur prior to a sale being finalized. For example, a customer may receive a direct mail that invites them to call for additional information. When they call, the company has the opportunity to convert the call into the sale, or they may take the information and forward it to a sales person. These are referred to as "leads" or responses. They do not result in a sale, at least not yet. However, there is a cost associated with soliciting their response. That cost is described as a cost per lead or cost per response. It is calculated by taking all the costs associated with generating the lead, and dividing them by the number of responses or leads.

It's important to understand the CPL or CPR for a campaign, because they are not directly correlated with conversion rates. For example, one campaign may generate a $2.58/CPL, while another may generate a $4.50/CPL. However, the latter CPL may result in a far higher conversion than the previous CPL.

[Ex. 4] Fill in the blanks with the words given below.

| methods | platforms | represent | message | measurement |
| visitors | techniques | advertisers | marketing | performance |

Online Marketing Platform

Online Marketing Platform (OMP) is an integrated web-based platform that combines the benefits of a business directory, local search engine, Search Engine Optimization (SEO) tool, Customer Relationship Management (CRM) package and Content Management System (CMS). EBay and Amazon are used as online marketing and logistics management ___1___. On Facebook, Twitter, YouTube, Pinterest, LinkedIn, and other social media, retail online marketing is also used. Online business ___2___ platforms such as Marketo, Aprimo, MarketBright and Pardot have been bought by major IT companies (Eloqua-Oracle, Neolane-Adobe and Unica-IBM).

Unlike television marketing in which Neilsen TV Ratings can be relied upon for viewing metrics, online ___3___ do not have an independent party to verify viewing claims made by the big online platforms.

- Compensation Methods

Advertisers and publishers use a wide range of payment calculation ___4___. In 2012, advertisers calculated 32% of online advertising transactions on a cost-per-impression basis, 66% on customer ___5___ (e.g. cost per click or cost per acquisition), and 2% on hybrids of impression and performance methods.

- CPM

Cost Per Mille, often abbreviated to CPM, means that advertisers pay for every thousand displays of their ___6___ to potential customers (mille is the Latin word for thousand). In the online context, ad displays are usually called "impressions". Definitions of an "impression" vary among publishers, and some impressions may not be charged because they don't ___7___ a new exposure to an actual customer. Advertisers can use technologies such as web bugs to verify if an impression is actually delivered.

Publishers use a variety of ___8___ to increase page views, such as dividing content across multiple pages, repurposing someone else's content, using sensational titles, or publishing tabloid or sexual content.

CPM advertising is susceptible to "impression fraud", and advertisers who want ___9___ to come to their sites may not find per-impression payments a good proxy for the results they desire.

- CPC

CPC (Cost Per Click) or PPC (Pay Per Click) means advertisers pay each time a user clicks on the ad. CPC advertising works well when advertisers want visitors to their sites, but it's a less accurate ___10___ for advertisers looking to build brand awareness. CPC's market share has grown each year since its introduction, eclipsing CPM to dominate two-thirds of all online advertising compensation methods.

Like impressions, not all recorded clicks are valuable to advertisers. GoldSpot Media reported that up to 50% of clicks on static mobile banner ads are accidental and resulted in redirected visitors leaving the new site immediately.

Text B

E-commerce Supply Chain Management: Reducing Cost and Inefficiency

The term supply chain management brings images to mind of warehouses, shipping containers, and people walking around in hard hats holding clipboards. It can seem complicated—and let's be honest, it is. A supply chain is the multi-faceted backbone of your retail or wholesale business whether you're selling online, in stores or doing a little bit of both.

As with any major aspect of your business, there are probably lots of areas where you're incurring more costs than necessary and some of these can definitely be streamlined. It's worth taking a look at your supply chain as a whole to recognize areas where there could be fewer costs, which also means higher profits.

If you're not sure where to start, here's a guide for cutting those costs and optimizing your supply chain.

1. Inventory Cost

(1) Bring Down Your TIC

Total Inventory Cost (TIC) is a large number that encompasses many aspects of one thing: the total cost of one of your most important assets. TIC is essentially all the costs that make up your inventory.

Calculate this number to have an idea of what the inventory is costing you overall. When you break the total cost figure down, you can figure out which areas need improvement.

TIC can be broken into 3 smaller costs: ordering costs, shortage costs, and carrying costs. Each of those three represent various aspects of the supply chain. Have a look into each part to identify where costs can be trimmed.

Ordering costs are, as you might guess, all costs associated with ordering your inventory. These are usually fixed costs. Landed costs make up the majority of this figure.

Landed costs equal the total price of your products including everything that happens up until the point when they arrive to you. They include the original price, transportation fees, taxes, insurance, handling and other fees.

If you run an international operation, take a particularly close look at your landed costs: these will include customs, international taxes, currency exchange differences and import duties that you're paying on your goods.

To bring the total inventory cost down, ask yourself: does the extra landed cost justify bringing in your products from an overseas supplier or should you look into finding a local supplier?

Shortage costs come from out of stock situations. Doing proper inventory forecasting and finding your economic order quantity and ideal reorder points can reduce these costs greatly. Shortage costs get high when you need to make last-minute orders from other suppliers with even more last-minute shipping charges attached.

Preventing this from happening in the first place is a good way to reduce these costs. Just be like the Boy Scouts: always prepared.

Finally, carrying costs are a big one when you're thinking about the total cost of your inventory. Ideally, they should only make up 20%–30% of your TIC.

Carrying costs include capital costs, non-capital costs and inventory risk costs. To reduce this cost to the recommended 20%–30%, examine if there's an alternative way to store your inventory with lower holding costs, change your service provider, or change your overall inventory management technique.

For example, you may consider changing from just-in-time inventory management to drop shipping for certain products that bring you a high carrying cost.

(2) Get Rid of Dead Stock

There's something else that could be causing high costs in your inventory, and it's something hidden down, deep down, in that one forgotten corner of your warehouse: dead stock.

The name is a little melodramatic, but it's a real problem for a lot of retailers.

Dead stock is product that hasn't sold for at least one year, and is slowly but surely becoming obsolete, out of season, or simply impossible to sell.

However, against your better judgment, it stays in your warehouse, hoping for better days. Dead stock is a problem because while it's not making any money, it's still costing money in the form of holding costs in your warehouse. It's also taking up space that you could be using to store your newer stock that actually will sell.

To get that stock moving you can just donate it all (in the US, and in several other countries, these donations are tax-deductible). Another option is to try product bundling, which will both get rid of existing dead stock and also reduce the risk of accumulating it again in the future. For example, if you have cameras and camera straps that fly off the shelves, but are left with too many camera bags, try creating a new product that bundles all three.

2. Inventory Valuation

Switching from external costs, another area to examine is your inventory valuation methods. Inventory valuation gives a value to all the items in your inventory and therefore, puts a value on the major assets of your business.

If you don't use the ideal valuation method for your product, your expenses and revenues at the end of the year may not reflect the reality of the situation.

There are two main methods of tracking your inventory: perpetual and periodic.

Periodic valuation keeps track of sales as they happen, but doesn't update inventory until the periodic stock take happens.

Perpetual valuation keeps routine, updated record of the inventory on hand at any point in time.

In the fast-paced world of retailing online, we highly recommend perpetual to keep your valuations accurate all the time.

When you go the perpetual route, there are three common ways to give value to your inventory:

1) First-in, first-out (FIFO[1]) in which older inventory is recorded as the first sold, regardless of whether the actual product itself was first or last in line on the shelf.

2) Last-in, first-out (LIFO[2]) in which the newest inventory is recorded as being sold first. The issue with the LIFO method is that it is rarely encountered in practice. If a company were to use the process flow embodied by LIFO, a significant part of its inventory would be very old, and likely obsolete.

3) Weighted average costs, which uses the average cost of the goods sold to determine inventory value.

This is the really short version of complex accounting processes, but it's enough to get the message across: choosing which of these inventory valuation method you (and your accountant) use has an impact on your overall supply chain and inventory costs. Each gives a different valuation to your inventory, and therefore, a different overall financial state of your supply chain and business.

As every business is different and financial reporting standards around the world differ, it's best to discuss your inventory valuation method with your accountant.

3. Quality Control

Quality issues cause delays in shipments, unhappy customers and loss of revenue when you have to send things back to the manufacturer. There are several ways to reduce this cost—mostly by preventing them from happening in the first place.

Establish your quality assurance standards when you first start looking for suppliers and manufacturers. Have a list of clear quality requirement that you have and make sure that the supplier you choose is capable of producing to meet this standard.

Once you've chosen your preferred suppliers, ask for samples, give feedback on samples, ask for samples again and only then agree to do business. You will also have to put in some quality time at the actual factory to ensure quality standards are met once full-scale production starts.

These are simple tips, but they are an effective way to ensure quality products from the beginning, which will help you cut costs associated with bad quality products over the long term.

4. Sales Channels

(1) Expanding to Wholesale

Let's move on to another way to optimize your supply chain—but in this section, rather than talking about cutting costs, we're talking about economies of scale and making more money!

How about expanding your sales channels? This is less about expanding to add another retail sales channel, and more about making a bigger sales channel expansion: from retail to wholesale.

---

1 FIFO and LIFO accounting are methods used in managing inventory and financial matters involving the amount of money a company has tied up within inventory of produced goods, raw materials, parts, components, or feed stocks. They are used to manage assumptions of cost sheet related to inventory, stock repurchases (if purchased at different prices), and various other accounting purposes.

2 "LIFO" stands for last-in, first-out, meaning that the most recently produced items are recorded as sold first.

In many cases, as a retailer, you may already have the foundation to expand into wholesale, such as a customer base, market knowledge and product knowledge.

But the real challenges are: scaling operations, taking production or sourcing into your own hands, and gaining customers for the wholesale market as well. However, these are surmountable, especially when taking into account the potential profits that this channel can bring.

What's the process for expanding into wholesaling? Start slow. If some of your products are doing extremely well and you have trouble finding quality suppliers, these could be good products to start with. Identify your target customers and work out the logistics such as storage, shipping and pricing.

Wholesale as another sales channel can open up new bigger, better revenue streams, scale operations such as warehousing, shipping and production, and expand your brand reach to new retailers.

(2) Warehousing & Fulfillment Logistics

Let's move to another part of your process—order fulfillment. This includes pick, pack and ship methods and your warehouse layout.

If your pick, pack and ship method has your warehouse employees running around like they're on a deluded scavenger hunt, it's time to rethink your process. Make sure your pick list is clear and detailed so that warehouse staff know exactly where to find things. Place products on shelves in an organized way that make sense within the overall layout of the warehouse.

Place your packing station in a logical position, probably somewhere near the last of your product shelves. Finally, make sure shipping labels are clear and detailed for quick shipping once your packages are ready to leave the warehouse.

Speaking of the "pick" bit, your warehouse layout should be organized and make sense. Make sure shelves and products are clearly labeled, items are accessible and it's easy to navigate between rows and aisles.

Pick, pack and ship and warehouse layout are some of the most basic aspects of order fulfillment, yet they can be the most time consuming and can incur big costs simply by being inefficient. Take the time to work out the optimal layout before you get started on anything else.

(3) Maybe Try a 3PL

Speaking of warehouse layouts, here's a thought: do you actually need a warehouse in the first place? Or will you hire a Third-Party Logistics(3PL) to do it for you? A 3PL, can make your dreams come true—if those dreams are of seamless fulfillment, shipping and taking care of your products all on their own.

While 3PLs do come with a cost of their own, hiring one can be worth it in the long run—the trick is to work out how much you will save with one, and if it will be worth it. In the end, you can save on costs such as warehousing, transportation, technology and staffing.

Along with potential cost savings, a 3PL can add a lot of value to your supply chain that leads to other cost savings, namely in the form of knowledge and expertise. As a company that specializes in this sort of thing, a good 3PL brings knowledge about the industry, techniques and other resources that could take you years to discover. They focus on optimizing their processes, and then you can focus on optimizing yours.

When you scale your business, a 3PL brings more flexibility to that growth, with the capacity to take on higher volumes, and lead to your cost savings, and ultimately, profit as the business grows.

When it comes to choosing a 3PL, you can save costs by selecting the one that is really right for your business. Ask yourself these 3 questions to help you narrow down your search:

1) What service level do I need? Figuring out exactly what you need guarantees you won't overpay for a service that is surplus to your requirements.

2) Does the technology the 3PL uses for operations match my technology—are they compatible?

3) What is the 3PL's reputation within the industry and do they have good references from other customers?

5. Conclusions

Your supply chain is a complex aspect of your retail business, which can incur a lot of costs and loss of time due to inefficiencies. To optimize your supply chain, it's simply a matter of stopping to analyze it section by section to see what is working and what is not. Then you can focus on getting your product off your virtual shelves and into the hands of happy customers.

New Words

warehouse	n.	仓库，货栈，大商店
	v.	贮入仓库
container	n.	集装箱
clipboard	n.	有纸夹的笔记板，剪贴板
incur	v.	招致
streamlined	adj.	最新型的，改进的
encompass	v.	包围，环绕，包含或包括某事物
asset	n.	资产
ordering	n.	订货，订购，排序，分类，调整
shortage	n.	缺货，不足，缺乏
import	n.	进口货(常用复数)，进口，输入
	v.	输入，进口
justify	v.	证明……是正当的
forecasting	n.	预测
reorder	v. & n.	再订购
prepared	adj.	准备好的，预先准备的
melodramatic	adj.	情节剧的
judgment	n.	判断
donation	n.	捐赠品
tax-deductible	adj.	可免税的
bundling	n.	打小包，集束，成束
accumulate	v.	积聚，堆积

valuation	n.	估价，评价，计算
expense	n.	费用，代价，损失，开支
perpetual	adj.	永久的
periodic	adj.	周期的，定期的
routine	n.	常规，日常事务，程序
rarely	adv.	很少地，罕有地
encounter	v.	遇到，相遇
shipment	n.	出货，装船
assurance	n.	保证，担保
standard	n.	标准
feedback	n.	反馈，反应
wholesale	n.	批发
	adj.	批发的
optimize	v.	使最优化
surmountable	adj.	可战胜的，可克服的
delude	v.	迷惑，蛊惑
shelf	n.	架子
aisle	n.	走廊，过道
inefficient	adj.	效率低的，效率差的
seamless	adj.	无缝的
overpay	v.	多付(钱财)
surplus	n.	剩余，过剩
	adj.	过剩的，剩余的
	v.	转让，卖掉
compatible	adj.	谐调的，一致的，兼容的

✎ Phrases

supply chain management	供应链管理
bring to mind	想起
walk around	绕……而走
a bit of	一点
inventory cost	存货成本，储存成本
figure down	算出，弄清，了解
ordering cost	订购成本，订货费
shortage cost	缺货成本
carrying cost	置存成本
fixed cost	固定成本
original price	原价
transportation fee	运费，运输费用

landed cost	到岸成本，登岸成本
import duty	进口税
shipping charge	运送费，装船费用
prevent from	阻止，妨碍
capital cost	资本成本，资本费用
risk cost	风险成本
holding cost	储备成本
just-in-time inventory management	零库存管理
drop shipping	转运配送，直接代发货
get rid of	摆脱，除去
dead stock	滞销商品
out of season	过时，不合时令
make money	挣钱
regardless of	不管，不顾
process flow	工作流程
weighted average cost	加权平均成本
financial reporting	财务报表
economy of scale	规模经济，规模效益
take into account	重视，考虑
target customer	目标客户
make sense	有意义，合情合理
take care of	照顾
along with	连同……一起，随同……一起
this sort of thing	这一类的事情
loss of time	立刻，马上

Abbreviations

TIC (Total Inventory Cost)	总存储成本
FIFO (First-In, First-Out)	先进先出
LIFO (Last-In, First-Out)	后进先出
3PL (Third-Party Logistics)	第三方物流

Exercises

[Ex. 5]   Answer the following questions according to the text.

1. What images does the term supply chain management bring to mind?
2. How many smaller costs can total inventory cost be broken into? What are they?
3. What is dead stock?
4. What can you do to get rid of dead stock?
5. How many main methods of tracking your inventory are there? What are they?

6. How many common ways are there to give value to your inventory when you go the perpetual route? What are they?

7. What should you do once you've chosen your preferred suppliers?

8. What can wholesale as another sales channel do?

9. What does order fulfillment include?

10. What are the 3 questions asked to help you narrow down your search?

Reading Material

Online Advertising

Online advertising, also called online marketing or Internet advertising or web advertising, is a form of marketing and advertising which uses the Internet to deliver promotional[1] marketing messages to consumers. It includes e-mail marketing, search engine marketing (SEM), social media marketing, mobile advertising and display advertising and so on. Like other advertising media[2], online advertising frequently involves both a publisher, who integrates advertisements into its online content, and an advertiser, who provides the advertisements to be displayed on the publisher's content. Other potential participants include advertising agencies[3] who help generate and place the ad copy, an ad server which technologically delivers the ad and tracks statistics, and advertising affiliates[4] who do independent promotional work for the advertiser.

1. E-mail Advertising

E-mail advertising is ad copy comprising an entire email or a portion of an email message. Email marketing may be unsolicited[5], in which case the sender may give the recipient an option to opt out of future emails, or it may be sent with the recipient's prior consent (opt-in[6]).

2. Search Engine Marketing

Search Engine Marketing, or SEM, is designed to increase a website's visibility in search engine results pages (SERPs). Search engines provide sponsored results and organic (non-sponsored) results based on a web searcher's query. Search engines often employ visual cues[7] to differentiate sponsored results from organic results. Search engine marketing includes all of an advertiser's actions to make a website's listing more prominent for topical keywords.

3. Social Media Marketing

Social media marketing[8] is commercial promotion conducted through social media websites.

1　promotional　　*adj.*　增进的，奖励的
2　media　　*n.*　媒体
3　advertising agency　　广告商，广告公司
4　affiliate　　*v.*　(使……)加入，接受为会员
5　unsolicited　　*adj.*　主动提供的
6　opt in　　决定参加
7　visual cue　　视觉线索，可视线索
8　social media marketing　　社交媒体营销

95

Many companies promote their products by posting frequent updates and providing special offers through their social media profiles.

4. Mobile Advertising

Mobile advertising[1] is ad copy delivered through wireless mobile devices such as smartphones[2], feature phones, or tablet computers. Mobile advertising may take the form of static or rich media display ads, SMS (Short Message Service[3]) or MMS (Multimedia Messaging Service[4]) ads, mobile search ads, advertising within mobile websites, or ads within mobile applications or games (such as interstitial ads, "advergaming", or application sponsorship[5]). Industry groups such as the Mobile Marketing Association have attempted to standardize mobile ad unit specifications, similar to the IAB's[6] efforts for general online advertising.

5. Display Advertising

Display advertising conveys its advertising message visually using text, logos, animations[7], videos, photographs, or other graphics. Display advertisers frequently target users with particular traits to increase the ads' effect. Online advertisers (typically through their ad servers) often use cookies, which are unique identifiers of specific computers, to decide which ads to serve to a particular consumer. Cookies can track whether a user leave a page without buying anything, so the advertiser can later retarget the user with ads from the site the user visited.

As advertisers collect[8] data across multiple external websites about a user's online activity, they can create a detailed picture of the user's interests to deliver even more targeted advertising. This aggregation[9] of data is called behavioral targeting. Advertisers can also target their audience by using contextual[10] to deliver display ads related to the content of the web page where the ads appear.

Retargeting, behavioral targeting, and contextual advertising all are designed to increase an advertiser's return on investment[11], or ROI, over untargeted ads.

Advertisers may also deliver ads based on a user's suspected geography through geotargeting. A user's IP[12] address communicates some geographic information (at minimum, the user's country or general region). The geographic information from an IP can be supplemented and refined with other proxies[13] or information to narrow the range of possible locations. For example, with mobile

---

1 mobile advertising 　　手机广告，移动广告
2 smartphone 　　*n.* 智能手机
3 Short Message Service 　　短信
4 Multimedia Messaging Service 　　彩信
5 sponsorship 　　*n.* 赞助，发起，倡议
6 IAB (Internet Architecture Board) 　　互联网架构委员会
7 animation 　　*n.* 动画
8 collect 　　*v.* 收集，聚集
9 aggregation 　　*n.* 集合，聚合
10 contextual 　　*adj.* 情景中的
11 return on investment 　　投资回报
12 IP (Internet Protocol) 　　网际协议
13 proxy 　　*n.* 代理

devices, advertisers can sometimes use a phone's GPS[1] receiver or the location of nearby mobile towers. Cookies and other persistent data on a user's machine may provide help narrowing[2] a user's location further.

(1) Web Banner Ads

Web banners or banner ads typically are graphical ads displayed within a web page. Many banner ads are delivered by a central ad server.

Banner ads can use rich media[3] to incorporate video, audio, animations, buttons, forms[4], or other interactive elements using Java applets, HTML[5], Adobe Flash, and other programs.

(2) Frame Ads (Traditional Banner)

Frame ads[6] are the first form of web banners. The colloquial usage of "banner ads" often refers to traditional frame ads. Website publishers incorporate frame ads by setting aside a particular space on the web page. The Interactive Advertising Bureau's Ad Unit Guidelines proposes standardized pixel[7] dimensions for ad units.

(3) Pop-Ups/Pop-Unders

A pop-up ad[8] is displayed in a new web browser window that opens above a website visitor's initial browser window. A pop-under ad[9] opens a new browser window under a website visitor's initial browser window.

(4) Floating Ads

A floating ad[10], or overlay ad, is a type of rich media advertisement that appears superimposed[11] over the requested website's content. Floating ads may disappear or become less obtrusive after a preset time period.

(5) Expanding Ads

An expanding ad[12] is a rich media frame ad that changes dimensions upon a predefined condition, such as a preset amount of time a visitor spends on a webpage, the user's click on the ad, or the user's mouse movement over the ad. Expanding ads allow advertisers to fit more information into a restricted ad space.

(6) Trick Banners

A trick banner is a banner ad where the ad copy imitates some screen element users commonly

---

1 GPS (Global Positioning System)　　全球定位系统
2 narrow　　*v.*　缩小，变窄
3 rich media　　富媒体
4 form　　*n.*　窗体
5 HTML (HyperText Markup Language)　　超文本标示语言
6 frame ad　　框架广告
7 pixel　　*n.*　像素
8 pop-up ad　　弹出广告
9 pop-under ad　　推出网页时弹出的广告
10 floating ad　　浮动广告
11 superimposed　　*adj.*　重叠的，叠加的
12 expanding ad　　扩张式广告

encounter, such as an operating system message or popular application message, to induce[1] ad clicks. Trick banners typically do not mention the advertiser in the initial ad, and thus they are a form of bait-and-switch[2]. Trick banners commonly attract a higher-than-average click-through rate, but tricked users may resent[3] the advertiser for deceiving them.

(7) News Feed Ads

"News Feed Ads[4]", also called "Sponsored Stories", "Boosted Posts", typically exist on Social Media Platforms that offer a steady stream of information updates ("news feed") in regulated formats (i.e. in similar sized small boxes with a uniform style). Those advertisements are intertwined with non-promoted news that the users are reading through. Those advertisements can be of any content, such as promoting a website, a fan page, an app, or a product.

Some examples are: Facebook's "Sponsored Stories", LinkedIn's "Sponsored Updates", and Twitter's "Promoted Tweets".

This display ads format falls into its own category because unlike banner ads which are quite distinguishable[5], News Feed Ads' format blends well into non-paid news updates. This format of online advertisement yields much higher click-through rates than traditional display ads.

6. Interstitial[6]

An interstitial ad displays before a user can access requested content, sometimes while the user is waiting for the content to load. Interstitial ads are a form of interruption[7] marketing.

A text ad displays text-based hyperlinks[8]. Text-based ads may display separately from a web page's primary content, or they can be embedded by hyperlinking individual words or phrases to advertiser's websites. Text ads may also be delivered through e-mail marketing or text message marketing. Text-based ads often render faster than graphical ads and can be harder for ad-blocking software to block.

7. Chat Advertising

As opposed to static messaging, chat advertising refers to real time messages dropped to users on certain sites. This is done by the usage of live chat software or tracking applications installed within certain websites with the operating personnel behind the site often dropping adverts on the traffic surfing[9] around the sites. In reality this is a subset of the e-mail advertising but different because of its time window.

8. Online Classified Advertising

Online classified advertising is advertising posted online in a categorical listing of specific

---

1 induce   *v.* 劝诱，促使，导致，引起
2 bait-and-switch   诱饵调包手法，引诱顾客购买高价商品
3 resent   *v.* 愤恨，怨恨
4 News Feed Ad   消息推送广告
5 distinguishable   *adj.* 可区别的，可辨识的
6 interstitial   *adj.* 插播式的
7 interruption   *n.* 中断，打断
8 hyperlink   *n.* 超链接
9 surfing   *n.* 网络冲浪

products or services. Examples include online job boards, online real estate[1] listings, automotive listings, online yellow pages, and online auction-based listings.

9. Adware

Adware is software that, once installed, automatically displays advertisements on a user's computer. The ads may appear in the software itself, integrated into web pages visited by the user, or in pop-ups/pop-unders. Adware installed without the user's permission is a type of malware[2].

10. Affiliate Marketing

Affiliate marketing[3] (sometimes called lead generation) occurs when advertisers organize third parties to generate potential customers for them. Third-party affiliates receive payment based on sales generated through their promotion. Affiliate marketers generate traffic to offers from affiliate networks, and when the desired action is taken by the visitor, the affiliate earns[4] a commission[5]. These desired actions can be an e-mail submission, a phone call, filling out an online form, or an online order being completed.

参 考 译 文

电子商务网站营销的五种方法

在电子商务行业，我们开始听到越来越多的术语，如"增长黑客"，我本人并不真的在意它。任何经验丰富的电子商务老手都会告诉你，需要可持续的长期营销计划——而不是短期的"增长黑客"。如龟兔赛跑寓言所说——"慢和稳定赢得比赛"，在商业中，特别是在电子商务中也是如此。

本文针对电子商务领域的任何小企业主——无论你刚刚开始、还是寻找更有效的方式来营销你的电子商务网站，都可从本文中有所得。本文中讨论的营销技术都可以为你所用。

1. 社交媒体

大多数大品牌和公司似乎都"热爱"社交媒体。然而，私下很多公司会抱怨社交媒体的投资回报率很低。我不大同意——并没有可靠的方法来计算社交媒体的整体投资回报率。为此，难以估量 ROI 实际效果的优劣。如果情况那么糟糕，并且社交媒体营销活动就是把钱往下水道扔，我想你就不会看到相当多的公司（有大有小）如此重视它。

你不必每天从早到晚都通过社交媒体宣传你的业务。一些最好的营销活动每天只需要不到一小时。必须首先选择要用的平台——电子商务企业的最佳平台通常是 Facebook（脸谱网）、Google +（谷歌+）、Pinterest（照片分享网站）和 Twitter（推特网）。

然后就是寻找要共享的有趣的、行业相关的新闻和趋势，建立链接。当然，你应该明确

1　real estate　　房地产

2　Malware, short for malicious software, is any software used to disrupt computer or mobile operations, gather sensitive information, gain access to private computer systems, or display unwanted advertising.

3　affiliate marketing　　联盟营销

4　earn　　*v.* 赚得，获得

5　commission　　*n.* 佣金

地分享你的网站的链接和特定功能的产品，但记住不能多。在我自己的社交媒体活动中，我的比率为 80/20——80％是主题行业新闻、20％插入我的网站或产品。如果在每个状态更新或发推文中都插入你的网站或产品，就会发现很难吸引粉丝并互动，而这才是社交媒体的最终目标。

2. PPC

　　PPC 是一个非常笼统的术语——它表示每次点击付费。PPC 中涉及许多不同的部分，从搜索网络广告到重定位，直到谷歌产品列表广告（PLA）。PPC 在过去几年已经走过了很长的路，这是一个真正好的方式，它以可持续、盈利的方式宣传电子商务网站。你会听到很多反对者声称"PPC 没利"——但它受大多数人的拥护。你不能简单地进行一个在线活动，希望它从第一天起就赚很多钱。如果你能这样做，那么每个人都会。使用 PPC，必须持续测试和改进广告系列。只有如此，才能真的从 PPC 中有所收获。

　　目前，最好的 PPC 选项是 Google PLA 和重定向。尽管传统文字广告在搜索网络和展示网络中的效果很好，但目前，对于我的电子商务网站来说，PLA 和再定位是目前最好的（也是最有利可图的）结果。PLA 专门用于电子商务网站——它们向搜索者提供他们在 SERPS 中查找的东西的图片。每次点击费用往往低于搜索文字广告，但转化率更高。其原因有许多种，包括买方在点击 PLA 之前是"有资格的"，他们可以看到该东西的图片，他们可以看到商家的名称，他们也可以看到价格。如果他们知道所有的信息，并继续点击，他们很有可能转换成买家。

　　重定向正变得越来越受欢迎——但这不是什么新鲜事。如果你曾经想过为什么会被以前访问过的网站的网络广告所轰炸，则重定向就是答案！如果广告网络从某个网站看到 Cookie，就可以把目标广告从该网站发给你。重定向流量往往相当便宜，但转化率却远高于从显示网络获得的其他标准流量。传统上，很难设置重定向广告系列，但现在有像 AdRoll 这样的灵巧工具，使得它很容易上手。

　　良好的老式搜索文字广告和图片展示广告仍然有效，但如果想要一个可持续的、有利可图的电子商务网站，就不能只用这两个"简单的选项"。你真的需要大张旗鼓地使用 PLA 和重定向。别只用 Google AdWords——也看看市面上的其他 PPC（应该考虑 Bing Ads、Facebook Ads 和 Twitter）。

3. 公共关系

　　我听到过人们一些可笑的说法，像"PR 是新的 SEO"。PR 基本上是指人们对你的品牌或网站的议论，这通常可以通过在报纸、电视、热门博客等上面宣传你的网站而实现。在某些场合，公关是建立声誉的一个重要方式——这是向你的目标受众营销的好方式。

　　你下一次打开报纸看到一个产品评论，可能该产品已经作为礼物送给了这家报纸。作为回报，他们得到了该产品的评论（好的或坏的）。PR 颇为简单但确实有效——PR 的问题在于从何开始。从电视或报纸随机接触人们看看他们是否想要评价你的产品，这似乎是令人生畏和毫无意义的。

　　如果你对 PR 的世界完全陌生，请参考我的建议，并尝试联系行业中的几个博主，看看他们是否愿意在帖子中评论你的产品或网站。有些人可能会说不，有些人不会回复你的电子邮件，但几乎肯定总有一些人会回应你。只要将你的网站刊登在热门博客中，就可以吸引成千上万名目标对象到你的电子商务网站。一旦你掌握了联系博主的公关艺术，你就可以通过新闻记者和其他途径（如报纸和电视）建立你的眼线。虽然 PR 基本上是免费的，但很耗时。需要时间来培育与公关行业的关系。不会一夜之间就有一个很棒的公关活动。

此处我们不可能讨论电视和印刷媒体公关的内容，但是当你的公司有了一些发展的时候，你会发布有关事实的新闻，你几乎肯定会收到来自记者需要后续信息的要求，并可能甚至根据他们的特点来评价产品。

4. 广播广告

我本可以很容易把本部分标为"离线广告"，但我认为那样有点含糊。相反，我决定锁定广播广告。广播广告的确非常有效，特别是在较小的地方广播电台。有时候，一个短广告时段花费低于 200 美元，而该广告能有成千上万的听众。

虽然不是在电子商务行业，我知道在保险业有人从广播广告中取得重大成功。通过 PPC 等营销方法，在某些保险市场中每次导入成本可能高于 200 美元。因此，如果用 200 美元在收音机上做广告，只要有一个或两个潜在客户，通过离线营销得到的结果比 PPC 更好。

广播广告被许多电子商务企业忽视。当然，你应该遵循规则并身体力行。广播广告不能全年盈利，如果在深夜做广告，就没有多少听众。重要的是选择正确的时机，当然，要让网站（包括电子商务网站广告）的无线广告高效，仍需试验和纠错。

5. 多渠道销售

营销电子商务网站又容易花费又少的方式是多个渠道销售。利用像亚马逊市场和 eBay（易见）等平台——包括一张名片或商品促销传单。在该传单上包含折扣代码，你会惊喜地发现将来买家会直接从你那里购买。电子商务企业必须多渠道销售的理由很多。事实上，其中一个理由就是可以从这些大市场获得客户。

我以前的一个帖子中提到过一些大品牌通过像 eBay 这样的市场进行销售——我当时就说他们这样做的原因是为了进一步扩大他们的品牌。所以如果大家伙都在做，你应该也这么做！永远不要低估把多渠道销售作为营销策略的重要性。它是可持续的、有利可图的并以最小的努力吸引新客户的好方式。

你可能想知道为什么我从营销方法列表中省略了 SEO 流量，对吗？按照我的看法，有机流量的"可持续"已经变得难以预测。我已经看到网站由于各种原因骤然放弃 SERPS。有时候很明显是网站管理员违反了谷歌的指南，其他时候则更加模糊。现在我根本不推动有机流量。我的网站收到的任何有机流量都是一个奖金。

有无数企业试图向电子商务网站所有者销售营销服务。有无数的"大师"和公司试图销售课程和材料，旨在使你一夜之间成为营销天才（如其所言）。简单的事实是，为了成功，你不需要购买任何这些东西。让你的网站持续经营下去和成功所需的信息都在互联网上。如果你要开展电子商务业务而经济拮据，那么你必须咬紧牙关并学习营销。如果你在电子商务网站的营销活动投入大量的时间和精力，就没有不成功的理由。如果营销电子商务业务很容易，那每个人都会这样做。如果不努力，就不会在电子商务中取得成功。

Unit 6

Text A

Web Traffic

Web traffic is the amount of data sent and received by visitors to a web site. This necessarily does not include the traffic generated by bots. Since the mid-1990s, web traffic has been the largest portion of Internet traffic. This is determined by the number of visitors and the number of pages they visit.

Sites monitor the incoming and outgoing traffic to see which parts or pages of their site are popular and if there are any apparent trends, such as one specific page being viewed mostly by people in a particular country. There are many ways to monitor this traffic and the gathered data is used to help structure sites, highlight security problems or indicate a potential lack of bandwidth.

Not all web traffic is welcomed. Some companies offer advertising schemes that, in return for increased web traffic (visitors), pay for screen space on the site. Sites also often aim to increase their web traffic through inclusion on search engines and through search engine optimization.

1. Analysis

Web analytics is the measurement of the behavior of visitors to a website. In a commercial context, it especially refers to the measurement of which aspects of the website work towards the business objectives of Internet marketing initiatives; for example, which landing pages encourage people to make a purchase. Notable web analytics software and services include Google Analytics, IBM Digital Analytics (formerly Coremetrics) and Adobe Omniture.

2. Measurement

Web traffic is measured to see the popularity of web sites and individual pages or sections within a site. This can be done by viewing the traffic statistics found in the web server log file, an automatically generated list of all the pages served. A hit is generated when any file is served. The page itself is considered a file, but images are also files, thus a page with 5 images could generate 6 hits (the 5 images and the page itself). A page view is generated when a visitor requests any page within the web site—a visitor will always generate at least one page view (the main page) but could generate many more. Tracking applications external to the web site can record traffic by inserting a small piece of HTML code in every page of the web site.

Web traffic is also sometimes measured by packet sniffing, thus gaining random samples of traffic data from which to extrapolate information about web traffic as a whole across total Internet usage.

The following types of information are often collated when monitoring web traffic:
- The number of visitors.
- The average number of page views per visitor—a high number would indicate that the average visitors go deep inside the site, possibly because they like it or find it useful.
- Average visit duration—the total length of a user's visit. As a rule, the more time they spend, the more they're interested in your company and are more prone to contact.
- Average page duration—how long a page is viewed for. The more pages viewed, the better it is for your company.
- Domain classes—all levels of the IP addressing information required to deliver web pages and content.
- Busy times—the most popular viewing time of the site would show when would be the best time to do promotional campaigns and when would be the most ideal to perform maintenance.
- Most requested pages—the most popular pages.
- Most requested entry pages—the entry page is the first page viewed by a visitor and shows which are the pages most attracting visitors.
- Most requested exit pages—the most requested exit pages could help find bad pages, broken links or the exit pages may have a popular external link.
- Top paths—a path is the sequence of pages viewed by visitors from entry to exit, with the top paths identifying the way most customers go through the site.
- Referrers. The host can track the (apparent) source of the links and determine which sites are generating the most traffic for a particular page.

Web sites produce traffic rankings and statistics based on those people who access the sites while using their toolbars and other means of online measurements. The difficulty with this is that it's not looking at the complete traffic picture for a site. Large sites usually hire the services of companies such as the Nielsen NetRatings or Quancast, but their reports are available only by subscription.

3. Control

The amount of traffic seen by a website is a measure of its popularity. By analyzing the statistics of visitors it is possible to see shortcomings of the site and look to improve those areas. It is also possible to increase the popularity of a site and the number of people that visit it.

(1) Limiting Access

It is sometimes important to protect some parts of a site by password, allowing only authorized people to visit particular sections or pages.

Some site administrators have chosen to block their page to specific traffic, such as by geographic location.

It is also possible to limit access to a web server both based on the number of connections and by the bandwidth expended by each connection. On Apache HTTP servers, this is accomplished by the limitipconn module and others.

(2) From Search Engines

The majority of website traffic is driven by the search engines. Millions of people use search engines everyday to research various topics, buy products, and go about their daily surfing activities. Search engines use keywords to help users find relevant information and each of the major search engines has developed a unique algorithm to determine where websites are placed within the search results. When a user clicks on one of the listings in the search results, they are directed to the corresponding website and data is transferred from the website's server, thus counting the visitors towards the overall flow of traffic to that website.

Search Engine Optimization (SEO), is the ongoing practice of optimizing a website to help improve its rankings in the search engines. Several internal and external factors are involved which can help improve a site's listing within the search engines. The higher a site ranks within the search engines for a particular keyword, the more traffic they will receive.

(3) Increasing Traffic

Web traffic can be increased by placement of a site in search engines and purchase of advertising, including bulk e-mail, pop-up ads, and in-page advertisements. Web traffic can also be increased by purchasing through web traffic providers or non-Internet based advertising.

Web traffic can be increased not only by attracting more visitors to a site, but also by encouraging individual visitors to "linger" on the site, viewing many pages in a visit.

If a web page is not listed in the first pages of any search, the odds of someone finding it diminishes greatly, especially if there is other competition on the first page. Very few people go past the first page, and the percentage that go to subsequent pages is substantially lower. Consequently, getting proper placement on search engines, a practice known as SEO, is as important as the web site itself.

4. Traffic Overload

Too much web traffic can dramatically slow down or prevent all access to a website. This is caused by more file requests going to the server than it can handle and may be an intentional attack on the site or simply caused by over-popularity. Large scale websites with numerous servers can often cope with the traffic required and it is more likely that smaller services are affected by traffic overload. Sudden traffic load may also hang your server or may result in shutdown of your services.

(1) Denial-of-Service Attacks

Denial-of-Service attacks (DoS attacks) have forced websites to close after a malicious attack, flooding the site with more requests than it could cope with. Viruses have also been used to coordinate large scale distributed denial-of-service attacks.

(2) Sudden Popularity

A sudden burst of publicity may accidentally cause a web traffic overload. A news item in the media, a quickly propagating e-mail, or a link from a popular site may cause such a boost in visitors, sometimes called a flash crowd or the Slashdot effect[1].

New Words

traffic	*n.*	流量
bot	*n.*	自动运行的程序
monitor	*n.*	监控程序，监控器
	v.	监控
gather	*n.*	集合，聚集
	v.	集合，聚集，使聚集，搜集，积聚
structure	*n.*	结构，构造
	v.	建筑，构成，组织
aim	*n.*	目标，目的，瞄准
	v.	对……瞄准，打算
inclusion	*n.*	包含，内含物
optimization	*n.*	最佳化，最优化
measurement	*n.*	测量法，度量
behavior	*n.*	举止，行为
initiative	*n.*	主动权
	adj.	主动的，自发的
encourage	*v.*	鼓励
section	*n.*	部分，节，项，区
server	*n.*	服务器
serve	*v.*	服务，供应，适合
code	*n.*	代码，密码，编码
	v.	编码
packet	*n.*	信息包
sniff	*v.*	嗅探
gain	*n.*	利润，收获
	v.	得到，赚到，获利，增加
extrapolate	*v.*	推断
collate	*v.*	整理，检查，比较
duration	*n.*	持续时间，为期
entry	*n.*	登录，进入，入口
attract	*v.*	吸引，有吸引力，引起注意
sequence	*n.*	次序，顺序，序列
identify	*v.*	识别，鉴别，确定

---

1 The Slashdot effect, also known as slashdotting, occurs when a popular website links to a smaller site, causing a massive increase in traffic. This overloads the smaller site, causing it to slow down or even temporarily become unavailable.

subscription	*n.*	订阅，签署
shortcoming	*n.*	缺点，短处
protect	*v.*	保护
authorized	*adj.*	认可的，审定的，经授权的
administrator	*n.*	管理人，网站管理员
connection	*n.*	连接，关系
determine	*v.*	决定，确定
corresponding	*adj.*	相应的
counting	*n.*	计算
rank	*n.*	等级
placement	*n.*	放置，布置
bulk	*n.*	大批，大多数
	v.	显得大，显得重要
linger	*v.*	逗留，闲荡，拖延，游移
diminish	*v.*	(使)减少，(使)变小
competition	*n.*	竞争，竞赛
percentage	*n.*	百分数，百分率，百分比
subsequent	*adj.*	后来的，并发的
substantially	*adv.*	充分地
overload	*v.*	使超载，超过负荷
	n.	超载，负荷过多
dramatically	*adv.*	戏剧地，引人注目地
handle	*v.*	处理，操作
intentional	*adj.*	有意图的，故意的
attack	*n. & v.*	攻击
sudden	*adj.*	突然的，意外的
shutdown	*n.*	关机，关门，停工
malicious	*adj.*	怀恶意的，恶毒的
flooding	*n.*	泛洪，泛滥
virus	*n.*	病毒
coordinate	*n.*	坐标
	v.	调整，整理
distributed	*adj.*	分布式的
burst	*v.*	爆发
accidentally	*adv.*	偶然地，意外地
propagate	*v.*	繁殖，传播，宣传
boost	*v.*	增加，促进，提高，推进

Phrases

landing page	登录页
log file	日志文件
main page	主页
random sample	随机抽样调查
be prone to	易于……，倾向于……
busy time	忙碌时间，被占时刻
external link	外部链接
direct to	把(注意力、精力)贯注在……上
pop-up ad	弹出式广告
in-page advertisement	页面内广告
flash crowd	瞬间拥挤，突发数据

Abbreviations

HTML (HyperText Markup Language)	超文本标识语言
DoS (Denial-of-Service)	拒绝服务

Exercises

[Ex. 1] Answer the following questions according to the text.

1. What is web traffic?
2. What is web analytics?
3. What is the purpose of measuring web traffic?
4. How is web traffic measured?
5. How do websites produce traffic rankings and statistics?
6. What is the result of analyzing the statistics of visitors?
7. How is the majority of website traffic driven? What do millions of people use them everyday to do?
8. What is Search Engine Optimization (SEO)?
9. What do Denial-of-Service attacks (DoS attacks) do?
10. What may a sudden burst of publicity accidentally cause?

[Ex. 2] Translate the following terms or phrases from English into Chinese and vice versa.

1. external link
2. landing page
3. main page
4. log file
5. pop-up ad
6. 随机抽样调查

7. 攻击	7. _____
8. 代码，密码，编码；编码	8. _____
9. 连接，关系	9. _____
10. 推断	10. _____

[Ex. 3] Translate the following passage into Chinese.

Conversion is a key element in your paid search strategy. If you're not actually turning lookers into buyers at a high rate, what are you advertising for? Conversion rate optimization enables you to maximize every cent of your PPC (PayPerClick) spend by finding that sweet spot that convinces the maximum percentage of your prospects to take action.

But what is a good conversion rate? If you're already achieving 3%, 5% or even 10% conversion rates, is that as high as you're going to go?

We recently analyzed thousands of AdWords accounts with a combined $3 billion in annual spend and discovered that some advertisers are converting at rates two or three times the average. Do you want to be average, or do you want your account to perform exponentially better than others in your industry?

Through our analysis of this massive amount of data on landing pages and conversion rates, we were able to identify some common traits of the top converting landing pages.

[Ex. 4] Fill in the blanks with the words given below.

attract	engines	ranking	particular	contains
number	pages	links	developed	content

What Is Google PageRank?

PageRank is what Google uses to determine the importance of a web page. It's one of many factors used to determine which ___1___ appear in search results. PageRank is also sometimes referred to by the slang term "Google juice".

PageRank was ___2___ by Google founders Larry Page and Sergey Brin at Stanford. In fact the name PageRank is a likely play on Larry Page's name. At the time that Page and Brin met, early search ___3___ typically linked to pages that had the highest keyword density, which meant people could game the system by repeating the same phrase over and over to ___4___ higher search page results. Sometimes web designers would even put hidden text on pages to repeat phrases.

PageRank attempts to measure a web page's importance.

The idea comes from academia, where citation counts are used to find the importance of researchers and research. The more often a ___5___ paper is cited by other papers, the more important that paper is deemed.

This makes sense because people do tend to link to relevant ___6___, and pages with more links to them are usually better resources than pages that nobody links. At the time it was developed, it was revolutionary.

PageRank doesn't stop at link popularity. It also looks at the importance of the page that ___7___ the link. Pages with higher PageRank have more weight in "voting" with their links than pages with lower PageRank. It also looks at the ___8___ of links on the page casting the "vote".

108

Pages with more links have less weight.

This also makes a certain amount of sense. Pages that are important are probably better authorities in leading web surfers to better sources, and pages that have more ___9___ are likely to be less discriminating on where they're linking.

PageRank is one of many factors that determines where your web page appears in search result ___10___, but if all other factors are equal, PageRank could potentially have a significant impact on your Google rankings.

Text B

Conversion Rate Optimization

1. Conversion Rate

Conversion rate is defined as the number of visitors to a website that complete a desired goal (a conversion) out of the total number of visitors. As one of the most important parts of paid inclusion campaigns, the conversion rate of a website is  the measurement of the success of a paid inclusion campaign. It is measured by the number of potential visitors performing the desired action, whether the action is buying a product, filling out a form, or some other goal of the web page. For example, if there are 100 visitors to a particular web page via a pay per click ad, and one of those 100 buys the product the website sells, then the conversion rate for that particular ad is one percent. The larger the conversion rate of a web page means the more successful the website will be as well as how successful the paid inclusion campaign is.

Measuring conversion rates can be very difficult for companies who are using paid inclusion to bring more business to the web page. Usually, web pages use web analytics programs to measure the conversion rates they are getting when they launch a new pay per click campaign. The web analytics software studies the behavior of website visitors, and collects data for use in many different research areas, including learning about current conversion rates. Data used to study conversion rates is compared against key performance indicators to determine if the conversion rate of the particular website is at the peak percentage or if there are changes that need to be made to the campaign to gather the desired results.

An important part of conversion rates is maximizing the chances of the visitor becoming a conversion. This can happen in a number of ways. One of the ways to make the visitor more susceptible to conversion is to match the right visitor with the right time and the right website. This is difficult to do, but that is where such things as paid inclusion and search engine optimization come into play. Web pages can also maximize chances of a visitor becoming a conversion by making the desired action, whether it is filling out a form or buying a product, as easy as possible. Visitors respond to the ease of the action, especially if it is also beneficial to the visitor. Offering a benefit to the visitor can also raise conversion rates of the particular website.

There are many different ways to raise conversion rates, most of which have to do with being everything a potential customer wants. Of course, improving conversion rates may just have something to do with recognizing the potential of the website. Some of the other ways to maximize the chances of a conversion include:
- knowing the unique selling point of the web page;
- being memorable with unique information;
- offering several payment options;
- having a clear returns policy;
- having clear policies on information protection;
- being clear and concise with information.

A conversion rate can be one of the most important factors in a paid inclusion campaign. The measure of whether the money poured into a marketing campaign is worth it or not is certainly something that any business will want to know.

2. Conversion Rate Optimization

In Internet marketing, conversion optimization, or Conversion Rate Optimization (CRO) is a system for increasing the percentage of visitors to a website that convert into customers, or more generally, take any desired action on a webpage. It is commonly referred to as CRO.

(1) Methodology

Conversion rate optimization seeks to increase the percentage of website visitors that take a specific action (often submitting a web form, making a purchase, signing up for a trial, etc.) by methodically testing alternate versions of a page or process. In doing so, businesses are able to generate more leads or sales without investing more money on website traffic, hence increasing their marketing return on investment and overall profitability.

A conversion rate is defined as the percentage of visitors who complete a goal, as set by the site owner. Some test methods, such as split testing or A/B testing[1], enable one to monitor which headlines, copy, images, social proof[2] elements and content help one convert more visitors into customers.

---

1 In marketing and business intelligence, A/B testing is a term for a randomized experiment with two variants, A and B, which are the control and variation in the controlled experiment. A/B testing is a form of statistical hypothesis testing with two variants leading to the technical term, two-sample hypothesis testing, used in the field of statistics. Other terms used for this method include bucket tests and split-run testing. These terms can have a wider applicability to more than two variants, but the term A/B testing is also frequently used in the context of testing more than two variants. In online settings, such as web design (especially user experience design), the goal of A/B testing is to identify changes to web pages that increase or maximize an outcome of interest (e.g., click-through rate for a banner advertisement). Formally the current web page is associated with the null hypothesis. A/B testing is a way to compare two versions of a single variable typically by testing a subject's response to variable A against variable B, and determining which of the two variables is more effective.

2 Social proof, also known as informational social influence, is a psychological phenomenon where people assume the actions of others in an attempt to reflect correct behavior for a given situation. This effect is prominent in ambiguous social situations where people are unable to determine the appropriate mode of behavior, and is driven by the assumption that surrounding people possess more knowledge about the situation.

There are several approaches to conversion optimization with two main schools of thought prevailing in the last few years. One school is more focused on testing as an approach to discover the best way to increase a website, a campaign or a landing page conversion rates. The other school is focused more on the pretesting stage of the optimization process. In this second approach, the optimization company will invest a considerable amount of time understanding the audience and then creating a targeted message that appeals to that particular audience. Only then would it be willing to deploy testing mechanisms to increase conversion rates.

(2) Elements of the Test Focused Approach to Conversion Optimization

Conversion optimization platforms for content, campaigns and delivery need to consist of the following elements.

1) Data collection and processing. The platform must process hundreds of variables and automatically discover which subsets have the greatest predictive power, including any multivariate relationship. A combination of pre- and post-screening methods is employed, dropping irrelevant or redundant data as appropriate. A flexible data warehouse environment accepts customer data as well as data aggregated by third parties.

Data can be numeric or text-based, nominal or ordinal. Bad or missing values are handled gracefully.

Data may be geographic, contextual, frequencial, demographic, behavioral, customer based, etc.

2) Hypothesis. After data collection, forming a hypothesis is the next step. This process forms the foundation of why changes are made. Hypotheses are made based on observation and deduction. It is important that each hypothetical situation be measurable. Without these no conclusions can be derived.

3) Optimization goals. The official definition of "optimization" is the discipline of applying advanced analytical methods to make better decisions. Under this framework, business goals are explicitly defined and then decisions are calibrated to optimize those goals. The methodologies have a long record of success in a wide variety of industries, such as airline scheduling, supply chain management, financial planning, military logistics and telecommunications routing. Goals should include maximization of conversions, revenues, profits or any combination thereof.

4) Business rules. Arbitrary business rules must be handled under one optimization framework. Using such a platform entails that one should understand these and other business rules, then adapt targeting rules accordingly.

5) Real-time decision making. Once mathematical models have been built, ad/content servers use an audience screen method to place visitors into segments and select the best offers, in real time. Business goals are optimized while business rules are enforced simultaneously. Mathematical models can be refreshed at any time to reflect changes in business goals or rules.

6) Statistical learning. Ensuring results are repeatable by employing a wide array of statistical methodologies. Variable selection, validation testing, simulation, control groups

and other techniques together help to distinguish true effects from chance events. A champion/challenger framework ensures that the best mathematical models are always deployed. In addition, performance is enhanced by the ability to analyze huge datasets and to retain historical learning.

New Words

conversion	n.	变换，转化
perform	v.	履行，执行
particular	n.	细节，详细
	adj.	特殊的，特别的，独特的，详细的，精确的
launch	n.	发行，投放市场
	v.	发动，发起，投入，开始
indicator	n.	指示符
maximize	v.	取……最大值
match	v.	相配，相称，匹配
action	n.	行动，举动，行为
memorable	adj.	值得纪念的，难忘的
concise	adj.	简明的，简练的
methodology	n.	方法学，方法论
methodically	adv.	有系统地，有方法地
alternate	adj.	交替的，轮流的，预备的
	v.	交替，轮流，改变
prevailing	adj.	占优势的，主要的，流行的
pretest	n.	预备考试，预备调查
	v.	进行预备考试
considerable	adj.	相当大(或多)的，值得考虑的，相当可观的
mechanism	n.	机制，机构
variable	n.	变量
	adj.	可变的，不定的，变量的
subset	n.	子集
predictive	adj.	预言性的，成为前兆的
multivariate	adj.	多变量的，多元的
irrelevant	adj.	不相关的
redundant	adj.	多余的
ordinal	n.	序数
	adj.	顺序的，依次的
hypothesis	n.	假设
observation	n.	观察，观测，观察资料(或报告)

deduction	n.	推论，演绎
situation	n.	情形，境遇
measurable	adj.	可测量的
conclusion	n.	结论，结束
decision	n.	决定，决策，结果
framework	n.	构架，框架，结构
calibrate	v.	校准
entail	v.	使必需，使承担
mathematical	adj.	数学的，精确的
reflect	v.	反映，表现，反射
repeatable	adj.	可重复的，可复验的
simulation	n.	仿真，模拟
distinguish	v.	区别，辨别
challenger	n.	挑战者
deploy	v.	展开，配置
enhanced	adj.	增强的，提高的
huge	adj.	巨大的，极大的
dataset	n.	数据集

Phrases

fill out a form	填表格
be beneficial to	有益于
selling point	卖点
pour into	注入，(使)川流不息地涌入
sign up	注册，签订
split testing	双方案测试
social proof	社交认证
post-screening method	筛选后的方法
pre-screening method	预筛选方法
as appropriate	视情况而定，酌情
missing value	遗漏值，漏测值
airline scheduling	航空调度，航线安排
supply chain management	供应链管理
telecommunications routing	电信路由
decision making	决策，判定
mathematical model	数学模型
validation testing	确认测试
control groups	控制组，对照组

Abbreviations

CRO (Conversion Rate Optimization)   转换率优化

Exercises

[Ex. 5]   Answer the following questions according to the text.

1. What is conversion rate defined as?

2. How is conversion rate measured?

3. What does the larger the conversion rate of a web page mean?

4. What is an important part of conversion rates?

5. How can web page maximize chances of a visitor becoming a conversion?

6. What are some of the other ways to maximize the chances of a conversion?

7. What is CRO?

8. What is a conversion rate?

9. What are the two main schools of thought about conversion optimization prevailing in the last few years?

10. What elements do conversion optimization platforms for content, campaigns and delivery need to consist of ?

Reading Material

PageRank

If you have ever done any reading about search engine optimization or are just curious[1] how you can get your site to the top of the Google search engine results, understanding PageRank is vital. I'm going to introduce you to the basics of PageRank and also provide a brief discussion on how much you should really worry about PageRank if you are running a website or Internet business.

Google's founders, Larry Page and Sergey Brin, invented PageRank and it forms the basis for how Google works. Google didn't become the best search engine in the world by chance, it became the best search engine because it provided the best results. PageRank is in fact the technology that gave Google its competitor-killing edge, a way to greatly improve the accuracy[2] and validity[3] of a search response to a user query.

In essence, PageRank provides a means to determine the value of a website for any given

---

1 curious   *adj.*   好奇的，求知的

2 accuracy   *n.*   精确性，正确度

3 validity   *n.*   有效性，合法性，正确性

search term or keyword phrase. This value is determined by how websites link together with the more popular (and theoretically better) sites receiving more links. It's these incoming links that help the site have a high PageRank value and thus display higher up in search results.

1. PageRank System

PageRank relies on[1] the uniquely democratic nature of the web by using its vast link structure as an indicator[2] of an individual page's value. Google interprets[3] a link from page A to page B as a vote, by page A, for page B. But, Google looks at more than the sheer volume of votes, or links a page receives; it also analyzes the page that casts the vote. Votes cast by pages that are themselves "important" weigh more heavily and help to make other pages "important".

Important, high-quality sites receive a higher PageRank, which Google remembers each time it conducts a search. Of course, important pages mean nothing to you if they don't match your query. So, Google combines PageRank with[4] sophisticated text-matching techniques to find pages that are both important and relevant to your search. Google goes far beyond the number of times a term appears on a page and examines all aspects of the page's content (and the content of the pages linking to it) to determine if it's a good match for your query.

The key rule to understand is that it is a combination of variables that determine how well your site performs in Google. These are the most important variables to worry about:

- Incoming[5] links to your site.
- The relevancy (to your site's theme) of the pages linking to your site and the PageRank of these pages.
- The keywords that other sites use to link to your site.
- The keywords on your website in particular in places like page titles and headlines[6].

You can control only some of those factors[7]. The important thing to understand regarding PageRank is that all those variables will determine how high your site shows up in search engine results. PageRank is the name for the technology that ranks sites and includes all those variables and many more.

2. PageRank Numbers—the Little Green Bar

If you install the Google Toolbar[8] into your browser you can choose to switch on the PageRank display (it's in the options). This will make a little green bar appear above the web pages you visit. The green bar represents[9] the PageRank of the page you are viewing in your browser. The

---

1　rely on　　　　依赖，依靠
2　indicator　　　*n.* 指示器
3　interpret　　　*v.* 解释，说明
4　combine with　　与……结合
5　incoming　　　*adj.* 引入的
6　headline　　　*n.* 大字标题，新闻提要；头条新闻
7　factor　　　　*n.* 因素，要素
8　toolbar　　　 *n.* 工具栏
9　represent　　　*v.* 代表，表示；表现，象征

ranking starts at 0 (no ranking) up to 10, the highest ranking and can be blanked out[1] completely if the page has been banned from Google. If you don't want to use the toolbar you can try this free PageRank lookup tool to find the ranking for any web address.

Google created quite a storm when it launched its green PageRank bar. Webmasters became obsessed[2] with methods to increase their PageRank and high PageRank sites started selling text links for hundreds of dollars. A link from a high PageRank page, from a PageRank 7, 8, 9 or 10, has been known to make lower PageRank pages increase a full number, even two if the incoming link is from a PageRank 10, and there is no doubt[3] it is good for search engine rankings.

The problem with PageRank being displayed in a little green bar is that it is very hard to really gauge[4] how valuable a ranking is. The Google PageRank technology is complex containing many variables. To interpret a number from 0–10, especially when only Google really knows how it works, is difficult. Worse still, the visible representation, the green bar that the public can see, only changes on a quarterly basis, while the real PageRank of a page changes on a daily basis. Most of the time you are looking at a very outdated[5] ranking value.

PageRank paranoia[6] is an issue that every webmaster may fall victim to. There are rumours[7] that Google will be changing the PageRank system because they are not happy with how it is being manipulated and interpreted. As a rule of thumb[8], watch the green bar with interest but don't take it too seriously[9] or spend too much time trying to force it to increase.

3. The Randomness of PageRank

Search engine optimization experts actively track PageRank and investigate[10] things like page backlinks[11] to try and work out what the top search engine ranked sites are doing right so they can replicate[12] and then surpass[13] them in the rankings. This is a very good strategy for any person running a web business looking to improve their search ranking. There is no need to reinvent the wheel—copy what works and do it slightly better than the competition.

This is all good in theory, but unfortunately there is a good amount of randomness in PageRank and search engine results. Google, of course, would argue[14] that it's not randomness and their

---

1　blank out　　　取消，作废
2　obsess　　*v.*　迷住，使困扰
3　no doubt　　　无疑地
4　gauge　　*v.*　测量
5　outdated　　*adj.*　过时的，不流行的
6　paranoia　　*n.*　妄想狂，偏执狂
7　rumour　　*n.*　谣言，传闻　*v.*　谣传
8　rule of thumb　　拇指规则，经验法则，凭感觉的方法，单凭经验的方法
9　seriously　　*adv.*　认真地，真诚地
10　investigate　　*v.*　调查，研究
11　backlink　　*n.*　后链
12　replicate　　*v.*　复制
13　surpass　　*v.*　超越，胜过
14　argue　　*v.*　争论，辩论；说服

PageRank system is merely using algorithms[1] that we don't understand, and no doubt that is true, but for the human webmaster trying to get traffic, PageRank and Google can be baffling sometimes.

There are instances of high PageRanked sites having little to no backlinks. Given that incoming links are one of the most important variables used in PageRank calculations[2], you have to scratch your head[3] and wonder how a site with no links could have a big green bar. Google's own backlink lookup[4] tool is another phenomenon[5] that search engine experts often choose to ignore rather than try and evaluate.

Thankfully the randomness of PageRank can result in positive outcomes as well, with your sites jumping high into search results in places where you wouldn't expect it. The only consistency is randomness but there is logic that can be followed. Just don't expect it to work precisely how or when you want it to.

4. What You Should Know and Do about PageRank

This advice I offer from experience as an avid PageRank chaser[6] and search engine optimizer. The key to gaining PageRank is to ignore it and focus on the variables that control it.

Having people link to your site has always been a good thing and PageRank was in fact a result of this. Don't get confused with the order of things, first came the Internet and links and then came PageRank. Focus on amassing[7] quality incoming links from quality sites relevant to your site. This practice will naturally improve your PageRank and also increase the amount of visitors coming to your site. Don't get bogged down chasing links from only high PageRank sites or waste energy adding links from just any site willing to link to you. Do things naturally and your site will grow naturally.

Learn about the importance of keywords. Keywords play a crucial role in bringing the right type of traffic to your site but you should never spend half an hour in front of[8] a computer trying to come up with the perfect title for your article. Name your content logically and think about what search words your audience would use to find your article and you can very quickly and easily develop good keywords without spending hours and hours tweaking[9] every little phrase and heading. See what your competitors[10] do in regards to keywords if you are completely lost.

If you build a good website with good content, always keep in mind[11] your important keywords and proactively work every day to earn and create new backlinks to your site you will improve your PageRank. The best sites with the highest PageRank never worry about PageRank, they simply keep churning out[12] content that people love to link to. This is a strategy that every

---

1 algorithm   *n.*   算法
2 calculation   *n.*   计算，考虑
3 scratch one's head   搔头皮，挠头，抓耳挠腮，对某事迷惑不解
4 lookup   *v.*   查找
5 phenomenon   *n.*   现象
6 chaser   *n.*   猎人
7 amass   *v.*   收集，积聚(尤指财富)
8 in front of   在……前面
9 tweak   *v.*   稍微调整
10 competitor   *n.*   竞争者
11 keep in mind   牢记
12 churn out   艰苦地做出

webmaster and Internet entrepreneur[1] should emulate[2] for success online.

参考译文

网 络 流 量

　　网络流量是访问者向网站发送和从网站接收的数据量。这必然不包括自动运行的程序所产生的流量。自 20 世纪 90 年代中期以来，网络流量一直是互联网流量的最大部分。这取决于访问者的数量和他们访问的页面数量。网站监控进出的流量，以查看其网站的哪些部分或哪些网页受欢迎，以及是否存在任何明显的趋势（例如，某个特定国家/地区的用户主要查看某个特定网页）。有许多方法来监控这些流量，收集的数据用于帮助构建站点，发现突出的安全问题或指明潜在的带宽不足。

　　并非所有的网络流量都受欢迎。一些公司提供广告计划，以增加网络流量（访问者），购买网站上的屏幕空间。网站还经常通过搜索引擎和搜索引擎优化来增加它们的网络流量。

1. 分析

　　网络分析是指测量网站访问者的行为。在商业背景下，尤指测量网站的哪些方面符合互联网营销的业务目标。例如，哪些着陆页鼓励人们购物。著名的网络分析软件和服务包括 Google Analytics（分析）、IBM Digital Analytics（以前称为 Coremetrics）和 Adobe Omniture。

2. 测量

　　测量网络流量以查看网站和网站中的各个页面或部分的受欢迎程度，这可以通过查看网络服务器日志文件在其中找到的流量统计信息来完成。该文件是一个自动生成的所有服务页面的列表。任何文件被投放时都会生成点击。页面本身被当作文件，但图像也是文件，因此一个具有 5 个图像的页面可以生成 6 个点击（5 个图像和页面本身）。当访问者请求网站中的任何页面时，会生成页面视图——访问者总是要生成至少一个页面视图（主页面），但可能会生成更多页面。网站外部的跟踪应用程序可以通过在网站的每个页面中插入一小段 HTML 代码来记录流量。

　　网络流量有时也通过分组嗅探来测量，以获得流量数据的随机样本，从而整体上推断关于整个互联网使用的网络流量信息。

　　在监控网络流量时，通常会整理以下类型的信息：

- 访客人数。
- 每位访问者的平均浏览量——较高的数字表示普通访问者深入网站内部，可能是因为他们喜欢或发现它有用。
- 平均访问持续时间——用户访问的总长度。通常，他们花费的时间越多，他们对你的公司越感兴趣，并且越容易联系。
- 平均网页持续时间——查看网页的时间长度。查看的页面越多，你的公司就越好。

1　entrepreneur　　*n.*　企业家，主办人
2　emulate　　*n.*　仿效

- 域类——传递网页和内容所需的所有级别的 IP 地址信息。
- 被占时间——网站最受欢迎的观看时间将显示何时是进行促销活动的最佳时间，以及最理想的维护时间。
- 最常请求的页面——最热门的页面。
- 最多请求的进入页面——进入页面是访问者查看的第一页，并显示哪些页面是最吸引访问者的页面。
- 最多请求的退出页面——请求最多的退出页面可以帮助找到错误的页面、断开的链接，或者可能有一个受欢迎的外部链接而退出页面。
- 顶级路径——路径是访问者从入口到出口查看的页面序列，其中顶级路径标识大多数客户经过网站的路线。
- 推荐者。主机可以跟踪链路的（明显的）来源并且确定哪些站点为特定页面带来了最多的流量。

根据访问网站的人员使用的工具栏和其他在线测量方法，网站生成流量排名和统计信息。这个问题的困难是，它不是看一个网站的完整流量图。大型网站通常会雇用 Nielsen NetRatings 或 Quancast 等公司来服务，但他们的报告只能通过订阅获得。

3. 控制

网站所看到的流量是其受欢迎度的度量。通过分析访客的统计数据，可以看到网站的缺点，并期待改善这些部分。还可以增加网站的受欢迎程度和访问者的数量。

（1）限制访问

有时候，通过密码保护网站的某些部分很重要，只允许授权的人访问特定的部分或页面。

某些网站管理员已选择对特定流量（如地理位置）屏蔽其网页。

还可以基于连接的数量和每个连接扩展的带宽来限制对网站服务器的访问。在 Apache HTTP 服务器上，这由 limitipconn 模块和其他模块完成。

（2）来自搜索引擎

大多数网站流量由搜索引擎驱动。每天数百万人使用搜索引擎来研究各种主题、购买产品并进行他们的日常冲浪活动。搜索引擎使用关键字来帮助用户找到相关信息，并且每个主要搜索引擎已经开发了唯一的算法来确定网站在搜索结果中的位置。当用户点击搜索结果中的列表项之一时，他们被引到相应的网站，并且从网站的服务器传送数据，从而计算访问者流向该网站的总流量。

搜索引擎优化（SEO）是优化网站以帮助提高其在搜索引擎中的排名的持续实践。它涉及几个内部和外部因素，可以帮助提高网站在搜索引擎中的排名。网站在特定关键字的搜索引擎中的排名越高，他们获得的流量就越多。

（3）增加流量

可以通过在搜索引擎中放置网站和购买广告（包括批量电子邮件、弹出广告和页内广告）来增加网络流量。还可以通过网络流量提供商来购买流量以增加网络流量，或购买非基于互联网的广告来增加流量。

不仅可以通过吸引更多访问者访问网站，还可以鼓励个人访问者在网站上"逗留"，以便让访问者查看多个页面来增加网络流量。

如果网页没有列在任何搜索的第一页，则发现它的可能性就大大减少，当在第一页上存在其他竞争时尤其如此。看过第一页后会读后续页面的人很少，并且百分比大大降低。因此，在搜索引擎上使用 SEO 与网站建设一样重要。

4. 流量过载

太多的网络流量可能会大大减慢或阻止大家访问网站。这是因为请求文件多到服务器难以处理，这可能是对网站的故意攻击或只是由于过度流行造成的。具有大量服务器的大规模网站通常能够处理所需的业务，而小网站更可能受到过载的影响。流量负载暴涨也可能会挤爆服务器或导致服务关闭。

（1）拒绝服务攻击

拒绝服务攻击（DoS 攻击）在恶意攻击后强制关闭网站，使网站淹没在其无法承受的请求中。病毒也已被用于协调大规模的分布式拒绝服务攻击。

（2）突然流行

突然爆发性的宣传可能会意外地导致网络流量过载。媒体中的新闻项目、快速传播的电子邮件或来自流行网站的链接可能导致访问者剧增，有时被称为瞬间拥挤或 Slashdot 效应。

Unit 7

Text A

Essential SEO Strategies for E-commerce Sites

Search Engine Optimization (SEO) may seem straightforward on the surface, but in practice, there are hundreds of interlocking pieces that must be monitored and adjusted in order to see positive results. The process is even more complicated for e-commerce sites, which operate under  a unique set of circumstances and must adhere to a distinct set of best practices. All the fundamentals still apply: publishing great content, earning quality inbound links, and maintaining an ongoing social media campaign. But in addition to these, you'll need to pursue these specific e-commerce strategies.

1. Create Unique Product Descriptions for Every Product

This is extremely important. It's tempting to use a manufacturer's description for your products, or to repeat sections of content for similar products, but the best strategy is to create a completely unique description for each of your products. It's a lot of work up front, but duplicate content can severely hinder your campaign, and all that extra unique content will pay off immediately.

2. Encourage User Reviews

Encourage your users to post reviews on each individual product page. Amazon executes this perfectly, so look at any product page on Amazon.com for a great example of how to implement user reviews. Google loves seeing unique, value-adding content, and with an e-commerce site, you have a key opportunity to generate free content from your user base. And you'll also boost sales by giving people more insight into the quality of the products you sell.

3. Establish Easy Site Navigation

This is crucial for both attaining higher search engine rankings and improving your site's user experience. Organize your product pages as intuitively as possible and separate them into easily searchable and easily understandable categories. Make your site map obvious and easy to follow, and design your site in a way that pleases the eye and immediately directs users where to go.

4. Optimize Your Site Load Times by Reducing the Size of Your Images

It's important to have high-quality images on your product pages, but don't go overboard. Having too many high-quality images on one page can slow down your site, which is bad for SEO.

Instead, reduce the size of your images, or build a feature that allows users to "zoom in" to see a larger version. This will keep your load speeds in check while still giving your users the quality they need to see.

5. Link between Pages Wherever Possible

Google prefers websites with value-adding internal linking. The fewer clicks a user has to make in order to get to any given page on your site, the better. Improve this by linking each page to several other similar, relevant pages in your domain.

6. Optimize Your Site for Mobile

This is essential for any site, but especially an e-commerce platform, which would otherwise be nearly impossible to navigate. Give your users a smooth mobile experience, either through a responsive design, a specific mobile design, or an interactive app that allows for a better mobile experience. This will become increasingly important in the coming years.

7. Integrate Your Product Pages with Social Sharing

In addition to basic social integration, your product pages should have social-share buttons so users can pass on information about your products with their friends and followers. This is a good business practice in general but it's particularly good for SEO because Google may use social signals as a measure of authority.

8. Keep Your Out of Stock and Discontinued Item Pages Up and Running

This might seem counterintuitive at first. After all, if you're no longer offering an item, why bother keeping the page up? It's worthwhile because it gives you more permanent pages, and a greater base of indexable content for Google bots to scour. All you need to do is add a headline or some other indication that the item is no longer available.

9. Create Seasonal Categories to Maximize Seasonal Attention

Seasonal items tend to have lower keyword competition, with the trade-off being a shorter period of relevance. To get the most out of your seasonal items, create specific seasonal category pages such as "Halloween Decor" or "Best in Fashion 2016".

10. Add a Community Forum and Encourage Growth

Another major content option for e-commerce platforms is a community forum where users can exchange information about their favorite products and make recommendations to one another. It will increase brand loyalty among your participants. Encourage community growth by starting conversations and responding to questions and complaints whenever possible.

11. Include Pictures and Videos for Every Product

E-commerce platforms serve as a perfect medium for visual content, which is increasingly important for SEO. Include videos and several high-quality pictures for every product you offer, tagged with relevant metadata, so each image has a chance of showing up for a relevant image-based search. Just keep them stored in a way that doesn't interfere with site loading times.

12. Make Your Site Secure

It's always been a best practice for e-commerce sites to have HTTPS encryption for user security. If you don't have it, get it now. In addition to providing an extra layer of user security, it also provides a significant ranking signal to Google.

13. Build Deep Inbound Links

Link building for e-commerce sites presents a significant opportunity: ample material for deep linking. When engaging in a link-building campaign, focus on attaining links to the deepest pages on your site that you can (such as niche product pages).

14. Check Your Pages for Errors Regularly

E-commerce sites can grow unwieldy fast, since they usually have a huge and growing number of pages. Perform routine checks to make sure none of your permalinks are generating 404 errors, and that all of your links to external content are still functional. You can do this using Google Webmaster Tools and a site-crawling[1] tool such as Screaming Frog.

15. Build Relevantly Titled URLs

Every URL on your e-commerce platform should be unique, relevant to the page, and keyword optimized. If you're using an automated means of page creation, you might be left with a URL ending in a long series of numbers and letters—change these immediately. For example, if you're offering a large red umbrella on a specific product page, end your URL with "/large-red-umbrella-v1" rather than "/10031490314180".

16. Use Catchy Meta Descriptions for Your Products

When a page appears on a Search Engine Ranking Page (SERP), the meta description appears as text under the hyperlink. Use this to your advantage by writing compelling copy for each of your products' meta descriptions. Your goal should be to immediately catch your user's attention, and draw him or her in.

17. Optimize Your Site's Internal Search Functionality

It's important to realize that Google isn't the only search engine you need to be thinking about. If you want your users to keep shopping on your site, you need to build and refine an internal search function that can efficiently scour your site and provide the most relevant results to your users. This means building an algorithm that can handle misspellings, offer predictive searches, and sort through every page on the site. It also means optimizing your product titles and categories to be searchable both internally and externally.

Put these strategies into effect immediately, and make regular updates as your business grows. E-commerce sites have unique challenges and differences from other websites, but with proper practices, SEO doesn't have to be difficult for them.

New Words

straightforward	adj.	简单的，易懂的，直接的
interlocking	adj.	相互关联的

---

[1] A web crawler is an Internet bot which systematically browses the World Wide Web, typically for the purpose of Web indexing (web spidering). Web search engines and some other sites use Web crawling or spidering software to update their web content or indices of others sites' web content. Web crawlers can copy all the pages they visit for later processing by a search engine which indexes the downloaded pages so the users can search much more efficiently.

complicated	*adj.*	复杂的，难解的
circumstance	*n.*	环境，详情，境况
distinct	*adj.*	清楚的，明显的，截然不同的，独特的
fundamental	*n.*	基本原则，基本原理
inbound	*adj.*	到达的
	n.	入站
pursue	*v.*	追求，继续，从事
duplicate	*adj.*	复制的，完全相同的
	n.	复制品，副本
	v.	复制，使加倍，使成双
hinder	*v.*	阻碍，打扰
review	*n.*	评论
implement	*v.*	贯彻，实现
	n.	工具，器具
value-adding	*n.*	增值
opportunity	*n.*	机会，时机
navigation	*n.*	导航，领航
intuitively	*adv.*	直观地
category	*n.*	种类，类别
mobile	*adj.*	可移动的，机动的
smooth	*adj.*	平滑的，平稳的，流畅的
	v.	使光滑，变平滑
responsive	*adj.*	做出响应的
app	*n.*	应用，应用程序，应用软件
integrate	*v.*	使成整体，使一体化
button	*n.*	按钮
follower	*n.*	追随者，粉丝
discontinue	*v.*	停止，废止，放弃
counterintuitive	*adj.*	违反直觉的，和直觉不同的
bother	*v.*	烦扰，打扰
	n.	麻烦，烦扰
permanent	*adj.*	永久的，持久的
seasonal	*adj.*	季节性的，周期性的
trade-off	*n.*	交换，协定，交易，平衡
community	*n.*	社区，团体
recommendation	*n.*	推荐，介绍(信)，劝告，建议
participant	*n.*	参与者，共享者
conversation	*n.*	会话，交谈

complaint	*n.*	诉苦，抱怨，牢骚，委屈
increasingly	*adv.*	日益，愈加
metadata	*n.*	元数据
encryption	*n.*	加密码
ample	*adj.*	充足的，丰富的
unwieldy	*adj.*	不实用的，难处理的，难使用的
functional	*adj.*	功能的
catchy	*adj.*	易记住的
meta	*n.*	元

❧ Phrases

on the surface	表面上
in practice	实际上
adhere to	坚持，信守，遵守
best practice	最优方法
inbound link	来自外部网站的链接
in addition to	除……之外
up front	前期，初期
pay off	还清(债务等)，付清，盈利
search engine ranking	搜索引擎排名
user experience	用户体验
site map	网站地图
load time	装入时间，加载时间
go overboard	过分爱好
zoom in	放大
out of stock	已脱销
brand loyalty	品牌忠诚
interfere with	妨碍，干涉，干扰
engage in	使从事于，参加
routine check	例行查核
be left with	被剩下，被留下
meta description	元描述，描述标签
to sb.'s advantage	对某人有利

❧ Abbreviations

HTTPS (HyperText Transfer Protocol over Secure Socket Layer) 带安全套接层的超文本传输协议
PermaLink (Permanent Link) 永久链接
URL (Uniform Resource Locator) 统一资源定位符

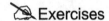 **Exercises**

[Ex. 1] Answer the following questions according to the text.

1. What is the best strategy when it comes to the description for each of your products?
2. How should you organize your product pages?
3. What is the result of having too many high-quality images on one page?
4. In addition to basic social integration, what should your product pages have? Why?
5. Why is it worthwhile to keep your out of stock and discontinued item pages up and running?
6. What should you do to get the most out of your seasonal items?
7. What should you do to encourage community growth?
8. What does e-commerce platforms serve as?
9. What should every URL on your e-commerce platform be?
10. If you want your users to keep shopping on your site, what do you need to do?

[Ex. 2] Translate the following terms or phrases from English into Chinese and vice versa.

1. best practice
2. engage in
3. inbound link
4. out of stock
5. site map
6. 搜索引擎排名
7. 用户体验
8. 会话，交谈
9. 加密码
10. 基本原则，基本原理

[Ex. 3] Translate the following passage into Chinese.

SEO vs. SEM

If you are an ecommerce professional that's not been living under a rock, you are plagued by the SEO vs. SEM debate. SEO as well as SEM are terms that can mean different things to different people. So let me clarify what I mean by those terms. By no means are these expected to be comprehensive definitions, but they serve the purpose of accuracy and simplicity.

What Is SEO?

Activities you undertake on your website, such as maintaining a certain keyword density, or on other websites, such as link building, with the intention of ranking higher on search engine results pages, is called Search Engine Optimization (SEO).

What Is SEM?

Paying search engines to send qualified traffic your way, probably using a pay-per-click mechanism, is Search Engine Marketing (SEM).

It can easily be argued that SEM is much broader than what I have just described and, in fact, includes the practice of SEO. So that we can come to some actionable conclusions, I am isolating SEO from other SEM activities.

It is easy to get stuck in an SEM-only approach, as that is what bears fruit initially. But price per click might soon rise to levels that your business may not be able to sustain. So it is good to build your organic leg too. Also, SEO is turning out to be an irritatingly moving target.

[Ex. 4]   Fill in the blanks with the words given below.

organized	visitors	search	strategy	particular
navigate	links	target	conversions	experience

Optimize Site Structure

Are the sections of your site appropriately themed? Namely, based on your keyword research, is your site's content organized well for both users to ___1___ across and search engines to deem relevant for a particular subject matter?

Creating a well-structured website defined by content and ___2___ around keyword research helps search engines in indexing your site's content. The easier it is for search engines to understand that your site is about a ___3___ subject matter, the more relevant you can become for a query.

As noted previously, a well organized, optimized website also helps visitors navigate it more easily to find the products they're seeking.

An integral part of an optimized site structure is internal linking. Search engine robots "crawl" the Web via links, so providing your website with a solid framework of internal ___4___ that logically lead from one page to another helps search engines in understanding the overall theme. Internal links also assist ___5___ with navigating your site—where do you want them to go next?

Part of an optimized internal linking strategy is using keywords where appropriate in the "anchor text"—the clickable words used in a link.

Optimize Usability

Essentially, "usability" refers to the ease with which visitors to your site can navigate it to find the information they're seeking.

Besides making your site easy to navigate, you can increase ___6___ with a clear "Call to Action" (CTA) that facilitates purchases: don't "hide" your sales pages or make it a complicated process for people to buy.

A second critical consideration when optimizing for usability is the growing trend toward mobile, as discussed by BrightEdge CEO Jim Yu at Search Engine Watch. Configuring your website for a mobile-friendly user ___7___ will assist consumers in their shopping and purchase decisions.

Social Media Integration

There is no doubt that social media influences the ___8___ results. Optimizing your site's content by integrating it with social media campaigns is a smart ___9___ that can help with your site's rankings and thereby, e-commerce sales.

When considering your social media integration strategy it's important to keep in mind the appropriate ___10___ audience. One size does not fit all: for some e-commerce businesses, especially those heavy with images, Pinterest may be the best social platform. For others, it may well be Google + or LinkedIn.

Text B

Best Practices That Could Double E-commerce Sales

1. Handling SEO for New Products

Good information architecture, website structure and internal link architecture are critical to rank new product pages well. Link categories from your home page, and your product pages from the category levels. This will ensure that Google finds, crawls and indexes your content fast. Also link to them from their parent category pages.

Optimize your website theme so that new products are always presented on your home page where they'll get found and indexed. A good internal link architecture will get your new product pages indexed and ranked quickly.

2. Presenting Product Descriptions from Manufacturers

Google doesn't like duplicate content. Reprinting product descriptions from manufacturers is duplicate content. But large e-commerce websites cannot rewrite all product descriptions and specifications.

You can get around this by adding unique content like user-generated comments and reviews around it. Invite user comments. Integrate social networking. Let users tell their stories. Happy customers will serve as your marketing helpers.

(1) Add Content to Product Pages

Raise the quality and uniqueness of your content by personalizing it to solve your users' problems. Add information, images, video or suggestions to your content.

(2) Add a "Psychology" Layer to Your Content

Typical product descriptions are dull and technical. People, however, buy on emotion and feelings. Bring your product descriptions to life by telling a story.

3. Dealing with Product Variations (Colors, Sizes, Etc.)

Some products are almost identical but exist in different colors or sizes. If not handled right, listing them can be considered duplicate content, which causes bad rankings and cannibalization between the different product variants. Products may rank for the wrong keywords (blue jeans rank for searches on red jeans). Adam Audette goes deeper into the nuances in this excellent report.

Review your website and you might find many products that may sell better if ranked for the right keywords.

4. Handling Category Pages

(1) Treat Category Pages As Individual Home Pages

Look at your categories as silos or niches that contain closely related product pages.

(2) Build Deep-Links to Product Categories

Guest blogging, content marketing and even paid ads work well, as does social media.

(3) Tag Socially Shared Content

Be strategic about sharing links on Google Plus, Twitter and other networks. Be specific with your tags.

(4) Take Charge of What's Being Shown/Presented

Design category pages to provide search engines and users the best service.

(5) Use Search-Friendly URLs

This often gets quick results because you are giving the search engines strong hints about what this URL is about while giving visitors help and valuable information—just make sure to avoid keyword stuffing. The most effective URL structure for category pages (and product pages) is:

- Category page: Website.com/category/.
- Sub-category page: Website.com/category/sub-category/.
- Product page: Website.com/category-sub-category/product-name/.

5. Managing Internal Link Building & Architecture

Internal link building helps with SEO and rankings. But to achieve better results, you need link architecture, not just "link building". Internal linking is not all about search engine spiders[1]. User friendliness also matters. Creating a solid internal link architecture needs planning and takes time.

(1) Offer Category Level Navigation

This makes it easier for your users to get an overview of what they will find in the subcategories and pages. Strive to keep things contextually relevant.

(2) Link to Category-Level Relevant Products

Look at this from a human perspective by taking intent and needs into consideration, but also optimize for the right keywords.

(3) Use Breadcrumbs on All Pages and Category Pages

This ensures that users and Google can navigate up one level to a parent category.

6. Weaving SEO into the Web Design Process

Web design isn't just about visual appeal. You need a specialist e-commerce web designer who's experienced and will work as a team with your SEO consultant, analyst, conversion rate optimizer and others. You must give them space and budgets to act as experts.

When your website design and information architecture work in tandem, with no pages/URLs breaking out of the structure, you'll boost the entire site every time you publish a new product page and ensure early crawling by search spiders. Good design and content along with a pleasant visitor experience will generate more sales.

(1) Failing to Plan Is Planning to Fail

SEO must be baked into the business/website early in the planning phase, before you even start

---

[1] A spider is a software program that travels the web (hence the name "spider"), locating and indexing websites for search engines. All the major search engines, such as Google and Yahoo!, use spiders to build and update their indexes. These programs constantly browse the web, traveling from one hyperlink to another.

129

working on your wireframes and design process—not after the site is launched. Making awesome category/section templates and having product pages promote them with internal links is very effective.

(2) SEO for E-commerce Websites Is Different from Traditional SEO

E-commerce SEO requires a consultant skilled in multiple disciplines, with a deep understanding of human psychology, conversion rate optimization, analytics, web design & development, social media marketing and communication, copywriting, economy, usability and user experience. The best e-commerce SEO specialists also have deep insight and understanding of commerce and how a retail business functions.

(3) E-commerce Web Design Is Never "Finished"

It's a continuous process of A/B testing to hunt down the best performing variations. The right "tools" are important, but the best consultant or company is more important. An expensive consultant is not expensive if she can generate many more sales than a "cheap" one.

7. Optimizing Product Pictures and Videos?

The quality of your pictures, photos and videos will influence how visitors feel about your product. Never underestimate the value of making prospective buyers feel the benefits of your product.

Interesting pictures get shared on Pinterest and social networks. Getting users to tag and comment on photos also makes your content unique. Your brand grows stronger as word of mouth spreads. With optimized images, you can even pull in more traffic from Google image search.

(1) Use High-Quality Pictures

Get photographs that create an atmosphere, that make prospects feel something. Those will make more sales. Though expensive, it's a good investment for your best products. Video can work even better.

(2) Optimize Your Images

File name, alt text, caption, etc., should be short yet descriptive. These are opportunities to provide search engines with clues as to what your image content is.

(3) A/B-Test Options

Try one picture against another to see which gives better conversion rates.

8. Designing for Mobile Devices

Mobile is too important to ignore in your e-commerce SEO strategy. An informal survey my colleague Kenneth Gvein ran for our e-commerce customers at Metronet and Vaimo Norway found that clients had 2 to 3 times higher growth rate on mobile e-commerce. Go mobile—or go home!

Offer desktop versions of all URLs. Some users prefer the standard web version, even on mobile. Offer the option to switch between versions. Don't return them to the home page like many e-commerce websites do.

9. Dealing with Security

Your customers are worried about online security—with good reason. They put their identity and financial data in your hands. You must reassure them that it's safe.

Leave visual clues. Display logos and text certifying that you comply with security standards. Show them your SSL/Visa/other security and encryption standards or certificates. Tell them that shopping at your e-commerce website is 100% safe. This boosts conversions.

Many e-tailers hide this information at the bottom of a page, or simply take it for granted. Don't make that mistake.

(1) Periodic SEO Analysis

SEO is not static, nor is your e-commerce website. Your site and code will change. A developer may, with the best intent at heart, fix one problem but create another. Use a strategic SEO framework to ensure that everything is in sync with your economic and strategic goals.

(2) Use Google Webmaster Tools

This free tool helps webmasters find and fix vexing SEO problems. Establish a routine in which you:

- Look for 404 errors, soft 404's and other problems.
- See how your website, products and pages are performing on the SERPs.
- Notice popular keywords and phrases, popular pages and more.

I recommend integrating Google Webmaster Tools, Google AdWords and Google Analytics to get access to valuable information for free.

(3) Take Action.

Just monitoring data isn't enough. You must identify the actionable items to keep improving. Know what to look for and why. Spot problems with indexing, duplicate content, manual penalties from Google and more. Fix the problems promptly.

(4) Invest in SEO Tools.

Tools like Moz, Search Metrics, Raven SEO Tools, Deep Crawl and others help you to identify problems and offer suggestions to fix them. Set up actionable reporting. Establish routines to address problems. Each tool has unique advantages. As a consultant, I recommend using a combination of tools for e-commerce SEO.

(5) Do Manual (Sample) Testing

Use Screaming Frog SEO Spider to identify problems with pages and sections of your e-commerce website. Pick one product segment that is important to you and perform an analysis within specific categories and subcategories. Often you'll track down site-wide problems caused by your CMS that can be quickly fixed.

(6) Do Data Analysis

Everything you do can be done better, but you don't have the resources to do it all. You need analysis to help prioritize areas for improvement. Build dashboards containing actionable information.

(7) Take the Mobile Revolution Seriously

Mobile devices are growing fast. Delays in developing your mobile site can kill your online business. What experience are you giving mobile users and how can you improve?

It's not possible to cover everything about SEO for e-commerce sites in one article. The advice above has helped many e-commerce websites increase sales and revenue by large multiples, but it is only the tip of the iceberg.

✍ New Words

index	n.	索引
	v.	编入索引中，做索引
rewrite	v.	重写，改写
specification	n.	详述，规格，说明书，规范
comment	n.	注释，评论，意见
	v.	注释，评论
uniqueness	n.	唯一性，独特性
suggestion	n.	提议，意见，暗示
psychology	n.	心理学，心理状态
dull	adj.	无趣的
technical	adj.	技术的，技巧的
emotion	n.	情绪，情感，感情
variation	n.	变更，变化，变异，变种
cannibalize	v.	(公司中一种产品)损害，冲击（其他产品的销量）
jeans	n.	牛仔裤，斜纹布裤
treat	v.	视为，对待，论述，交涉，谈判，协商
silo	n.	筒仓，地窖
stuffing	v.	填充
	n.	填充物
spider	n.	爬行程序，蜘蛛
subcategory	n.	亚类，子种类，子范畴
contextual	adj.	文脉上的，前后关系的
perspective	n.	观点，看法
breadcrumb	n.	面包屑导航
weave	v.	编织，组合，编排
consultant	n.	顾问，商议者，咨询者
wireframe	n.	线框图
usability	n.	可用性
continuous	adj.	连续的，持续的
influence	v.	影响，改变
atmosphere	n.	气氛
prospect	n.	景色，前景，前途，期望
	v.	寻找
caption	n.	标题，说明，字幕

	v.	加上标题，加上说明
ignore	*v.*	不理睬，忽视
informal	*adj.*	不正式的
reassure	*v.*	使……安心，使……恢复信心，打消……的疑虑
clue	*n.*	线索
certificate	*n.*	证书
	v.	发给……证书，以证书形式授权给……
static	*adj.*	静态的
sync	*n.*	同时，同步
fix	*v.*	修理，准备，安装
vex	*v.*	使烦恼，恼怒
actionable	*adj.*	可行动的
prioritize	*v.*	把……区分优先次序
dashboard	*n.*	主控面板，仪表板，挡泥板
advice	*n.*	忠告，建议

✍ Phrases

home page	主页
take charge of	负责，看管，担任，照管，监理
user friendliness	用户友好
in tandem	协力地
break out of	摆脱(束缚等)，突破
content with	满足于……
be different from…	与……不同
skill in…	对……熟练
hunt down	搜索直至找到（某物），穷追直至抓获
prospective buyer	可能的买主，潜在的买家
pull in	吸引，招引
even better	更胜一筹
alt text	替换文本，替换文字，替代文本
be worried about	为……忧虑，烦恼的
take it for granted	视为当然，想当然
invest in	投资于，买进
tip of the iceberg	露出水面的冰山顶，事物的表面部分

✍ Abbreviations

CMS (Content Management System)　　　内容管理系统

Exercises

[Ex. 5] Answer the following questions according to the text.

1. What critical to rank new product pages well?
2. How can you raise the quality and uniqueness of your content?
3. Why does using search-friendly URLs often get quick results?
4. What does creating a solid internal link architecture need and take?
5. When your website design and information architecture work in tandem, with no pages/URLs breaking out of the structure, what will you do?
6. What kind of consultant does e-commerce SEO require?
7. What should you never underestimate?
8. What should file name, alt text, caption, etc., be?
9. What did the author's colleague Kenneth Gvein find in an informal survey for their e-commerce customers at Metronet and Vaimo Norway?
10. What tools help you to identify security problems and offer suggestions to fix them?

Reading Material

Top Ten SEM Optimization Tips for E-commerce Sites

Earlier this week, we hosted a webinar[1] with Francis Shovlin and Ally Malick from SEER Interactive[2] on Search Engine Marketing (SEM) optimization for e-commerce. There's no denying it, it, those cats know their stuff. We wanted to pass along a few things we learned from them and share some insights[3]. By doing a few simple things, you can gain insights to performance that you wouldn't have available just by running Adwords.

1. Tag[4] Your URLs

The easiest thing to do in Google AdWords is to go into "my account" and enable the auto-tag feature. If you want to get really granular, make sure you are tagging manually by setting tags up in Google URL builder. It is better to start off with[5] too much detail and have all of the information in your analytics than to not tag and not be able to retroactively[6] figure out where traffic is coming from.

2. Modify[7] Your Google Analytics Codes to Track Revenue

Adwords can show you that your brand name[8] is driving the majority of your sales. That's

---

1　webinar　　　*n.*　在线研讨会
2　SEER Interactive　　成立于 2002 年的搜索公司。
3　insight　　*n.*　洞察力，见识
4　tag　　*n.*　标签　*v.*　加标签于
5　start off with　　从……开始，用……开始
6　retroactively　　*adv.*　追溯地
7　modify　　*v.*　更改，修改
8　brand name　　商标，品牌

great, but when people search your brand, what are they looking for? When you look in Google Analytics, you can see what exactly that term is driving people to purchase.

If it turns out that most people that search "your brand name" are buying one product, or one type of product, you can adjust your ad copy, landing pages and maybe even highlight a featured product on your homepage(Figure 7-1).

Product	Keyword	Quantity	Unique Purchases	Product Revenue
		1,869	1,328	$95,857
1. Shirt	[your brand term]	1	1	$4,800.00
2. Pants	+non +brand +term	1	1	$4,013.99
3. Shirt	nonbrand term	1	1	$3,600.00
4. Shirt	[your brand term]	1	1	$3,600.00
5. Pants	[your brand term]	1	1	$3,400.00
6. Socks	nonbrand term	1	1	$3,200.00

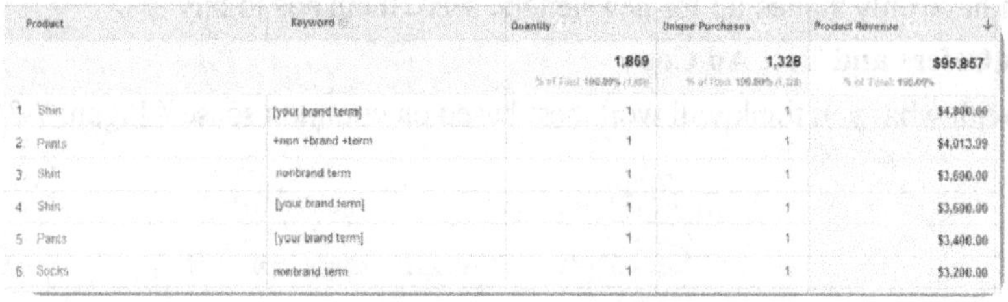

Figure 7-1

3. Update Your Ads to Match Your Inventory

Driving people to product pages that have no inventory is not a good user experience. Take the time to turn ad groups on and off depending on availability[1], or make it clear when the item will be back in stock. Unless you can promise a specific date of restock[2] and allow the customer to order it right then, don't advertise what you can't sell.

4. Test Bids on Research Keywords

Assign[3] unique strategies based on intent of query. Some people are searching with intent to buy and some people are searching the Internet just to do a little research. While it is tempting to eliminate research terms altogether, why sabotage the very top of your funnel? The research crowd might not have a high return value initially, but one day, they'll be ready to buy. By using the conversion assist report, you can calculate the true value of each keyword over time, even if they seem like lower return keywords to start(Figure 7-2).

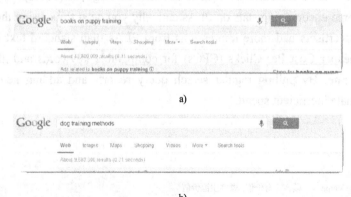

a)

b)

Figure 7-2

1 availability　*n.* 可用性，有效性，实用性

2 restock　*v.* 重新进货，再储存

3 assign　*v.* 分配，指派

5. Remarket to Both Converted and Haven't-Bought-Yet Users

There are many user situations that you can use for remarketing: First, target users who abandoned their shopping cart, reminding them that they should buy what they were looking for. If customers from a certain channel have a lower CLV(customer lifetime value[1]), target that channel and give them more opportunities to buy. Upsell[2] users that have previously converted. Don't forget about users that have only signed up for newsletters, serve them ads to buy!

6. Always Test Offers and Test Ad Copy

Don't go with what you think will work best based on common sense[3](Figure 7-3).

Figure 7-3

When testing, make sure you have your ads set to rotate indefinitely[4], not optimize for clicks. Do your own testing, as you don't want the most clicks, you want the ad that brings in the most revenue. This is a very important difference for e-commerce sites!

7. Learn How to Use Ad Extensions & Targeting

If you go back to point #2, we list a great reason to use sitelink extensions. If people searching for your brand typically end up buying a couple of[5] items, you can highlight those product pages with sitelink extensions. If you are running mobile campaigns, or often get calls about online purchases, use the call extension to put your phone number directly in the ad. The newest extension that Google offers is the offer extension. Give your users the opportunity to hand over their e-mail directly in your ad.

8. Take Advantage of the Prominent Placing of Product Listing Ads (PLAs)[6]

SEER gave some encouraging stats on PLAs and why you need to be using them. 8 out of the top 20 Adwords advertisers had more impressions from PLAs than standard text ads. One SEER client saw 33% cheaper Cost Per Clicks (CPCs) for comparable keywords and also had an 11% higher conversion rate. By pulling regular search query reports and adding negatives, you can optimize and eliminate inefficient spend.

---

1 Customer Lifetime Value   顾客终身价值，顾客生涯价值
2 upsell   v. 提升销售，向上销售，增销
3 common sense   常识
4 indefinitely   adv. 不确定地
5 a couple of   两个，几个
6 Product Listing Ads(PLAs)   产品列表广告，产品目录广告

Figure 7-4

9. If You Are Running Mobile Ads, Optimize Your Site for Mobile

Are you opted into[1] mobile? Product images should be large and clear on a smartphone and it should be easy to go from the product page through the checkout process. Think about making the add to cart button thumb-clickable. Remember, if you are sending ad traffic to mobile and you haven't optimized for it, your ad quality score will plummet[2]. Best case scenario, make everything mobile friendly, but if you can't do that, make sure you opt out of mobile ads!

10. Create Specific Product Landing Pages[3] to Maximize Conversion Rates

Say someone is searching for a red shirt. Do you send them to a page that only has a red shirt, or do you send them to a page that shows them many shirts? You might have more conversions by sending them directly to the item they've searched for, but you might have a higher AOV[4] by sending them to a page with shirts in every color(Figure 7-5).

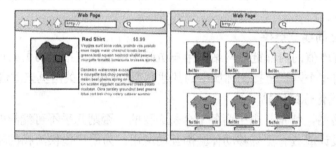

Figure 7-5

参 考 译 文

电子商务网站的基本 SEO 策略

搜索引擎优化（SEO）表面上看起来很简单，但在实践中，有许许多多相互关联的部分必须被监管和调整才有效。对于电子商务网站来说，这一过程更为复杂。电子商务网站在一系列独特的情况下运作，必须遵循一套独特的最佳做法。所有基本原则仍然适用：发布精彩内容、获得优质的内容链接以及维持不断的社交媒体宣传活动。除此之外，还需要采取下述

---

1 opted into　　选择使用
2 plummet　　*n.* 重荷　*v.* 垂直落下
3 landing page　　登录页，着录页
4 AOV (Average Order Value)　　平均客单价

137

这些具体的电子商务策略。

1. 为每个产品创建唯一的产品描述

这是非常重要的。对你的产品使用制造商的说明很有吸引力，或者重复类似产品的内容部分，但最好的策略是为每个产品创建完全独特的说明。这需要做很多前期工作，但重复的内容可以严重影响你的销售活动，每个额外的独特内容都立竿见影地有所回报。

2. 鼓励用户评论

鼓励你的用户在每个产品页上发布评论。亚马逊完美地执行了这一操作，是一个很好的范例。查看亚马逊网站上的任何产品页面，了解如何实施用户评论。谷歌喜欢看到独特的增值内容。有了电子商务网站，你就有机会从用户群中生成免费内容。你还可以通过让用户更深入地了解你销售的产品的质量，从而提高销量。

3. 建立轻松的网站导航

这对于获得更高的搜索引擎排名和改善你的网站的用户体验至关重要。尽可能直观地组织产品页面，并将其分为容易搜索和易于理解的类别。使你的网站地图更明显和容易跟随，并以这种方式设计网站；网站悦目并立即引导用户去其目标处。

4. 通过减小图像的大小来优化网站的加载时间

在产品页面上提供高品质的图片很重要，但不要过度使用。在一个网页上有太多高品质的图片可能会拖慢你的网站，这对 SEO 不利。相反，减少图片的大小，或建立一个功能，让用户用"放大"功能看到一个更大的图片，这将保持载入速度同时仍能让用户看到他们需要的高质量的图片。

5. 尽可能在页面之间建立链接

谷歌喜欢具有增值的内部链接网站。用户访问网站上任何指定网页的点击次数越少，效果就越好。通过将每个网页链接到你域中的其他几个类似的相关网页来改进此功能。

6. 针对移动设备优化你的网站

这对于任何网站，特别是电子商务平台是必要的，否则几乎不可能导航。通过响应式设计、特定的移动设计或具有更好移动体验的互动应用，为用户提供流畅的移动体验。这将在未来几年变得越来越重要。

7. 将你的产品页面与社交共享集成

除了基本的社交整合，你的产品页面应该有社交分享按钮，这样，用户可以把你的产品信息传递给他们的朋友和粉丝。总体来说，这是一个很好的商业惯例，但它对于 SEO 特别好，因为谷歌可能把社交信号作为对权威的度量。

8. 保留缺货和停售产品的页面

这似乎违反直觉。毕竟，如果你不再提供一个物品，为什么还要保留页面？这是值得的，因为它给你更多的永久页面和更大、更基本的可索引内容供谷歌机器人抓取。你需要做的只是添加一个标题或标明该物品已经停售。

9. 创建季节性类别以最大限度地提高季节性注意力

季节性物品的关键字往往竞争力较低，销售时段相对较短。要充分利用季节性商品，建立特定的季节性类别页面，如"万圣节装饰"或"2016年最佳时尚"。

10. 添加社区论坛并力求不断增加

电子商务平台的另一个主要内容选项是社区论坛，其中用户可以交换他们喜欢产品的信息并且互相提建议。它将提高参与者之间对你的品牌忠诚度。通过开始对话和尽可能回答问题和应对投诉来鼓励社区增长。

11. 为每个产品制作图片和视频

电子商务平台是视觉内容的完美媒介，它对于搜索引擎优化越来越重要。为每个产品都添加视频和几个高质量图片并标记相关的元数据，这样每个图片都有机会展示给相关的基于图片的搜索。只要存储方式得当就不会影响网站加载时间。

12. 让你的网站安全

对于电子商务网站来说，为了用户安全而采用 HTTPS 加密是一种最佳做法。如果你还没有，现在开始使用它吧。除了提供额外的用户安全层，它还向谷歌提供了重要的排名信号。

13. 建立深度入站链接

建立电子商务网站的链接可以提供一个重要的机会：用于深度链接的丰富材料。在构建链接时，可以专注于网站上最深的网页（如特定产品页）的链接。

14. 定期检查你的网页是否有错误

电子商务网站可以快速增长，因为它们通常有巨大的和不断增长的页数。执行例行检查，以确保没有任何永久链接正在生成 404 错误，并且所有指向外部内容的链接仍然有效。你可以使用谷歌网站管理员工具和网站抓取工具（如 Screaming Frog）执行此操作。

15. 构建相关标题的 URL

你的电子商务平台上的每个网址都应该是唯一的、与网页关联并且进行了关键字优化。如果使用自动创建页面的方式，则可能会看到以一系列数字和字母结尾的网址——请立即更改这些网址。例如，如果你在特定产品页上提供大型红色雨伞，请使用"/ large-red-umbrella-v1"而不是"/ 10031490314180"作为网址的结尾。

16. 对你的产品使用易于记忆的元描述

当页面出现在搜索引擎排名页面（SERP）上时，元描述在超链接下显示为文本。通过为每个产品的元描述撰写引人注目的副本，从而为你带来优势。目标应该是立即吸引用户的注意力，吸引他或她。

17. 优化你的网站的内部搜索功能

请注意，谷歌不是你唯一需要考虑的搜索引擎。如果你希望用户在你的网站上继续购物，则需要构建和优化内部搜索功能，以便用户能有效地浏览你的网站，并向用户提供最相关的结果。这意味着建立一种算法，可以处理拼写错误，提供预测搜索和对网站上的每一个页面进行排序。它还意味着优化产品标题和类别，以便在内部和外部都可搜索。

立即采用这些策略，并随着业务的增长定期更新。电子商务网站不同于其他网站且有独特的挑战性，但如果做法得当，则 SEO 并不困难。

Unit 8

Text A

The Ways to Track Online to Offline Conversions (and Vice Versa)

In the real world, what marketers need are discrete ways to track discrete actions. That's why I think a roundup of some methods of tracking online to offline conversions (and back again) might be useful.

扫一扫，听课文

1. Tracking Online Marketing to Offline Sales

(1) Tracking Estimated Store Visits from PPC Ad Clicks

An estimate of store visits was introduced to Google's conversion tracking in AdWords at the end of 2014.

The concept is simple, link a verified store location from Google Maps with your AdWords account and Google will give an estimated number of store visits within 30 days of your PPC ads being clicked.

Google does this by aggregating data from smartphone users who have location history enabled and are signed in to Google.

Although only an estimate, this method will reveal which PPC campaigns are driving more traffic to store and hence are likely to be more impactful than their mere online conversion rate suggests.

(2) Importing Offline Conversions That Start with a PPC Ad Click

This is a method of tracking, again within AdWords, that involves capturing customer details on your website (perhaps via a contact form or a phone call) and saving these details alongside the globally unique tracking parameter (Gclid) generated by their incoming PPC ad click.

When a sale is closed off the back of this customer contact, it's up to the advertiser to regularly upload these conversions and Gclids back into AdWords, which will register a sale against the appropriate campaign and keyphrases[1].

(3) Call Tracking

Call tracking solutions allow each caller to be assigned a unique phone number, so leads and

---

[1] Phrases or a search term that is made up of multiple keywords, or a specific combination of keywords, that a user would enter into a search engine. In SEO (search engine optimization), optimizing your site for specific keyphrases will yield a smaller number of more specific and relevant traffic.

sales can be assigned to site visitors who move offline and pick up the phone.

These solutions allow the marketer to look at page visits and keyword referral. Call tracking is particularly important for considered purchases where a sale is completed offline.

From mobiles, the click-to-call functionality in Google search is becoming more common. This is enabled in AdWords as a call extension.

A recent study by Econsultancy and Response Tap showed only 18% of respondents were using call tracking.

(4) Coupons

In marketing, a coupon is a ticket or document that can be redeemed for a financial discount or rebate when purchasing a product.

Customarily, coupons are issued by manufacturers of consumer packaged goods or by retailers, to be used in retail stores as a part of sales promotions. They are often widely distributed through mail, coupon envelopes, magazines, newspapers, the Internet (social media, e-mail newsletter) and mobile devices such as cell phones directly from the retailer. Since only price conscious consumers are likely to spend the time to claim the savings, coupons function as a form of price discrimination, enabling retailers to offer a lower price only to those consumers who would otherwise go elsewhere. In addition, coupons can also be targeted selectively to regional markets in which price competition is great.

There are different types of values applied to coupons such as discounts, free shipping, buy-one get-one, trade-in for redemption, first-time customer coupons, free trial offer, launch offers, festival offers, and free giveaways. Similarly, there are different uses of coupons which include: to incentive a purchase, to reduce the price of a particular item or items, provide a free sample, or to help allow marketers better-understand the demographics of their customer.

Coupon is the oldest trick in the book. Of course, the rub here is that a discount is necessary as the incentive. A coupon's success is usually used at the campaign level.

(5) Ask the Customer How They Heard about You

If all else fails, simply ask the customer how they heard about you. This may not give any detailed insight and will probably work better for considered purchases where interaction with the customer is increased.

(6) Click and Collect

Click and collect is obviously not solely a tracking method, it's a customer expectation in many sectors, which will improve the experience for online and offline shoppers.

However, it's also obvious that click and collect creates data around customers and products, and shows which customers shop where and when.

This may help to tailor future messaging to customers based on store locations.

2. Tracking Offline Marketing to Online Sales

(1) Adding UTM parameters to links

Using Google's URL builder, you can append a link with information about its source. Traffic from these links is then shown as a unique campaign within Google Analytics.

Of course, for offline campaigns, you'll want to use a catchy URL.

You can shorten your appended link and customize it. However, bear in mind that this involves a number of redirects and can be unreliable.

It's probably better to create a custom landing page, with UTM parameters mostly used for tracking across digital channels.

(2) Creating Custom Landing Pages

Using landing pages for offline campaigns is a time-tested way of measuring engagement and ultimately sales. Simply use a catchy URL in your offline marketing.

Remember not to allow indexing of the landing pages within search.

Deciding not to index will prevent search traffic hitting the page and should give a clearer picture of campaign success.

Using analytics to also account for social visits to your landing pages may be appropriate, although it's arguable this falls within the context of an offline campaign as customers share it among themselves.

(3) Using Redirect Domains

For services marketed at a local level, marketers may want to use a more relevant domain that is then redirected to the appropriate page on their "real" website.

For example, if I happened to be the owner of Marquees.com but wanted to run a campaign aimed at the mill town in North West England where I grew up, I might purchase the domain BuryMarquees.com in the belief that this would drive more website visitors.

Redirecting BuryMarquees.com to my main website and using tracking code to set the redirecting domain as the referrer, I could keep tabs on success.

(4) QR Codes

This is essentially a method of directing users to a URL. It is just a delivery method for custom landing pages or tracked URLs.

QR codes are a *bête noire* for many marketers, often used in the worst way conceivable. NFC is similarly controversial.

(5) Direct Traffic Increase

If offline campaigns are big enough, for example a big Christmas TV advert, the increase in direct web traffic and sales is usually visible as a very obvious correlation.

This is, of course, only a comfort to those with big above-the-line media budgets.

3. Joining Up Online and Offline Sales Data

Honorable mention must be made here for two tactics that don't fall into either of the camps above—loyalty cards and e-receipts.

These are techniques to unite sales data and give a single customer view.

Both can allow a retailer to unite a customer's online and offline sales data and build a more accurate picture of customer value and behavior.

E-receipts, in particular, are surprisingly uncommon. Shoe retailer Schuh uses them to improve the customer experience (makes 365-day returns easier).

It's conceivable that e-receipts would allow retailers to match e-mail addresses given in store to their CRM, to give a similar view to that provided by loyalty card data.

New Words

conversion	n.	转化，变换
marketer	n.	市场商人
discrete	adj.	不连续的，离散的
roundup	n.	集拢，赶拢，摘要，综述
concept	n.	观念，概念
aggregate	n.	合计，总计，集合体
	adj.	合计的，集合的，聚合的
	v.	聚集，集合，合计
enable	v.	使能够
reveal	v.	展现，显示，揭示
suggest	v.	建议，提出，使想起
parameter	n.	参数，参量
advertiser	n.	登广告者，广告客户
keyphrase	n.	关键短语
caller	n.	呼叫者，传唤员，访客
referral	n.	提名，推举
coupon	n.	商家的优待券
redeem	v.	补偿，兑换
rebate	n.	回扣，折扣
	v.	减少，打折扣，给……回扣，打折扣
envelope	n.	信封，封套，封袋
newsletter	n.	通信
conscious	adj.	在意的，自觉的，有意的
festival	n.	节日
	adj.	节日的，快乐的
giveaway	n.	免费样品
sample	n.	样品
	v.	取样，采样，抽取……的样品
demographic	adj.	人口统计学的
shopper	n.	购物者
tailor	v.	制作
customize	v.	定制，用户化
redirect	v.	重新定向，使改变方向
unreliable	adj.	不可靠的

time-tested	adj.	经受时间考验的，久经试验的
arguable	adj.	可辩论的，可论证的
domain	n.	域
referrer	n.	来源页面地址
conceivable	adj.	可能的，想得到的，可想象的
controversial	adj.	争论的，争议的
correlation	n.	相互关系，相关性
tactics	n.	战术，策略
e-receipt	n.	电子收条，电子收据
surprisingly	adv.	令人惊讶地
uncommon	adj.	不凡的，罕有的，难得的

Phrases

online to offline	线上到线下
vice versa	反之亦然
sign in	签到，登记
close off	结账
pick up	捡起，获得
consumer packaged good	大众消费品，快速消费品
retail store	零售店
sales promotion	促销
price conscious consumer	对价格敏感的消费者
price discrimination	价格歧视，因人而异的售价
price competition	价格竞争
free shipping	免费送货
buy-one get-one	买一送一
free trial	免费试用
bear in mind	记住
grow up	长大
mill town	磨坊小镇，工业城
bête noire	眼中钉，非常不受人喜欢的人或事
honorable mention	荣誉奖，优秀奖，鼓励奖

Abbreviations

QR (Quick Response)	快速反应
NFC (Near Field Communication)	近距离通信
CRM (Customer Relationship Management)	客户关系管理

 **Exercises**

[Ex. 1] Answer the following questions according to the text.
1. How does Google track estimated store visits?
2. What is importing offline conversions that start with a PPC ad click?
3. What does tracking solutions allow?
4. What did a recent study by Econsultancy and Response Tap show?
5. What is a coupon in marketing?
6. What are the different types of values applied to coupons?
7. What is using landing pages for offline campaigns?
8. What may marketers want to do for services marketed at a local level?
9. What are loyalty cards and e-receipts? What can both of them allow a retailer to do?
10. What does shoe retailer Schuh use e-receipts to do?

[Ex. 2] Translate the following terms or phrases from English into Chinese and vice versa.

1. buy-one get-one		1.	_____
2. consumer packaged good		2.	_____
3. free shipping		3.	_____
4. retail store		4.	_____
5. sales promotion		5.	_____
6. 价格竞争		6.	_____
7. 对价格敏感的消费者		7.	_____
8. 商家的优待券		8.	_____
9. 电子收条，电子收据		9.	_____
10. 免费样品		10.	_____

[Ex. 3] Translate the following passage into Chinese.

Social Media Marketing

Social Media Marketing (SMM) is a form of Internet marketing that utilizes social networking websites as a marketing tool. The goal of SMM is to produce content that users will share with their social network to help a company increase brand exposure and broaden customer reach.

One of the key components of SMM is Social Media Optimization (SMO). Like Search Engine Optimization (SEO), SMO is a strategy for drawing new and unique visitors to a website. SMO can be done in two ways: adding social media links to content, such as RSS feeds and sharing buttons—or promoting activity through social media by updating statuses or tweets, or blog posts.

SMM helps a company get direct feedback from customers (and potential customers) while making the company seem more personable. The interactive parts of social media give customers the opportunity to ask questions or voice complaints and feel they are being heard. This aspect of SMM is called social Customer Relationship Management (social CRM).

SMM became more common with the increased popularity of websites such as Twitter, Facebook, Myspace, LinkedIn, and YouTube. In response, the Federal Trade Commission (FTC) has

145

updated its rules to include SMM. If a company or its advertising agency provides a blogger or other online commenter with free products or other incentives to generate positive buzz for a product, the online comments will be treated legally as endorsements. Both the blogger and the company will be held responsible for ensuring that the incentives are clearly and conspicuously disclosed, and that the blogger's posts contain no misleading or unsubstantiated statements and otherwise complies with the FTC's rules concerning unfair or deceptive advertising.

[Ex. 4] **Fill in the blanks with the words given below.**

| socialize | reach | loyalty | profitable | discounts |
| successful | store | cultural | promoted | conscious |

Tactics to Make Group Buying More Profitable

The group buying concept started in China, where retailers provided discounts and special offers for customers to come in and purchase certain products and services. It was later adopted by sites such as Groupon, which offered the deals and __1__ on merchants' behalf. At first, the approach was successful, and retailers capitalized on a surge of customers to their stores to buy the specially __2__ products. Offers on group buying sites started to go viral, further increasing the returns on these one-time sales.

With the right approach, group buying can be __3__ in not only creating leads, but also in generating revenue. Here are a few recommended tactics:

1. Customize It

Customer behavior is key in crafting any offer. What type of group do you aim to attract? Do you target customers with specific __4__ backgrounds, genders, style preferences, and lifestyles? Do you sell a product or service that friends might purchase together? Groups of friends are the most __5__ about the purchases they make; a friend has more influence over a choice than a family member, for example. Or perhaps a special offer combining one product or service with another would have the most appeal. Retailers who control the type of visitors when planning a group buying offer typically have better sales. Mass selling doesn't work; customer preference is what builds customer __6__ and frequency.

2. Make It Mobile

The best way to __7__ today's customers is through their mobile phones. Apps and social media sites are part of their daily lives, so using this technology is a great way to boost engagement and sales. Inviting different groups of individuals to __8__ through your app and meet in your store can be an innovative way to sell products. Customizing offers and sending them at the time the customer requests or prefers can also have successful results.

3. Promote a Cause

Another way to make group buying more __9__ is to tie offers to something that benefits the community. The better you do, the more your sales will increase and the stronger your brand will become. Donating a portion of the sale of a product for a social cause will encourage your customers to visit your __10__ or website beyond a special offer—they will want to be part of that cause

146

and will feel good when buying your products. This approach also distinguishes you from other retailers; it shows you are a real part of the community. Reaping the benefits of that is a win-win.

Text B

Benefits of Social Media Marketing

To some entrepreneurs, social media marketing is the "next big thing", a temporary yet powerful fad that must be taken advantage of while it's still in the spotlight. To others, it's a buzzword with no practical advantages and a steep, complicated learning curve.

Because it appeared quickly, social media has developed a reputation by some for being a passing marketing interest, and therefore, an unprofitable one. The statistics, however, illustrate a different picture. According to Hubspot, 93% of marketers in 2016 claimed that social media marketing was important for their business, with 85% indicating their efforts increased traffic to their websites. And according to Social Media Examiner, 97% of marketers are currently participating in social media—but 85% of participants aren't sure what social media tools are the best to use.

This demonstrates a huge potential for social media marketing to increase sales, but a lack of understanding on how to achieve those results. Here's a look at just some of the ways social media marketing can improve your business.

1. Increased Brand Recognition

Every opportunity you have to syndicate your content and increase your visibility is valuable. Your social media networks are just new channels for your brand's voice and content. This is important because it simultaneously makes you easier and more accessible for new customers, and makes you more familiar and recognizable for existing customers. For example, a frequent Twitter user could hear about your company for the first time only after stumbling upon it in a newsfeed. Or, an otherwise apathetic customer might become better acquainted with your brand after seeing your presence on multiple networks.

2. Improved Brand Loyalty

According to a report published by Texas Tech University, brands who engage on social media channels enjoy higher loyalty from their customers. The report concludes "Companies should take advantage of the tools social media gives them when it comes to connecting with their audience. A strategic and open social media plan could prove influential in morphing consumers into being brand loyal". Another study published by Convince & Convert found that 53% of Americans who follow brands in social life are more loyal to those brands.

3. More Opportunities to Convert

Every post you make on a social media platform is an opportunity for customers to convert.

When you build a following, you'll simultaneously have access to new customers, recent customers, and old customers, and you'll be able to interact with all of them. Every blog post, image, video, or comment you share is a chance for someone to react, and every reaction could lead to a site visit, and eventually a conversion. Not every interaction with your brand results in a conversion, but every positive interaction increases the likelihood of an eventual conversion. Even if your click-through rates are low, the sheer number of opportunities you have on social media is significant. And as I pointed out in my article, "The Four Elements of Any Action, And How To Use Them In Your Online Marketing Initiative," "opportunity" is the first element of any action.

4. Higher Conversion Rates

Social media marketing results in higher conversion rates in a few distinct ways. Perhaps the most significant is its humanization element; the fact that brands become more humanized by interacting in social media channels. Social media is a place where brands can act like people do, and this is important because people like doing business with other people; not with companies.

Additionally, studies have shown that social media has a 100% higher lead-to-close rate than outbound marketing[1], and a higher number of social media followers tends to improve trust and credibility in your brand, representing social proof. As such, simply building your audience in social media can improve conversion rates on your existing traffic.

5. Higher Brand Authority

Interacting with your customers regularly is a show of good faith for other customers. When people go to compliment or brag about a product or service, they turn to social media. And when they post your brand name, new audience members will want to follow you for updates. The more people that are talking about you on social media, the more valuable and authoritative your brand will seem to new users. If you can interact with major influencers on Twitter or other social networks, your visible authority and reach will skyrocket.

6. Increased Inbound Traffic

Without social media, your inbound traffic is limited to people already familiar with your brand and individuals searching for keywords you currently rank for. Every social media profile you add is another path leading back to your site, and every piece of content you syndicate on those profiles is another opportunity for a new visitor. The more quality content you syndicate on social media, the more inbound traffic you'll generate, and more traffic means more leads and more conversions.

7. Decreased Marketing Costs

According to Hubspot, 84% of marketers found as little as six hours of effort per week was enough to generate increased traffic. Six hours is not a significant investment for a channel as large as social media. If you can lend just one hour a day to develop your content and syndication strategy, you could start seeing the results of your efforts. Even paid advertising through Facebook and

---

[1] Inbound marketing is the promotion of a company or other organization through blogs, podcasts, video, eBooks, newsletters, whitepapers, SEO, physical products, social media marketing, and other forms of content marketing which serve to attract customers through the different stages of the purchase funnel. In contrast, buying attention, cold-calling, direct paper mail, radio, TV advertisements, sales flyers, spam, telemarketing and traditional advertising are considered "outbound marketing".

Twitter is relatively cheap (depending on your goals, of course). Start small and you'll never have to worry about going over budget—once you get a better feel for what to expect, you can increase your budget and increase your conversions correspondingly.

8. Better Search Engine Rankings

SEO is the best way to capture relevant traffic from search engines, but the requirements for success are always changing. It's no longer enough to regularly update your blog, ensure optimized title tags and meta descriptions, and distribute links pointing back to your site. Google and other search engines may be calculating their rankings using social media presence as a significant factor, because of the fact that strong brands almost always use social media. As such, being active on social media could act as a "brand signal" to search engines that your brand is legitimate, credible, and trustworthy. That means, if you want to rank for a given set of keywords, having a strong social media presence could be almost mandatory.

9. Richer Customer Experiences

Social media, at its core, is a communication channel like e-mail or phone calls. Every customer interaction you have on social media is an opportunity to publicly demonstrate your customer service level and enrich your relationship with your customers. For example, if a customer complains about your product on Twitter, you can immediately address the comment, apologize publicly, and take action to make it right. Or, if a customer compliments you, you can thank them and recommend additional products. It's a personal experience that lets customers know you care about them.

10. Improved Customer Insights

Social media also gives you an opportunity to gain valuable information about what your customers are interested in and how they behave via social listening. For example, you can monitor user comments to see what people think of your business directly. You can segment your content syndication lists based on topic and see which types of content generate the most interest—and then produce more of that type of content. You can measure conversions based on different promotions posted on various social media channels and eventually find a perfect combination to generate revenue.

These are the benefits of sustaining a long-term social media campaign, but if you're still apprehensive about getting started, consider these points:

1) Your competition is already involved. Your competitors are already involved on social media, which means your potential social media traffic and conversions are being poached. Don't let your competitors reap all the benefits while you stand idly by. If, somehow, your competition is not involved on social media, there's even more of a reason to get started—the field is open.

2) The sooner you start, the sooner you reap the benefits. Social media is all about relationship building, and it tends to grow exponentially as your followers tell their friends, and their friends tell their friends, and so on. The sooner you start, the sooner you'll be able to start growing that audience.

3) Potential losses are insignificant. Realistically, you don't have anything to lose by getting involved in social media. The amount of time and money it takes to create your profiles and start

posting is usually minimal, compared to other marketing channels. Just six hours a week or a few hundred dollars is all it takes to establish your presence.

The longer you wait, the more you have to lose. Social media marketing, when done right, can lead to more customers, more traffic, and more conversions, and it's here to stay.

New Words

fad	*n.*	时尚，一时流行的狂热，一时的爱好
spotlight	*n.*	聚光灯
buzzword	*n.*	时髦词，流行词
curve	*n.*	曲线，弯曲
	v.	弯，使弯曲，成曲形
unprofitable	*adj.*	无利益的，不赚钱的，没有用的
illustrate	*v.*	举例说明，图解于，阐明，举例
indicating	*n.*	指示，标志
demonstrate	*v.*	示范，证明，论证
recognition	*n.*	赞誉，承认，辨识度
syndicate	*n.*	企业联合
recognizable	*adj.*	可认识的，可公认的，可认知的
newsfeed	*n.*	消息推送，新闻推送
apathetic	*adj.*	缺乏兴趣的，缺乏感情的，无动于衷的
influential	*adj.*	有影响的，有势力的
reaction	*n.*	反应，反作用
positive	*adj.*	肯定的，积极的，正的
likelihood	*n.*	可能，可能性
eventual	*adj.*	最后的，结局的
humanize	*v.*	人性化，使通人情
compliment	*n.*	称赞，致意，问候
	v.	称赞，褒扬
brag	*n. & v.*	吹牛
skyrocket	*v.*	飙升，飞速上升，猛涨
correspondingly	*adv.*	相对地，比照地
credible	*adj.*	可信的，可靠的
trustworthy	*adj.*	可信赖的
mandatory	*adj.*	命令的，强制的
enrich	*v.*	使富足，使肥沃
apologize	*v.*	道歉，辩白
recommend	*v.*	推荐，介绍，劝告
sustaining	*adj.*	支持的，持续的
apprehensive	*adj.*	有理解力的

poach	*v.*	侵入偷猎，窃取

Phrases

social media marketing	社交媒体营销
learning curve	学习曲线
participate in	参加，参与，分享
stumble upon	偶然发现
connect with	连接，将……连起来
click-through rate	点进率，点通率，广告点击率
sheer number	大数字，数量之多
point out	指出
humanization element	人性化元素
outbound marketing	推式营销
good faith	真诚，善意
significant factor	重要因子，重要因素
brand signal	品牌信号

Exercises

[Ex. 5] Fill in the following blanks according to the text.

1. To some entrepreneurs, social media marketing is _____, a temporary yet powerful fad that must be taken advantage of while it's still _____. To others, it's a buzzword _____ and a steep, complicated learning curve.

2. Your social media networks are _____. This is important because it simultaneously makes you easier and more accessible _____, and makes you more familiar and recognizable _____.

3. Another study published by Convince & Convert found that _____ of Americans who follow brands in social life are _____.

4. Every post you make on a social media platform is an opportunity _____. Although not every interaction with your brand results in _____, every positive interaction increases _____.

5. Social media is a place _____, and this is important because people like doing business with other people; not _____.

6. Interacting with your customers regularly is a show of _____. The more people that are talking about you on social media, the more _____ your brand will seem to new users.

7. The more _____ you syndicate on social media, the more inbound traffic you'll _____ and more traffic means _____.

8. According to Hubspot, _____ of marketers found_____ per week was enough to generate increased traffic.

151

9. Social media, at its core, is _____ like e-mail or phone calls. Every customer interaction you have on social media is an opportunity to _____ and _____.

10. Social media also gives you an opportunity to gain _____ about what your customers are interested in and how they behave via social listening. Social media marketing, when done right, can lead to _____, _____, and _____.

Reading Material

E-commerce Legals and Law

E-commerce transactions should be legally straightforward. You get money up front for the sale, in return for[1] delivery of a product as described within the timeframe[2] specified. A standard set of terms and conditions should cover the vast majority of transactions.

Your terms and conditions should outline that buyers are entering into a contract to when they purchase goods from your website. Outline the terms of delivery, shipping, refunds and payments, exclusions of liability and terms of use for your website. Finally, specify the choice of law and jurisdiction[3] of wherever you're based—this will shift the case to your own legal system, so you don't find yourself negotiating some unknown foreign law interpreting your terms in the event of legal issues.

1. Shipping and Delivery Policy

A clear, defined delivery policy is a must-have, so that customers know when to expect their products and how their packages will be delivered. You will need to specify the expected delivery timeframes and costs, as well as detailed terms on any shipping promotions. A number of merchants use shipping discounts and promotions to encourage a higher average spend—for example, free shipping on orders over ￡200. Policies like this can help squeeze[4] extra revenue into the bargain[5].

By making your shipping information clear on your product pages, and within your terms and conditions, you can prevent any problems from arising with disgruntled customers. This means customers are more likely to understand the shipping terms you offer, with the security of their agreement to your terms in the event of [6]disputes.

2. Refunds Policy

Refunds are an important part of building trust with customers, and you will hamper[7] conversions if you don't recognise that refunds will sometimes be required. It is wise to be liberal in

---

1 in return for 作为……的回报
2 timeframe *n.* 时间表
3 jurisdiction *n.* 权限
4 squeeze *n. & v.* 压榨，挤
5 bargain *n.* 契约，合同，成交商品，便宜货 *v.* 议价
6 in the event of 如果……发生
7 hamper *v.* 妨碍，牵制

your refunds policy, and you must refund cancelled purchases within the statutory[1] "cooling off" period[2]—14 days. You can ask the customer to pay the cost of returns, and you are entitled to[3] expect goods to be returned to you in a merchantable[4] condition.

Accepting that refunds are a natural part of the business, and responding promptly in handling refund requests will help assure customers that you care, while ensuring you don't end up shy of consumer selling regulation.

Include your refunds policy prominently on your website, and certainly within your terms and conditions so that buyers can see what they are getting into. By getting the customer to read, agree to these terms and conditions before their purchase, you can be sure they understand and accept the terms of refunds beyond their statutory rights.

You can keep refunds low by using better photos on your product pages, improving the accuracy of your descriptions, and making sure your products are well packages and promptly dispatched[5]. Try to make it easy for your customers to keep your product, by limiting the potential reasons they could request a refund.

Ultimately, refunds can hit your bottom line[6], and this can become a problem as you try to your your shop if you don't keep a grip on the reasons your customers are refunding. Track refund activity and the reasons for refund requests, so you can work on getting the percentage down.

3. Protecting Your Interests

Terms and conditions are essential for protecting your business, and possibly your personal, interests when selling online. In an ideal world, you would never encounter[7] disputes or difficulties in e-commerce. In the real world, it's an absolute guarantee with scale. By taking care over drafting your terms and conditions, and consulting a lawyer where the budget allows, you can clearly set out the terms of business, and secure agreement from your customers at the point the contract of sale is created.

4. Standard E-commerce Terms and Conditions

There are a number of clauses[8] that can be found in most terms and conditions, either by virtue virtue of legal necessity or to protect the merchant in the selling process. The following is a non-exhaustive[9] list of some of the things you might want to include within your e-commerce terms and conditions:

1) Information commensurate with latest Consumer Contract Regulations. The latest Consumer

---

1 statutory   *adj.*   法令的, 法定的
2 cooling off' period   冷静期
3 be entitled to   有……的资格, 有权
4 merchantable   *adj.*   可买卖的, 有销路的
5 dispatch   *v.*   分派, 派遣   *n.*   派遣, 急件
6 bottom line   底线
7 encounter   *v.*   遭遇, 遇到, 相遇
8 clause   *n.*   条款
9 non-exhaustive   *adj.*   不彻底的, 非全面的

Contract Regulations stipulate[1] that information must be made clear to consumers purchasing online via your terms and conditions. These include your contact details, including clarification[2] of your business identity, the products you sell, and how you can be contacted by your customers. This is not optional, so it pays to do your homework on what must be included when drafting up[3] your terms and conditions.

2) Liability limitations. Limited liability[4] is a standard practice across most contracts, in a bid to limit any future claims that may arise from the transaction. There are some claims to liability you can't contract away from—such as those causing death or personal injury[5]—broad exclusions of other types of damages can be effective in reducing your future obligations[6] (and keeping legal costs to an absolute minimum).

3) What happens and who pays for returns? Returns are a fact of life[7] in e-commerce, and it's useful to be upfront about how your returns process works, and who bares the costs of return shipping. Specify this within your terms and conditions, even if you have an external refunds policy in place.

4) Jurisdiction/Choice of law. Under which laws will the contract of sale be interpreted? This matters particularly in e-commerce, where you may end up resorting to the lottery[8] of legal systems systems when selling across the EU, or indeed the world, if you don't seize[9] the initiative.

5) Delivery terms. It's also useful to take into account your delivery terms, or to directly reference your shipping policy if you have one in place. When your customers accept these terms, you can solve so many support issues or refund requests, simply by referring to the terms and processes laid down in your delivery terms. Provided they are fair and reasonable, as you must be at all times in drafting terms relating to consumers, you will likely cover your back for more situations.

Terms and conditions generators and templates[10] are available, which model on some of the most common terms used in e-commerce contracts. Alternatively, for maximum protection, speak to a lawyer.

5. Data Protection

Data protection is an area of the law all website owners should be mindful of[11]. If you intend to collect personal information about your website visitors, you will need to be registered under the *Data Protection Act*[12], and to handle your data in compliance with[13] the law at all times.

You are not allowed to migrate information collected from your customers or website visitors

---

1 stipulate   v.   规定, 保证
2 clarification   n.   澄清, 净化
3 draft up   起草
4 limited liability   有限责任
5 injury   n.   伤害, 侮辱
6 obligation   n.   义务, 职责
7 fact of life   无法更改的事实
8 lottery   n.   彩票
9 seize   v.   抓住，占领
10 template   n.   模板(=templet)
11 be mindful of   注意
12 *Data Protection Act*   数据保护法
13 in compliance with   遵守

outside of the EU, and you can only hold information relevant to the needs of your business. If a customer asks for their information to be removed from your records, or to be revealed to them, you are required by law to do so.

Failure to adhere to data protection laws can land you in[1] hot water, with fines likely if you get get taken to task. Be mindful of your responsibilities—it is helpful to keep up to date with legal goings-on relevant to the e-commerce sector, if you're not engaging[2] the services of a lawyer to manage this on your behalf. As with all matters legal and accounting, it's best either way over time if you move to outsource.

When starting a small business e-commerce site, retail is one type business that many people lean toward. While it may seem that the requirements for conducting retail business online are easier than those for a brick-and-mortar store, it's important to know you still have rules, regulations and standards to comply with[3].

In the United States, the Federal Trade Commission (FTC) is the primary agency that regulates[4] e-commerce activities. This includes regulations for a number of e-commerce activities such as commercial e-mail, online advertising and consumer privacy. Another organization that e-commerce site owners should become familiar with is the PCI (Payment Card Industry) Security Standards Council. This organization provides security standards and regulations for handling and storing your customer's financial data.

6. Protecting Your Customer's Privacy Online

Online privacy is a big issue as many e-commerce sites collect and retain personal information about customers. Some of the personal data you will likely obtain would include a customer's name, address, e-mail address, and possibly their credit card and other types of financial information. As the e-commerce site owner it is your responsibility to ensure this personally identifiable information is protected, and that when you collect such data you comply with federal and state privacy laws.

E-commerce site owners should provide a privacy policy and post it on the e-commerce website. This policy should clearly identify what kinds of personal information you will collect from users visiting your website, who you will share the information you collect with, and how you will use and store that information.

Most small business e-commerce site owners approach a privacy policy like any business requirement. You could have a lawyer draft a privacy policy document for your business, or secure a trusted service provider to manage and host your privacy policy. Once you have privacy policy in place, be sure to remain in compliance with it—if not your business can face costly legal fees.

---

1 land in [口]使处于，使陷入(困境等)
2 engaging *adj.* 动人的，有魅力的，迷人的
3 comply with 照做
4 regulate *v.* 管制，控制，调节

参 考 译 文

跟踪线上到线下（反之亦然）的转化方法

在现实世界中，营销人员需要用不连续的方式来跟踪不连续的行为。这就是为什么我认为一些跟踪线上到线下转化（和再回来）的一些方法可能是有用的。

1. 跟踪线上营销到线下销售

（1）跟踪来自 PPC 广告点击的商店访客估计次数

2014 年年底，商店访客估算被引入 AdWords 中的谷歌转化跟踪中。

这个概念很简单，将谷歌地图中的已验证商店位置与你的 AdWords 账户相关联，谷歌会根据点击你的 PPC 广告估计 30 天内商店访客次数。

谷歌通过汇总来自启用了位置记录并登录谷歌的智能手机用户的数据来做到这一点。

虽然只是一个估计，这种方法将揭示哪些 PPC 活动为商店带来更多的流量，因此可能比仅仅线上转换率更有效。

（2）导入以点击 PPC 广告开始的线下转化

这是一种跟踪方法，也使用 AdWords，它获取你网站上的客户详情（可能通过联系表单或致电），并将这些详细信息与 PPC 广告点击生成的全球唯一跟踪参数（Gclid）一起保存。

当客户结账后，由广告商定期将这些转化和 Gclids 传回 AdWords，AdWords 会根据相应的销售活动和关键字记录销售。

（3）呼叫跟踪

呼叫跟踪解决方案允许为每个呼叫者分配唯一的电话号码，这样可以把线索和销售分配给已经到线下和接听电话的网站访问者。

这些解决方案允许营销人员查看网页访问和关键字引荐。对于通过线下销售完成的重大购买尤其重要。

来自移动设备的谷歌搜索中的点击通话功能变得越来越普遍。即在 AdWords 中激活，成为电话的扩展。

Econsultancy 和 Response Tap 最近的一项研究显示，只有 18% 的调查对象使用呼叫跟踪。

（4）优惠券

在营销中，优惠券是在购买产品时可以兑换财务折扣或打折的票据或文件。

通常，优惠券由大众消费品制造商或零售商发放，作为销售的一部分在零售商店中使用。他们通常通过邮件、优惠券信封、杂志、报纸、互联网（社交媒体、电子邮件通信）和直接来自零售商的移动设备（如手机）广泛分发。由于只有具有价格意识的消费者可能花费时间索要优惠券，所以优惠券是一种价格歧视，使零售商只能向那些原本要去其他地方的消费者提供更低的价格。此外，优惠券也可以有针对性地用于价格竞争激烈的区域市场。

优惠券的价值多种多样，如折扣、免费运送、买一送一、换购折扣、首次客户优惠券、免费试用、优惠活动、节日优惠和免费样品。类似地，优惠券有不同用途，包括激励购买，降低某一特定物品或一些物品的价格，提供免费样品或帮助营销人员更好地理解他们的客户的人口统计。

优惠券是本书中最古老的窍门。当然,通过打折刺激销售是必要的。在销售活动中使用优惠券通常都会成功。

(5) 倾听客户的意见

如果失败了,只要问问客户,倾听他们的意见。这样做可能不会得到任何详细的见解,但可能提高购买意向,增加与客户互动。

(6) 点击并收集

点击并收集显然不仅仅是一个跟踪方法。在许多方面,它是一个客户期望,这将提高线上和线下购物者的体验。

但是,也很明显,点击并收集会创建客户和产品的数据,并表明客户是谁、他们在哪里、他们何时购物。这可以帮助以后基于商店位置定制消息发送给客户。

2. 跟踪线下营销到线上销售

(1) 在链接中添加 UTM 参数

使用谷歌的 URL 制作工具,可以附加一个包含其来源信息的链接。来自这些链接的流量会在 Google Analytics 中显示为唯一活动。

当然,对于线下活动,需要使用易于记忆的网址。

可以缩短附加的链接并定制。但是,请记住,这涉及一些重定向并且可能不可靠。

创建客户着陆页也许更好,其中 UTM 参数主要用于对数字渠道的跟踪。

(2) 创建客户着陆页

在线下活动中使用着陆页是久经考验后得出的作法,可以衡量预约和最终销售。在线下营销中应直接使用易于记忆的网址。

记住不要在搜索中使用着陆页索引。

如果不使用索引,就能阻止搜索流量进入此页,并且能更清楚地了解活动的成功与否。

使用分析方法来解释社交性访问你的着陆页可能是合适的,尽管有人认为这属于线下活动,因为客户们互相分享。

(3) 使用改向域

对于在本地市场销售的服务,营销人员可能想使用更相关的域,然后将其定向到他们的"实际"网站上的适当页面。

例如,如果我碰巧是 Marquees.com 的所有者,但想要在英格兰西北的工业城(我长大的地方)开展一个活动,我可能购买域名 BuryMarquees.com,相信这会带来更多的网站访客。

将 BuryMarquees.com 定向到我的主要网站,并使用跟踪代码将定向域设置为来源网址,我可以保持成功。

(4) QR 码

这本质上是一种将用户定向到 URL 的方法。它只是客户着陆页或跟踪网址的发布方式。

QR 码是许多营销人员的眼中钉,经常以相当糟糕的方式来使用。NFC 也有类似的争议。

(5) 直接增加流量

如果线下活动足够大,例如一个大的圣诞节电视广告,通常可以增加直接网络流量和销售，因为这很有关联。

当然，这对那些拥有大规模媒体预算的人来说只是一种安慰。

3. 连接线上和线下销售数据

在这里必须提到不属于上述范畴的两个战术——会员卡和电子收据。

这些是统一销售数据并提供单个客户查看的技术。

两者都可以允许零售商整合客户的线上和线下的销售数据，并更准确地了解客户价值和行为。

特别是电子收据，异常少见。鞋子零售商 Schuh 使用它们来改善客户体验（使 365 天退货更容易）。

可以想象，电子收据将允许零售商把商店中的电子邮件地址与其 CRM 匹配，以便给出与会员卡数据所提供的类似的查看报告。

Unit 9

Text A

E-commerce Payment System

1. Basic

An e-commerce payment system facilitates the acceptance of electronic payment for online transactions. Also known as a sample of Electronic Data Interchange (EDI)[1], e-commerce payment systems have become increasingly popular due to the widespread use of the Internet-based shopping and banking.

扫一扫，听课文

Over the years, credit cards have become one of the most common forms of payment for e-commerce transactions. In North America almost 90% of online retail transactions were made with this payment type. It would be difficult for an online retailer to operate without supporting credit and debit cards due to their widespread use. Increased security measures include use of the Card Verification Number (CVN) which detects fraud by comparing the verification number printed on the signature strip on the back of the card with the information on file with the cardholder's issuing bank. Also online merchants have to comply with stringent rules stipulated by the credit and debit card issuers (Visa and MasterCard). This means that merchants must have security protocol and procedures in place to ensure that transactions are more secure. This can also include having a certificate from an authorized Certification Authority (CA)[2] who provides PKI (Public-Key Infrastructure)[3] for securing credit and debit card transactions.

---

1 Electronic Data Interchange (EDI) is an electronic communication method that provides standards for exchanging data via any electronic means. By adhering to the same standard, two different companies or organizations, even in two different countries, can electronically exchange documents (such as purchase orders, invoices, shipping notices, and many others).

2 In cryptography, a certificate authority or Certification Authority (CA) is an entity that issues digital certificates. A digital certificate certifies the ownership of a public key by the named subject of the certificate. This allows others (relying parties) to rely upon signatures or on assertions made about the private key that corresponds to the certified public key. In this model of trust relationships, a CA is a trusted third party—trusted both by the subject (owner) of the certificate and by the party relying upon the certificate. The most commonly encountered Public-Key Infrastructure (PKI) schemes are those used to implement https on the world-wide web.

3 A Public-Key Infrastructure (PKI) is a set of roles, policies, and procedures needed to create, manage, distribute, use, store, and revoke digital certificates and manage public-key encryption. The purpose of a PKI is to facilitate the secure electronic transfer of information for a range of network activities such as e-commerce, Internet banking and confidential e-mail. It is required for activities where simple passwords are an inadequate authentication method and more rigorous proof is required to confirm the identity of the parties involved in the communication and to validate the information being transferred.

Despite the widespread use in North America, there are still a large number of countries such as India and Pakistan that have some problems to overcome in regard to credit card security. In the meantime, the use of smartcards has become extremely popular. A smartcard is similar to a credit card; however it contains an embedded 8-bit microprocessor and uses electronic cash which transfers from the consumers' card to the sellers' device. A popular smartcard initiative is the VISA Smartcard. Using the VISA Smartcard you can transfer electronic cash to your card from your bank account, and you can then use your card at various retailers and on the Internet.

There are companies that enable financial transactions to take place over the Internet, such as PayPal. Many of the merchants permit consumers to establish an account quickly, and to transfer funds into their on-line accounts from a traditional bank account (typically via ACH[1] transactions), and vice versa, after verification of the consumer's identity and authority to access such bank accounts. Also, the larger merchants further allow transactions to and from credit card accounts, although such credit card transactions are usually assessed a fee (either to the recipient or the sender) to recoup the transaction fees charged to the merchants.

The speed and simplicity with which cyber-merchant accounts can be established and used have contributed to their widespread use, although the risk of abuse, theft and other problems—with disgruntled users frequently accusing the merchants themselves of wrongful behavior—is associated with them.

2. Methods of Online Payment

Credit cards constitute a popular method of online payment but can be expensive for the merchant to accept because of transaction fees primarily. Debit cards constitute an excellent alternative with similar security but usually much cheaper charges. Besides card-based payments, other forms of payment have emerged and sometimes even claimed market leadership. Wallets like PayPal and Alipay are playing major roles in the ecosystem. Bitcoin payment processors are a cheaper alternative for accepting payments online which also offer better protection from fraud.

(1) Net Banking

This is a system, well known in India, that does not involve any sort of physical card. It is used by customers who have accounts enabled with Internet banking. Instead of entering card details on the purchaser's site, in this system the payment gateway allows one to specify which bank they wish to pay from. Then the user is redirected to the bank's website, where one can authenticate oneself and then approve the payment. Typically there will also be some form of two-factor authentication.

It is typically seen as being safer than using credit cards, with the result that nearly all merchant accounts in India offer it as an option.

A very similar system, known as iDEAL, is popular in the Netherlands.

(2) PayPal

PayPal is a global e-commerce business allowing payments and money transfers to be made

---

[1] Automated Clearing House (ACH) is an electronic network for financial transactions in the United States. ACH processes large volumes of credit and debit transactions in batches. ACH credit transfers include direct deposit, payroll and vendor payments. ACH direct debit transfers include consumer payments on insurance premiums, mortgage loans, and other kinds of bills.

through the Internet. Online money transfers serve as electronic alternatives to paying with traditional paper methods, such as cheques and money orders. It is subject to the US economic sanction list and other rules and interventions required by US laws or government. PayPal is an acquirer, a performing payment processing for online vendors, auction sites, and other commercial users, for which it charges a fee. It may also charge a fee for receiving money, proportional to the amount received. The fees depend on the currency used, the payment option used, the country of the sender, the country of the recipient, the amount sent and the recipient's account type. In addition, eBay purchases made by credit card through PayPal may incur extra fees if the buyer and seller use different currencies.

(3) Paymentwall[1]

Paymentwall is an e-commerce solutions providing company launched in 2010. It is headquartered in San Francisco, with offices in Istanbul, Berlin, Kiev, Manila, Amsterdam, Las Vegas, Hanoi, Beijing, São Paulo, Tokyo, Lisbon, Seoul, Sofia, Poznan and Moscow. It started as an international e-commerce payment platform for Facebook games, but has since shifted to other services, such as MMORPG and browser games, SaaS companies, video streaming, dating sites, and more. It offers a wide range of online payment methods that its clients can integrate on their website.

(4) Google Wallet

Google Wallet was launched in 2011, serving a similar function as PayPal to facilitate payments and transfer money online. It is a peer-to-peer payments service developed by Google that allows people to send and receive money from a mobile device or desktop computer at no cost to either sender or receiver. It also features a security that has not been cracked to date, and the ability to send payments as attachments via e-mail.

(5) Mobile Money Wallets

In undeveloped countries the banked population is very less, especially in some small cities. Taking the example of India, there are more mobile phone users than people with active bank accounts. Telecom operators, in such areas, have started offering mobile money wallets which allows adding funds easily through their existing mobile subscription number by visiting physical recharge points close to their homes and offices and converting their cash into mobile wallet currency. This can be used for online transaction and e-commerce purchases.

New Words

facilitate	v.	使容易，使便利，推动
acceptance	n.	接受，承诺
retail	n.	零售
	adj.	零售的
	v.	零售

---

1 Paymentwall 是一个全球在线支付平台，主要涉及跨境支付和虚拟货物支付两方面的业务，为游戏厂商、社交网站以及更多的在线服务与虚拟货物提供全面、完善的全球支付渠道和解决方案。

widespread	adj.	分布广泛的，普遍的
detect	v.	察觉，发觉，探测
verification	n.	确认，查证，作证
signature	n.	签名，署名，信号
cardholder	n.	持有信用卡的人，持卡人
stringent	adj.	严厉的，迫切的
stipulate	v.	规定，保证
issuer	n.	发行者
overcome	v.	克服，解决
smartcard	n.	智能卡
assess	v.	评定，估价，确定
recoup	v.	偿还；补偿，收回，[法] 扣除，扣留
	n.	获得补偿
charge	v.	索价，收费；控告
	n.	收费，负责，负担，费用，管理
simplicity	n.	简单
contribute	v.	捐助，贡献
embedded	adj.	嵌入的，植入的，内含的
microprocessor	n.	微处理器
abuse	n. & v.	滥用
theft	n.	偷盗，偷窃，被盗，失窃，盗窃之物，赃物
disgruntled	adj.	不满的，不高兴的
accuse	v.	指控，指责，谴责
wrongful	adj.	不正当的
constitute	v.	制定(法律)，建立(政府)，组成，任命
emerge	v.	显现，浮现，形成
ecosystem	n.	生态系统
Bitcoin	n.	比特币
processor	n.	处理机，处理器
protection	n.	保护
specify	v.	指定
authenticate	v.	鉴别
approve	v.	批准，通过
authentication	n.	鉴别
cheque	n.	支票
sanction	n. & v.	批准，同意，支持，认可
incur	v.	招致，引起，产生，遭受
intervention	n.	干涉

proportional	*adj.*	成比例的，相称的，均衡的
currency	*n.*	流通
subsidiary	*adj.*	辅助的，补充的
headquarter	*v.*	以……作总部，设总公司于……
wallet	*n.*	钱包，钱夹
attachment	*n.*	附件
fund	*n.*	资金，基金
	v.	支助，投资

Phrases

e-commerce payment system	电子商务支付系统
online transactions	在线交易
credit card	信用卡
security measure	安全措施，保密措施
security protocol	安全协议
contribute to	有助于，促成
accuse sb. of sth.	因某事指控某人，因某事指责某人，因某事谴责某人
issuing bank	发卡银行，开卡银行
comply with	遵循，照做
in regard to	关于
in the meantime	在……期间，同时
electronic cash	电子现金
bank account	银行账户
cyber-merchant account	网络商务账户
money order	汇票，邮政汇票
be subject to	受支配，从属于
peer-to-peer payments service	点对点支付服务
at no cost	不花钱
telecom operator	电信运营商
mobile money wallet	移动钱包

Abbreviations

EDI (Electronic Data Interchange)	电子数据交换
CVN (Card Verification Number)	信用卡验证码，信用卡校验码
CA (Certification Authority)	证书授权
PKI (Public-Key Infrastructure)	公钥基础设施
ACH (Automated Clearing House)	自动清算房，自动清算系统，自动清算所

Exercises

[Ex. 1] Answer the following questions according to the text.

1. What does an e-commerce payment system facilitate?
2. Why have e-commerce payment systems become increasingly popular?
3. What has happened to credit cards over the years? What happened in North America?
4. What is a smartcard?
5. Credit cards constitute a popular method of online payment. But why can it be expensive for the merchant to accept?
6. What is net banking?
7. What is PayPal?
8. What is Paymentwall? Where is its headquarters?
9. When was Google Wallet launched? What is it?
10. What have telecom operators started doing in undeveloped countries?

[Ex. 2] Translate the following terms or phrases from English into Chinese and vice versa.

1. bank account
2. comply with
3. cyber-merchant account
4. electronic cash
5. e-commerce payment system
6. 点对点支付服务
7. 安全协议
8. 确认，查证，作证
9. 签名，署名，信号
10. 鉴别

[Ex. 3] Translate the following passage into Chinese.

A payment system is any system used to settle financial transactions through the transfer of monetary value, and includes the institutions, instruments, people, rules, procedures, standards, and technologies that make such an exchange possible. A common type of payment system is the operational network that links bank accounts and provides for monetary exchange using bank deposits.

What makes a payment system a system is the use of cash-substitutes; traditional payment systems are negotiable instruments such as drafts (e.g., checks) and documentary credits such as letters of credit. With the advent of computers and electronic communications a large number of alternative electronic payment systems have emerged. These include debit cards, credit cards, electronic funds transfers, direct credits[1], direct debits[2], Internet banking and e-commerce payment systems. Some payment systems include credit mechanisms, but that is essentially a different aspect of payment. Payment systems are used in lieu of tendering cash in domestic and international transactions and consist of a major service provided by banks and other financial institutions.

Payment systems may be physical or electronic and each has its own procedures and protocols. Standardization has allowed some of these systems and networks to grow to a global scale, but there are still many country- and product-specific systems. Examples of payment systems that have become globally available are credit card and automated teller machine networks. Specific forms of payment systems are also used to settle financial transactions for products in the equity markets, bond markets, currency markets, futures markets, derivatives markets, options markets and to transfer funds between financial institutions both domestically using clearing and real-time gross settlement (RTGS) systems and internationally using the SWIFT network.

The term electronic payment can refer narrowly to e-commerce—a payment for buying and selling goods or services offered through the Internet, or broadly to any type of electronic funds transfer.

[Ex. 4] Fill in the blanks with the words given below.

| range | institution | statements | connect | account |
| report | previously | protection | allocate | register |

Online Banking

Online banking, also known as Internet banking, e-banking or virtual banking, is an electronic payment system. It enables customers of a bank or other financial ___1___ to conduct a range of financial transactions through the financial institution's website. The online banking system will typically ___2___ to or be part of the core banking system operated by a bank and is in contrast to branch banking which was the traditional way customers accessed banking services.

To access a financial institution's online banking facility, a teacher with Internet access would need to ___3___ with the institution for the service, and set up a password and other credentials for customer verification. The credentials for online banking is normally not the same as for telephone or mobile banking. Financial institutions now routinely ___4___ customers numbers, whether or not customers have indicated an intention to access their online banking facility. Customer numbers are normally not the same as ___5___ numbers, because a number of customer accounts can be linked to the one customer number. Technically, the customer number can be linked to any account with the financial institution that the customer controls, though the financial institution may limit the ___6___ of accounts that may be accessed to, say, cheque, savings, loan, credit card and similar accounts.

The customer visits the financial institution's secure website, and enters the online banking

---

1 In banking, a direct credit is a deposit of money by a payer directly into a payee's bank account. Direct deposits are most commonly made by businesses in the payment of salaries and wages and for the payment of suppliers' accounts, but the facility can be used for payments for any purpose, such as payment of bills, taxes, and other government charges. Direct deposits are most commonly made by means of electronic funds transfers effected using online, mobile, and telephone banking systems but can also be effected by the physical deposit of money into the payee's bank account.

2 A direct debit or direct withdrawal is a financial transaction in which one person withdraws funds from another person's bank account.

facility using the customer number and credentials ___7___ set up. The types of financial transactions which a customer may transact through online banking are determined by the financial institution. Most banks also enable a customer to download copies of bank ___8___, which can be printed at the customer's premises (some banks charge a fee for mailing hard copies of bank statements). Some banks also enable customers to download transactions directly into the customer's accounting software. The facility may also enable the customer to order a cheque book, statements, ___9___ loss of credit cards, stop payment on a cheque, advise change of address and other routine actions.

Today, many banks are Internet-only institutions. These "virtual banks" have lower overhead costs than their brick-and-mortar counterparts. In the United States, many online banks are insured by the Federal Deposit Insurance Corporation (FDIC) and can offer the same level of ___10___ for the customers' funds as traditional banks.

Text B

Understanding Online Payment Services

1. Why Bother with Online Payments?

If you're like many small organizations, you collect payments mainly through cash or checks. While this might be working for you at the moment, adding online payments provides a number of advantages to you and your supporters.

扫一扫，听课文

(1) Meet Expectations

People are increasingly comfortable paying online. When members or supporters are ready to sign up, register for an event, or make a donation, they want to do it quickly and easily. In fact, websites that don't support online payment can be seen as being out of step.

(2) Speed up the Process

Online payments are faster than manual payments, since you don't have to wait for the check to arrive or for it to clear. The whole process—from submitting an online payment to updating your bank account—can take a matter of seconds. The end result is improved cash flow for your organization, and almost immediate confirmation of transactions. Prospective members won't have to wait to join your organization, and participants will know right away whether they have successfully registered for an event.

In addition, the online payment service lets you know right away if the person making the online payment has sufficient funds to cover the transaction—rather than finding out a week later when the check bounces.

(3) Save You the Trouble

Automated payments also save you the trouble of depositing the check and recording the payment manually. Once you set up online payments for your website, they are automatically processed. You don't handle or store any credit card information. Any updates to member records are handled automatically.

(4) But at a Price

Of course, anything of value comes with a cost, and in this case, your payment provider will charge you a fee per transaction, and some charge other fees as well—such as setup fees or monthly fees. But if online payment helps you grow your membership or your fundraising, they'll be taking a slice out of your much larger pie, and everyone's a winner.

We'll explore the costs later, but now, before you start thinking about selecting a particular payment provider, it's important to understand some online payment terminology.

2. Understanding Online Payment Terminology

There are several terms that are used almost interchangeably when describing online payments:

- payment gateway;
- payment processor;
- payment provider;
- payment service or payment system;
- merchant account.

Though they are distinct, with subtle differences, they all refer to a company, service, or application that acts as a financial middleman between your website and your customer, and between both of you and your bank accounts. Each facilitates the completion of online transactions, and the processing of online payments.

(1) Payment Gateway

A payment gateway is a service that receives the online payment request from your website and directs it to the payment processor.

(2) Payment Processor

A payment processor is a service that validates the purchaser's credit card details (e.g., those of your member, donor, or supporter) and checks if they have sufficient funds in their account to cover the payment. If the customer has sufficient funds, the transaction is authorized, and the funds are transferred from the customer's account. The status of the transaction is transmitted back to the payment gateway which then sends a status message to your website (Figure 9-1).

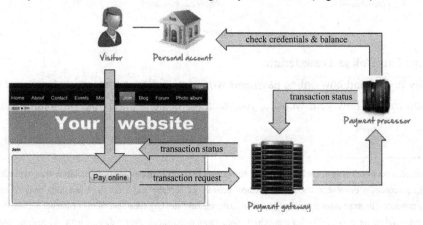

Figure 9-1

(3) Payment Provider

A payment provider (or payment service provider) is the company that operates the payment gateway or payment processor services. In some cases, the payment gateway and payment processor are combined into a single service known by either name.

(4) Payment Service or Payment System

Where a payment provider offers multiple types of payment gateways—with different features and pricing—each type is referred to as a payment service or payment system. For example, PayPal is a payment service provider that offers a number of payment services or payment systems such as PayPal Payflow Pro and PayPal Express Checkout.

(5) Merchant Account

A merchant account is another important term to understand. When an online transaction is successfully completed, the funds are transferred from the purchaser's account to your merchant account, a special kind of bank account used exclusively to hold funds received from credit and debit card transactions. To accept online payments, you usually need to set up a merchant account[1] with your payment provider. Funds accumulating in your merchant account are transferred to your organization's bank account on a regular basis (Figure 9-2).

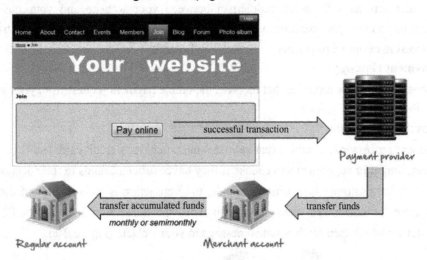

Figure 9-2

3. Anatomy of an Online Transaction

To fully understand how online payments work, let's follow a transaction from start to finish. In this way, you can see how your website, your member or donor, and your payment service provider all interact.

---

[1] A merchant account is a type of bank account that allows businesses to accept payments in multiple ways, typically debit or credit cards. A merchant account is established under an agreement between an acceptor and a merchant acquiring bank for the settlement of payment card transactions. In some cases a payment processor, Independent Sales Organization (ISO), or Member Service Provider (MSP) is also a party to the merchant agreement. Whether a merchant enters into a merchant agreement directly with an acquiring bank or through an aggregator, the agreement contractually binds the merchant to obey the operating regulations established by the card associations.

To get started with online payments, you typically need:
- a merchant account—though some payment systems (such as PayPal) do not require a merchant account or can provide you with one;
- an account with a payment service provider;
- a web page with a button (e.g. Join, Donate, Buy) that initiates the transaction process—you can use code provided by your service provider or specialized shopping cart software.

Once you've set up your web page and connected it to an online payment service, visitors to your site will be able to pay online for products or services. The online payment process begins when the visitor clicks the button to pay online for membership fees or an event registration, or to make a donation or purchase something from your online store.

On the online payment form that appears, the visitor enters their credit card information then submits the transaction request. Depending on your online payment service provider, the form may appear on your website, or your purchaser may be redirected to a form on your service provider's website (Figure 9-3).

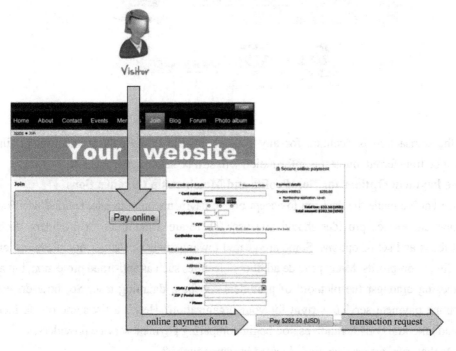

Figure 9-3

The transaction request, along with the credit card information entered by the purchaser, is securely transmitted to the payment gateway operated by your payment service provider. The information is encrypted so that no one—including you—can view the purchaser's personal and financial information.

Your payment service provider will use a secure payment processing service—either their own or one provided by another company—to verify the purchaser's credit card details and confirm whether the purchaser has sufficient funds to complete the transaction.

If the purchaser's credentials are valid and there are sufficient funds to complete the transaction, your payment service provider will initiate a transfer of funds from the purchaser's bank account to the merchant account associated with your website, and notify your website that the transaction has been approved. Depending on how your website is set up, that information can be used to automatically update records on your site (e.g., update your membership management or event registration database) (Figure 9-4).

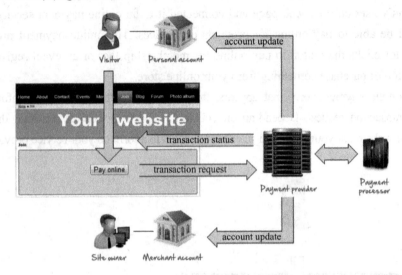

Figure 9-4

If the transaction is declined for any reason—invalid credentials or insufficient funds—no funds will be transferred, but status information will still be sent to your website.

4. Online Payment Options for Non-Profits and Membership Organizations

Once you've made the decision to accept online payments on your site, another decision looms: which payment service provider should you use? There are a multitude of providers, each with a different focus and set of options. Some are geared toward smaller or larger organizations, and some specifically to non-profits. Many provide additional features such as anti-fraud protection, but at a cost.

Choosing amongst the plethora of providers can be a daunting task. So, how do you know which online payment service is right for your organization? Here's a list some of the factors that you should take into consideration as you begin comparing payment service providers:

- Do they support organizations located in your country?
- Do they support the currencies you want to use in your transactions?
- What kind of fees do they charge—per transaction, monthly, or setup?
- What volume of transactions do you expect on your website?
- Are payments processed on your website or theirs? Do you care?
- What kind of payments do they accept—credit card, debit card, or PayPal?
- Do they support recurring payments?

New Words

supporter	n.	支持者，拥护者
comfortable	adj.	舒适的
register	n.	记录，登记，注册
	v.	登记，注册
manual	adj.	手动的，手工的
	n.	手册，指南
submit	v.	提交，递交
bounce	v.	(指支票)被银行退票
membership	n.	成员资格，成员人数
interchangeably	adv.	可交替地
gateway	n.	网关，门，通路
subtle	adj.	微妙的，精细的
sufficient	adj.	充分的，足够的
status	n.	情形，状况
purchaser	n.	买方，购买者
anatomy	n.	剖析，解剖学
initiate	v.	开始，发起
encrypt	v.	加密，将……译成密码
confirm	v.	确定，批准
credential	n.	凭据，证明书
notify	v.	通报
approved	adj.	经核准的，被认可的
decline	v.	拒绝
non-profit	adj.	非营利的
loom	v.	隐现，若隐若现
multitude	n.	多数
specifically	adv.	特定的，明确的
plethora	n.	过剩，过多

Phrases

at the moment	现在，当前
bother with…	为……而费心，因……而烦恼
be ready to	预备，即将
be out of step	落伍，跟不上脚步，步伐不一致，不协调，不一致
speed up	加速
cash flow	现金流
check bounce	支票被退票

at a price	以很高代价
monthly fee	月费，按月收费
payment service provider	支付服务提供者
merchant account	商户账户，商业账户，商家账户
shopping cart software	购物车软件
anti-fraud protection	防欺诈保护
at a cost	有代价，有花费
daunting task	令人生畏的任务
take into consideration	考虑到
recurring payment	自动扣款，自动扣除

Exercises

[Ex. 5] Answer the following questions according to the text.

1. How do people feel when paying online? Why?
2. Why are online payments faster than manual payments?
3. What are the several terms that are used almost interchangeably when describing online payments?
4. What is a payment gateway?
5. What is a payment processor?
6. What is a payment provider?
7. What happens when an online transaction is successfully completed?
8. What do you need to get started with online payments?
9. What will your payment service provider do if the purchaser's credentials are valid and there are sufficient funds to complete the transaction?
10. What are the factors that you should take into consideration as you begin comparing payment service providers?

Reading Material

Safe Online Payment Methods

You always take a risk when you shop online: there's a chance that thieves[1] could steal your payment information and make purchases on your dime (or pay themselves fraudulently). That risk isn't exclusive to online shopping—it can and does happen at brick-and-mortar stores as well—but it's especially easy to put sensitive information in the wrong hands online.

You can rely on[2] technology to a large degree.

Your information is usually scrambled[3] (or encrypted) into a hard-to-read format. But even

---

1　thief　　*n.*　小偷
2　rely on　　*v.*　依赖，依靠
3　scramble　　*n.*　混乱　*v.*　使混杂

when you do everything right—even at large, reputable websites—there's a chance of a data breach or intercepted[1] traffic. It's even possible that the trouble is on your end: something as simple as a keystroke[2] logger can grab your card number or PayPal password.

It's obviously important to keep your device secure and up to date, but what about the method of payment you use when shopping online—does that matter?

1. Payment Method Choices

You usually have a choice when it comes to paying: will you use a credit card, debit card, a payment service like PayPal, or some other options? Depending on your concerns, one of those choices might be better than another. Let's look at the pros and cons[3] of each payment method.

2. Credit Cards

The pros: A credit card is often a good choice for shopping online. Fraud protection with credit cards is quite strong, and getting charges reversed is pretty simple. Just report the suspicious[4] activity to your card issuer or let them know you never received what you paid for.

No money comes out of[5] your bank account—it's the card issuer's money that gets spent. As long as you act quickly, your liability[6] can belimited to $50, and in many cases you won't pay anything for fraudulent[7] charges.

The cons: You might think of your credit card as a tool of everyday life. Perhaps you use it regularly for personal and business expenses[8], and you might pay automatic or recurring charges with the card.

If your card number is stolen, you'll need a new card (and card number), you'll have to update billing information in numerous places, and you may have to live without your card for a while[9] as you wait for a replacement[10].

Tips: Use your credit card only when you're confident that it's safe to do so and when you want the strongest consumer protection available. You can also get a one-time-use credit card number (depending on your card issuer) for online purchases, so it won't matter if that number is stolen. Finally, consider getting an additional credit card that you only use online (or at sites you aren't familiar with); you can keep a closer eye on that account and you won't be inconvenienced[11] if you have to ditch the card number.

1　intercept　　*v.*　中途阻止，截取
2　keystroke　　*n.*　按键
3　the pros and cons　　赞成与反对的理由，优点和缺点
4　suspicious　　*adj.*　可疑的，怀疑的
5　come out of　　*v.*　由……产生，从……出来
6　liability　　*n.*　债务，负债
7　fraudulent　　*adj.*　欺诈的，欺骗性的，骗得的
8　expense　　*n.*　费用，代价，开支
9　for a while　　暂时
10　replacement　　*n.*　交换，代替，置换
11　inconvenience　　*n.*　麻烦，不方便之处

2. Payment Services

The pros: Third-party payment services are also a good option for online shopping (PayPal is the most popular payment method, but others such as Google Wallet exist). These services can provide an extra layer of safety: instead of giving your credit card number or bank account information to every website you shop with, you can keep that information in one central location.

If you shop at numerous sites or sites you're unfamiliar[1] with, you can reduce the number of places that hackers can find your information. These services may also offer some level of "buyer protection" in case your goods never arrive or you get swindled[2].

The cons: When things go bad (if you have a dispute with a seller) these accounts can get frozen[3] while the company investigates[4]. If you make a habit of[5] disputing charges (and the disputes don't end up in your favor), your account might even get closed and you could be banned from using the service. You can certainly live without a PayPal account—there are plenty of places to shop online with other payment methods—but PayPal is sometimes the easiest way to pay.

Tips: When you shop online, use a credit card as the funding source for purchases (if possible). That way, if there's a dispute and the payment service doesn't decide in your favor, you can dispute the charges again with your credit card company where you might have better luck.

3. Debit Cards

The pros: Debit cards are inexpensive payment cards that pull funds directly from your checking account. You don't need to apply, get approved, pay annual fees[6], or risk racking up debt[7] like you do with a credit card. Although it's not required by law, debit card issuers often offer "zero liability" protection similar to credit card protection.

The cons: A debit card is linked directly to your bank account. If the card number is used without your permission[8] (or if there's simply an error somewhere), money comes out of your checking account—and you might not be able to pay bills and expenses with a drained account. Yes, there are fraud protections in place, but it can take 10 long days for the bank to return money to your account.

Tips: Unless you're extremely vigilant[9] and have set up alerts[10] on your checking account[11] (and you have plenty of[12] extra cash available), avoid using debit cards if possible. If you simply can't use a credit card or a payment service, a prepaid[13] card can help insulate[14] your checking

---

1 unfamiliar   *adj.*   不熟悉的, 没有经验的
2 swindle   *v. & n.*   诈骗
3 frozen   *adj.*   冻结的
4 investigate   *v.*   调查, 研究
5 make a habit of   使……形成一种习惯
6 annual fee   年费
7 debt   *n.*   债务
8 permission   *n.*   许可, 允许
9 vigilant   *adj.*   警惕着的, 警醒的
10 alert   *adj.*   提防的, 警惕的   *n.*   警惕, 警报
11 checking account   经常账户
12 plenty of   许多
13 prepaid   *adj.*   先付的, 已支付的
14 insulate   *v.*   使绝缘, 隔离

account from any problems.

参 考 译 文

电子商务支付系统

1. 基本

　　电子商务支付系统促进接受在线交易的电子支付，也被称为电子数据交换（EDI）的样本。由于基于互联网的购物和银行的广泛使用，电子商务支付系统已经变得越来越流行。

　　多年来，信用卡已经成为电子商务交易最常见的支付形式之一。在北美，几乎 90% 的在线零售交易都是采用这种付款方式。由于其广泛使用，在线零售商难以在不支持信用卡和借记卡的情况下运营。增加的安全措施包括使用通过比较印在卡背面的签名条上的卡验证号码（CVN）与持卡人的发行银行的文件信息来检测欺诈。此外，网上商家必须遵守信用卡和借记卡发卡机构（Visa 和 MasterCard）规定的严格规则。这意味着商家必须具有安全协议和程序，以确保交易更安全。这还包括具有来自授权认证机构（CA）的证书，CA 提供 PKI（公钥基础设施）以保护信用卡和借记卡交易。

　　尽管北美地区广泛使用，仍然有许多国家（如印度和巴基斯坦）在信用卡安全方面有一些问题需要克服。同时，智能卡的使用已变得非常受欢迎。智能卡类似于信用卡，然而它包含一个嵌入式 8 位微处理器，并使用电子现金进行消费者卡到卖家设备的资金转移。流行的智能卡起源于 VISA 智能卡。使用 VISA 智能卡，可以从你的银行账户把电子现金转移到你的卡中，然后可以在各个零售商和互联网上使用你的卡。

　　有些公司（如 PayPal）允许通过互联网进行金融交易。许多商家允许消费者快速建立账户，并且在验证消费者的身份和获得该银行的授权之后，允许客户从传统的银行账户（通常通过 ACH 交易）将资金转入他们的在线账户，反之亦然。此外，尽管这种信用卡交易通常会收费（对接收者或发送者收费）以弥补收取商家的交易费用，一些较大的商家还会允许信用卡账户往来。

　　网络商家账户的建立和使用的快速和简易促进了其广泛使用，尽管有滥用、盗窃和其他问题的风险。不满的用户经常指责商人的不法行为。这都与其息息相关。

2. 网上支付方式

　　信用卡构成了流行的在线支付方法，但是商人要承受昂贵的交易费用。借记卡是一个很好的选择，具有类似的安全性，但费用通常更便宜。除了基于卡的支付，还出现了其他形式的支付，它们有时甚至宣称占据了市场领导地位。像 PayPal 和 Alipay 这样的钱包在生态系统中扮演着重要的角色。比特币支付处理器是在线支付的另一个更便宜的方案，也提供了更好的免欺诈保护。

　　（1）网络银行

　　这是一个在印度众所周知的系统，不涉及任何种类的物理卡。它由启用了网上银行账户的用户使用。在该系统中，不用在购买者网站输入卡的详细信息，支付网关允许用户指定支付银行。然后，用户被改向到该银行的网站，在银行网站上可以验证自己的身份，然后批准付款。通常还将存在某种形式的双因素认证。

它通常被视为比使用信用卡更安全,结果几乎所有印度的商家账户都把它作为一个选项。

一个非常类似的系统,被称为 iDEAL,在荷兰很受欢迎。

(2) PayPal

PayPal 是一个全球电子商务企业,允许通过互联网进行支付和汇款。在线汇款是传统纸张方法(如支票和汇票)支付的电子替代方式。它受美国经济制裁名单以及美国法律或政府要求的其他规则的支配。PayPal 是收单方,对在线供应商、拍卖网站和其他商业用户进行有效的支付处理,并收取费用。它也可能根据收到的金额按比例收费。费用取决于所使用的货币,使用的付款方式,汇款人所在国家,收款人所在国家或地区,发送金额和收款人账户类型。此外,如果买家和卖家使用不同的货币,通过 PayPal 用信用卡在 eBay 上购买可能会产生额外的费用。

(3) Paymentwall

Paymentwall 是一家于 2010 年推出的电子商务解决方案提供公司。总部设在旧金山,在伊斯坦布尔、柏林、基辅、马尼拉、阿姆斯特丹、拉斯维加斯、河内、北京、圣保罗、东京、里斯本、首尔、波兹南和莫斯科设有办事处。它开始是 Facebook 游戏的一个国际电子商务支付平台,但已经转移到其他服务,如 MMORPG 和浏览器游戏、SaaS 公司、视频流、约会网站等。它提供了广泛的在线支付方法,客户可以在其网站上加以集成。

(4) Google 电子钱包

Google 电子钱包于 2011 年推出,提供与 PayPal 类似的功能,能方便付款和在线转账。它是 Google 开发的对等支付服务,允许人们从移动设备或台式计算机向发送方或接收方免费发送和接收资金。到目前为止它的安全性最高,无人破解,并且能够通过电子邮件以附件形式发送付款。

(5) 手机钱包

在欠发达国家,银行客户非常少,特别是在一些小城市。以印度为例,手机用户比拥有活跃银行账户的用户多。在这些地区的电信运营商已经开始提供移动钱包,这就可以通过他们现有的移动订阅号轻松地添加资金。其方法是通过访问他们家庭和办公室附近的物理充值点,将他们的现金转换成移动钱包货币。这也可以用于在线交易和电子商务购买。

Unit 10

Text A

The Basics of Website Security for E-commerce Retailers

For e-commerce retailers, website security is the cornerstone of a successful online business. Why? Because people only want to give their money and their business to companies and organizations that they can trust.

扫一扫，听课文

If a retailer has an insecure website, then, all other marketing and inbound efforts simply won't bring results. Here, we run through some basic security practices that all e-commerce retailers should employ to make sure that their website is a secure, successful online destination.

1. PCI Compliance

The PCI Security Standards Council[1] is a global group formed to develop, enhance and maintain security standards for payment account security. Its founding members include American Express, Discover Financial Services, JCB International, MasterCard and Visa Inc.

Together, the members of this group has come up with a set of security requirements, known as the Payment Card Industry Data Security Standard (PCI DSS) that all merchants or organizations that process, store, or transmit credit card information must adhere to. There is good reason for this: these guidelines ensure that all stored credit card data is protected and that sensitive information is secure throughout the transaction process.

Many companies meet these guidelines through the use of tokenization.

Tokenization, when applied to data security, is the process of substituting a sensitive data element with a non-sensitive equivalent, referred to as a token that has no extrinsic or exploitable meaning or value. When sensitive information, such as digits in a credit card number, is replaced by non-sensitive information, or tokens, it cannot be read. This is an effective means of encrypting data because it's extremely secure: the tokenized information can only be detokenized to redeem the sensitive data under strict security controls and the storage of tokens and payment card data must comply with PCI standards, including the use of strong cryptography.

---

1 The PCI Security Standards Council is an organization created by the major credit card companies in an effort to better protect Credit card holder data. The PCI SSC was formed in response to an increase in data security breaches, which not only put customers at risk, but also increase the credit card companies' costs.

Staying PCI compliant and ensuring that all stored credit card data is fully tokenized in this way greatly reduces the risk of this sensitive information being stolen and used. Keeping this data secure is extremely important for all online retailers. If a cardholder's data is stolen, their credit can be negatively affected and they could lose credibility, money, and even their business.

2. SSL Certificate

The SSL certificate, also mandatory per PCI, works to ensure that the sensitive information that is sent over the Internet is encrypted and secure as well. When retailers or site visitors send information or data over the Internet, it passes through multiple computers before reaching its destination server. At any point during this chain, it could get stolen if it is not encrypted with an SSL certificate.

How does the certificate work? It essentially makes all sensitive information, which includes passwords, credit card information, and user names, unreadable for everyone except the destination server, thereby protecting all communication from eavesdropping and theft.

The SSL certificate is particularly valuable for e-commerce retailers not just for security reasons but also to build trust with site visitors and prospective customers. Attaining an SSL certificate essentially verifies an entity's credentials, certifying that they are who they say they are and that their site is safe to visit.

Make sure to watch for changes in requirements, such as the recent change from SHA-1[1] encryption to SHA-2[2] encryption, to make sure your company stays compliant.

3. Use HTTPS[3]

Hypertext Transfer Protocol with Secure Sockets Layer, or HTTPS, is a protocol to transfer data over the web that should be used instead of HTTP on all pages where data is created. Once again, the issue here is all about encryption. With HTTP, information is not encrypted—instead, it is sent as plain text, which means that anyone can intercept it and read what has been sent.

---

1 In cryptography, SHA-1 (Secure Hash Algorithm 1) is a cryptographic hash function designed by the United States National Security Agency and is a US Federal Information Processing Standard published by the United States NIST. SHA-1 produces a 160-bit (20-byte) hash value known as a message digest. A SHA-1 hash value is typically rendered as a hexadecimal number, 40 digits long. SHA-1 is no longer considered secure against well-funded opponents. In 2005, cryptanalysts found attacks on SHA-1 suggesting that the algorithm might not be secure enough for ongoing use,and since 2010 many organizations have recommended its replacement by SHA-2 or SHA-3. Microsoft, Google and Mozilla have all announced that their respective browsers will stop accepting SHA-1 SSL certificates by 2017.

2 SHA-2 (Secure Hash Algorithm 2) is a set of cryptographic hash functions designed by the National Security Agency (NSA). Cryptographic hash functions are mathematical operations run on digital data; by comparing the computed "hash" (the output from execution of the algorithm) to a known and expected hash value, a person can determine the data's integrity. For example, computing the hash of a downloaded file and comparing the result to a previously published hash result can show whether the download has been modified or tampered with. A key aspect of cryptographic hash functions is their collision resistance: nobody should be able to find two different input values that result in the same hash output. SHA-2 includes significant changes from its predecessor, SHA-1. The SHA-2 family consists of six hash functions with digests (hash values) that are 224, 256, 384 or 512 bits: SHA-224, SHA-256, SHA-384, SHA-512, SHA-512/224, SHA-512/256.

3 HTTPS (also called HTTP over SSL, and HTTP Secure) is a protocol for secure communication over a computer network which is widely used on the Internet. HTTPS consists of communication over Hypertext Transfer Protocol (HTTP) within a connection encrypted by Transport Layer Security or its predecessor, Secure Sockets Layer. The main motivation for HTTPS is authentication of the visited website and protection of the privacy and integrity of the exchanged data.

Furthermore, many customers know about this insecurity and tend to avoid e-commerce websites that use HTTP. This means that keeping HTTP could hurt a retailer's security and their business over time.

It's important to note, though, that HTTPS isn't necessary on every page of a website. Why? If retailers try to include it everywhere, it will slow their page load speed and likely hurt their business. HTTPS should just be used on pages that collect and store data so that customers can feel secure sending their information. That means skipping the homepage, about us page, etc.

4. DoS and DDoS protection

DoS (Denial of Service) and DDoS (Distributed Denial of Service) protection work to guard against denial of service and distributed denial of service attacks.

During both attacks, attackers attempt to block legitimate users from accessing information or services by flooding a network with requests, thereby overwhelming the bandwidth of the targeted system and preventing legitimate requests from coming through.

While both attacks work in the same way, the key difference is that a DoS attacker usually uses a single computer and Internet connection, while a DDoS attacker uses multiple connected devices, making the flood of information much larger and harder to deflect.

There are many ways to protect from DoS and DDoS attacks. The easiest and most expensive way is to buy more bandwidth. Assume that during these attacks, they're trying to flood your space. If you have a ton of space it will be more difficult for attackers to overwhelm you. However, this is a largely impractical solution, especially for DDoS attacks, since the attacks are just too large to overcome.

However, there are more inexpensive and effective other ways to mitigate attacks. Setting up effective, well-configured firewalls, for example, can prevent this attack traffic from reaching your computer.

5. Use a Firewall

As the name suggests, a firewall is a hardware or software system that essentially works as a wall or gateway between two or more networks. It permits authorized traffic and blocks unauthorized or potentially malicious traffic from accessing a network or system. Just like an actual wall.

A firewall essentially protects what is inside a network from the outside—a.k.a from other networks or from threats on the Internet like backdoor and DDoS attacks. Since e-commerce websites have a lot of inbound traffic, they need firewalls to protect themselves against malicious entry.

There are many different kinds of firewalls, but two very effective firewalls for online retailers are application gateways and proxy firewalls. Both function as intermediary programs between two or more networks, meaning that incoming traffic has no direct connection or access to a retailer's network.

6. Application Gateways

With an application gateway in place, there are two lines of communication: one between your computer and the proxy, the other between the proxy and the destination computer or network. It's essentially a checkpoint that all network information has to stop at. By serving as this middle point, the application gateways help hide and protect your network from others', and only let in traffic (or packets) that have been authorized.

7. Proxy Firewalls

Proxy firewalls are among the most secure. Why? Like the application gateway, the proxy serves as an intermediary connection. However, they take it one step further. Instead of your network connection going all the way through, a new network connection is started at the proxy firewall. This means that there is no direct connection between systems at all, which makes it even harder for attackers to discover your network and get in.

It is important to note that, it has to be properly configured to have a firewall to be effective. What does this mean? Well, firewalls don't automatically know which traffic is malicious, and they need to be programmed with this information. Make sure, then, that whoever sets up the firewall is properly configuring it so that all of the right information gets through.

By staying on top of all these security measures, online retailers can effectively build their customers' trust and their own company's reputability.

New Words

website	n.	网站
cornerstone	n.	基础
insecure	adj.	不可靠的，不安全的
employ	v.	雇用，使用，利用
destination	n.	目的地
compliance	n.	兼容
organization	n.	组织，机构，团体
guideline	n.	方针
tokenization	n.	标记，标记化
token	n.	令牌，标记，代币
equivalent	n.	等价物，相等物
	adj.	等价的，相等的，同意义的
extrinsic	adj.	外在的，外表的，外来的
exploitable	adj.	可开发的，可利用的
encrypt	v.	加密，把……加密
tokenize	v.	标记，使令牌化
extremely	adv.	极端地，非常地
detokenize	v.	去令牌，脱令牌
redeem	v.	恢复
strict	adj.	严格的，严谨的，精确的
cryptography	n.	密码使用法，密码系统，密码术
affected	adj.	受到影响的，受侵袭的

mandatory	*adj.*	命令的，强制的，托管的
multiple	*adj.*	多样的，多重的
	n.	倍数，若干
	v.	成倍增加
chain	*n.*	链(条)，一连串，一系列
essentially	*adv.*	本质上，本来
unreadable	*adj.*	不可读的，难以理解的
eavesdrop	*v.*	偷听
valuable	*adj.*	有价值的
prospective	*adj.*	预期的
attain	*v.*	获得，达到
intercept	*v.*	中途阻止，截取
insecurity	*n.*	不安全
hurt	*v.*	危害，损害
attacker	*n.*	攻击者
overwhelming	*adj.*	压倒性的，无法抵抗的
device	*n.*	装置，设备
deflect	*v.*	使中止，使放弃，偏离，偏转
overwhelm	*v.*	淹没，制服，压倒
solution	*n.*	解决办法，解决方案
firewall	*n.*	防火墙
block	*v.*	妨碍，阻塞
backdoor	*n.*	后门
	adj.	秘密的
proxy	*n.*	代理，代理人
intermediary	*adj.*	中间的，媒介的
	n.	中间物
application	*n.*	应用，应用程序，应用软件
checkpoint	*n.*	检查站，检查点
configure	*v.*	配置，设定
automatically	*adv.*	自动地，机械地
reputability	*n.*	声誉

Phrases

run through	匆匆查阅；贯穿
Security Standards Council	安全标准委员会
come up with	提出，拿出
a set of	一组，一套

pass through	经过，通过
instead of	代替，而不是……
plain text	纯文本
tend to	注意，趋向
application gateway	应用网关
proxy firewall	代理防火墙
get in	进入，到达
set up	建立，设立
stay on top of	知道，掌握

Abbreviations

PCI (Payment Card Industry)	支付卡行业
DSS (Data Security Standard)	数据安全标准
SSL (Security Socket Layer)	加密套接字协议层
SHA (Secure Hash Algorithm)	安全哈希算法
DDoS (Distributed Denial of Service)	分布式拒绝服务
a.k.a. (also known as)	又名……，也叫作

Exercises

[Ex. 1] Answer the following questions according to the text.

1. Why is website security the cornerstone of a successful online business for e-commerce retailers?

2. What is the PCI Security Standards Council?

3. What is tokenization when applied to data security?

4. What does the SSL Certificate ensure?

5. What does HTTPS stand for? What is it?

6. What is the key difference between a DoS attacker and a DDoS attacker?

7. What is a firewall? What does it do?

8. What are the two very effective firewalls for online retailers?

9. What are the two lines of communication with an application gateway in place?

10. Why are proxy firewalls the most secure?

[Ex. 2] Translate the following terms or phrases from English into Chinese and vice versa.

1. application gateway   1. _____
2. proxy firewall   2. _____
3. set up   3. _____
4. application   4. _____
5. attain   5. _____

6. 自动地，机械地	6. _____
7. 妨碍，阻塞	7. _____
8. 装置，设备	8. _____
9. 防火墙	9. _____
10. 中间的，媒介的；中间物	10. _____

[Ex. 3] Translate the following passage into Chinese.

Security Measures and Protocols in Internet

Following are the popular measures and protocols used over the Internet which ensures security of transactions made over the Internet.

1. Major Security Measures

• Encryption: It is a very effective and practical way to safeguard the data being transmitted over the network. Sender of the information encrypt the data using a secret code and specified receiver only can decrypt the data using the same or different secret code.

• Digital Signature: Digital signature ensures the authenticity of the information. A digital signature is an e-signature authentic authenticated through encryption and password.

• Security Certificates: Security certificate is unique digital id used to verify identity of an individual website or user.

2. Security Protocols in Internet

(1) Secure Socket Layer (SSL)

It is the most commonly used protocol and is widely used across the industry. It meets following security requirements:

• authentication;
• encryption;
• integrity;
• non-reputability.

"https://" is to be used for HTTP urls with SSL, whereas "http:/" is to be used for HTTP urls without SSL.

(2) Secure Hypertext Transfer Protocol (SHTTP)

SHTTP extends the HTTP Internet protocol with public key encryption, authentication and digital signature over the Internet. Secure HTTP supports multiple security mechanism providing security to end users. SHTTP works by negotiating encryption scheme types used between client and server.

(3) Secure Electronic Transaction

It is a secure protocol developed by MasterCard and Visa in collaboration. Thereoritically, it is the best security protocol. It has following components:

• Card Holder's Digital Wallet Software: Digital Wallet allows card holder to make secure purchases online via point and click interface.

- Merchant Software: This software helps merchants to communicate with potential customers and financial institutions in secure manner.
- Payment Gateway Server Software: Payment gateway provides automatic and standard payment process. It supports the process for merchant's certificate request.
- Certificate Authority Software: This software is used by financial institutions to issue digital certificates to card holders and merchants and to enable them to register their account agreements for secure electronic commerce.

[Ex. 4] Fill in the blanks with the words given below.

| customer | redirected | payment | authorize | non-hosted |
| secure | complete | sensitive | require | accomplished |

Payment Gateways

Online payments can be made in a variety of ways, but majority of the online financial transactions are done through secured payment gateways. Secure payment gateways, as the name suggests, are application service providers for e-commerce websites that ___1___ various financial transactions taking place on online stores for ensuring safety for both the retailers and the online buyers. The key goal of payment gateways is to ___2___ personal information like consumers' credit card numbers by encrypting their personal and confidential information.

A payment gateway is a software layer that helps pass ___3___ information between an online store and a bank by encrypting the confidential information so that online transactions can be ___4___ safely in real time. A payment gateway is like an online version of POS (Point of Sale), which stores use for taking payments from their customers.

There are two major types of payment gateway categories—hosted and non-hosted. With a hosted payment gateway, when a ___5___ checks out, he/she is directed away from that website to the payment gateway website page. At the payment page, the customer is asked to enter the transaction details or credit card details on the payment service provider page. Once the customer makes the ___6___, he/she is again redirected to the merchant's website. The advantage of these types of payment gateways, used by such companies as PayPal, Worldpay and Nochex, is that this payment gateway does not ___7___ the merchant ID because any of the client's important or vulnerable information is not gained in the merchant's website.

Some merchants do not like to divert their customers' attention from their website and, therefore, may choose ___8___ payment gateways. In a non-hosted payment gateway such as eWay's website, customers can directly enter their transaction information on payment page while the payment page is controlled by the payment protection gateway with ___9___ safety assurance. Once the customer has entered the card details and other important transaction information, he/she is taken back to the merchant's site. This type of payment gateway can save customers time due to not being ___10___ to another website.

Text B

How to Stay Safe When Shopping Online

E-commerce isn't just increasing, it's evolving. The exponential rate of e-commerce growth has far surpassed mainstream security measures set in place to properly regulate online commerce and prevent consumer identity fraud. Every time a new e-commerce innovation is released, a new security risk is posed for consumers.

Today's consumers are confronted by a maze of different online commerce opportunities, choices and decisions, none of which were available or even fathomable 20 years ago. E-commerce is gaining momentum and acceptance; previously risky online activities such as banking are now considered safe and reliable, yet popular methods used to access sensitive information online present serious security risks. Most consumers accept terms and conditions too easily and without a second thought, compromising online anonymity and privacy.

Although online commerce does present security risks, the consumer's benefits of e-commerce far outweigh a return to in-store shopping. After all, driving to the shopping center introduces the risk of a car accident; swiping a credit card at a checkout places us at risk of credit card skimming. There will always be risks, but as the e-commerce world evolves, we should embrace this dynamic industry and keep the following five fundamental security tips in mind.

1. Share with Caution

Share only what is required. You should never share more than absolutely required, particularly when it comes to highly sensitive personal information such as national insurance or driver's license numbers. Sellers create online checkout forms with fields for irrelevant details to gather customer data—but don't require such fields be completed. Skip the questions that aren't marked "required" with an asterisk and you'll significantly improve your shopping anonymity.

Think before sharing devices. Reassess how freely you share the devices you use to make purchases. If you have a digital wallet app, it's not the best idea to let a stranger use your phone to make a call. If you keep yourself logged into shopping sites on your home devices, simply ask the guests to use a different browser. Consider any device you use to make purchases comparable to your wallet. Sharing without thinking twice or taking basic precautions is just asking for a problem down the road.

Extra caution is advised if you use your mobile phone for any e-commerce activity. Jailbroken phones are generally not suitable for secure commerce usage, as rogue downloads are likely to lack reliable security features. Be wary of storing usernames, passwords, banking numbers, and other sensitive information on your phone, including within apps assumed to be secretive. If e-mail is connected to your phone, never send highly sensitive information to others or even to yourself. Treat

185

your phone like your credit card; if it's lost or stolen, one of the first steps to reduce collateral damage should be contacting your financial institution or credit card provider.

Furthermore, if you actively shop on a mobile device, you may want to consider a password manager, or other mobile security tool for advanced protection.

Shared Wi-Fi is equal to unsecure Wi-Fi. As a rule of thumb, assume all shared Wi-Fi networks are unsafe for your sensitive data. Everything from an online bank statement to a Gmail account can be compromised when surfing the web on a shared Wi-Fi network. It's nearly impossible to accurately gauge how secure a Wi-Fi network is, and thus it's best to err on the side of caution.

You also want to ensure you are not connected to a shared Wi-Fi when making mobile transactions. Saved network passwords within your phone settings will automatically connect to previously used Wi-Fi networks without any notification. As a precaution, it's best to disable Wi-Fi on your phone before beginning any type of mobile transaction.

2. Verify All URLs

Verify URLs for secure connections. Regular online shoppers know to check URLs for "https" security when making transactions online, but many don't know how frequently to check. In every step of the checkout process, the URL of the site should be encrypted, that is, it should read "https" rather than "http".

It's also important to check for "https" when making purchases on the mobile web. Mobile purchases thrive off ease-of-use and convenience, making it even more important to take the time to check the URL.

Use URLs to verify site legitimacy. Verifying URLs is especially important in deciphering the legitimacy of sites discovered through advertisements and hyperlinks. Any link presented in an e-mail, social media comment, or advertisement can bring you to a fraudulent website. To make matters worse, deceitful sites are often virtually indistinguishable from the legitimate sites. Regardless of how you come to a website or how clean-cut it appears, examine the URL. You don't need to understand all parts of it, but if the root domain name (the part following "www") does not match the site content, chances are you should purchase elsewhere.

3. Question before You Buy, Save without Question

Question every site. One of the easiest ways to avoid online scams is to ensure you're shopping with a legitimate site. Beyond checking the URL for validity, a simple two-step process will help ensure the site is authentic. First, check that the site you plan to make a purchase on has a valid "About us" or "Contact us" page with contact information listed. Second, confirm the company has some type of social media presence.

Google the site's domain; its Twitter, Facebook and/or LinkedIn accounts should be present on the first few result pages. Genuine companies will have active social accounts and an online conversation in place with consumers, whereas fraudulent sites are likely to show Google results of consumer complaints, warnings, or other scam indications.

Record all purchase details. After every purchase, make sure you have proof the transaction took place. You should always receive a confirmation number or emailed receipt along with tracking information for shipments. Keep all receipts and confirmation numbers, along with a copy of the site's contact information.

If you are uncertain about a transaction from the get-go, screenshot your confirmation page and any post-purchase information you receive on screen. Screenshots allow you to save details you don't yet know you need, such as opt-in boxes left checked for ongoing payments or membership activation. Overall, the more documentation you have, the better.

4. Keep Payment Methods Separate from Bank Accounts

Opt for credit, not debit card payments. Although both credit cards and debit cards can be used as a plastic payment method in-store, credit cards are best for shopping online thanks to the online fraud protection most offer. When you pay via credit card, the payment is technically coming from the credit card company as a loan, rather than a monetary payment deducted directly from your bank account. Any processing errors or excess charges can be easily caught on your credit card statement, if not even sooner by the credit card company's standard fraud protection measures in place.

Alternatively, debit card payments deduct money directly from your bank account, and can be much more difficult to retrieve or correct after the event. Debit card information is also a prime target for hackers, as it provides an easy route for accessing and draining your accounts.

Use virtual credit cards as needed. Some financial institutions and credit card companies offer Virtual Credit Cards (VCC) for certain online purchases. Virtual credit cards are temporary payment cards, and come in the form of a physical plastic card, or as a generated credit card number, and they're separate from your bank information. This type of disposable credit card payment method contains a preset spending amount, has a shorter-than-usual expiration date, and is equivalent to a regular credit card for most payments purposes.

Virtual credit card payments are usually charged to your credit or debit card, rather than directly to your bank account, essentially offering an additional layer of protection. When you pay with a virtual credit card, your banking information remains separate from your individual purchase, thus ensuring if the card number is stolen, hackers cannot access your accounts or reuse the card fraudulently.

5. You Only Have One Online Identity, So Protect It

If you think you don't have an online identity, you're wrong. All you need is one e-mail address or a Facebook account, and you already have an online identity formed. No matter how cautious you are in the e-commerce sphere, the best way to protect yourself is to monitor your online identity actively.

Protect your online identity on the social front. Online purchasing is getting more and more social, with 50 percent of web sales projected to occur via social media by 2015. Each time you join a new site through the "Login with Facebook" option, you're extending your online identity further. In fact, an abundance of sites will first prompt you to become a member not by e-mail, but by connecting a social media account. When you then go on to transact on these third-party sites while logged in via Facebook or Twitter, you are essentially connecting the account with a credit card.

Is it a direct connection? Technically, no. Will it be used to shape your online identity?

Absolutely. Your social media presence defines your digital footprint to the point where companies are looking to use your social media identity to combat online payment fraud and your social signals to tackle identity fraud in the near future.

Once you realize that the majority of your online activity is interconnected, you can better defend yourself from making thoughtless choices that may endanger your data. Just like you shouldn't post something you don't want your employer to see on Facebook, you shouldn't post anything you don't want a hacker to see, like a picture of your driver's license or passport, anything with a home address and any snapshots that include a visible credit card or credit card number. It's also smart to choose passwords, passphrases, and answers to security questions that cannot be derived from your online social presence.

New Words

mainstream	n.	主流
regulate	v.	管制，控制，调节
pose	v.	形成，引起，造成
maze	n.	迷宫，迷津，迷惘，迷惑，糊涂
	v.	使迷惘，使混乱，迷失
fathomable	adj.	可测的，看得透的
momentum	n.	动力，要素
risky	adj.	危险的
serious	adj.	严肃的，认真的，严重的
compromise	v.	妥协，折衷，危及……的安全
anonymity	n.	匿名，作者不明(或不详)
outweigh	v.	在重量(或价值等)上超过
accident	n.	意外事件，事故
embrace	v.	拥抱，包含
asterisk	n.	星号
reassess	v.	再估价，再评价
stranger	n.	陌生人，门外汉
comparable	adj.	可比较的，比得上的
advised	adj.	考虑过的，细想过的
jailbroken	adj.	已经越狱的；破解的
rogue	n.	流氓，无赖
	v.	欺诈
reliable	adj.	可靠的，可信赖的
username	n.	用户名
collateral	adj.	附属的，间接的
unsecure	adj.	不安全的，不可靠的
impossible	adj.	不可能的

notification	n.	通知，布告，告示
precaution	n.	预防，警惕，防范
disable	v.	使无效，使失去能力
thrive	v.	兴旺，繁荣
convenience	n.	便利，方便
legitimacy	n.	合法(性)，正确(性)，合理(性)
decipher	v.	译解(密码等)，解释
	n.	密电译文
fraudulent	adj.	欺诈的，欺骗性的
deceitful	adj.	欺诈的
indistinguishable	adj.	不能辨别的，不能区别的
authentic	adj.	可信的
genuine	adj.	真实的，真正的，诚恳的
complaint	n.	诉苦，抱怨，牢骚
indication	n.	迹象，暗示
proof	n.	证据
receipt	n.	收条，收据
uncertain	adj.	不确定的，不可预测的，靠不住的
screenshot	n.	屏幕截图
documentation	n.	文件
plastic	n.	塑胶，塑料制品
loan	n.	（借出的）贷款，借出
	v.	借，借给
disposable	adj.	可任意使用的
preset	v.	预先设置，事先调整
spending	n.	开销，花费
sphere	n.	范围，领域，方面，圈子
project	n.	计划，方案，事业，工程
	v.	设计，计划
abundance	n.	大量，丰富，充裕
define	v.	定义，详细说明
footprint	n.	足迹，脚印
combat	n.	战斗，格斗
	v.	战斗，搏斗，抗击
tackle	v.	处理，解决，抓住；捉住，扭住，扭倒
interconnect	v.	使互相连接
endanger	v.	危及
snapshot	n.	快照，简单印象

Phrases

exponential rate	指数比率
be confronted by	面临，面对，碰上
credit card skimming	信用卡盗刷
keep in mind	牢记，谨记，记住
national insurance	国民保险，国家保险
driver's license	驾驶执照
digital wallet	数字钱包
be likely to	可能
collateral damage	附带损害
rule of thumb	拇指规则，经验法则，单凭经验的方法
bank statement	银行结单，银行报表
root domain name	根域名
err on the side of caution	宁求稳妥，不愿涉险
as ever	依旧，仍然
opt-in box	选择框
separate from	分离，分开
opt for	选择
deduct from	扣除
financial institution	金融机构
credit card number	信用卡号
shorter-than-usual	比正常短一点
expiration date	有效期
be equivalent to…	相当于……，等同于，与……等效
no matter how	不管如何
be derived from	来自，源于

Abbreviations

Wi-Fi (Wireless Fidelity)   高保真无线网络

VCC (Virtual Credit Cards)   虚拟信用卡

Exercises

[Ex. 5] Fill in the following blanks according to the text.

1. Today's consumers are confronted by a maze of _____, choices and decisions, none of which were _____ 20 years ago.

2. You should never share more than absolutely required, particularly when it comes to highly sensitive personal information such as _____ or _____.

3. If you keep yourself logged into shopping sites on your home devices, simply ask the guests to _____.

4. Shared Wi-Fi is equal to _____. As a precaution, it's best to _____ before beginning any type of mobile transaction.

5. In every step of the checkout process, the URL of the site should _____, that is, it should read "https" rather than _____. It's also important to check for "https" when making purchases _____.

6. One of the easiest ways to avoid online scams is to ensure you're shopping with _____. After every purchase, make sure _____.

7. If you are uncertain about a transaction from the get-go, _____ and _____ on screen. _____ allow you to save details you don't yet know you need.

8. When you pay via credit card, the payment is technically coming from _____ as a loan, rather than _____ deducted directly from your bank account. Alternatively, debit card payments deduct money _____, and can be _____ or correct after the event.

9. When you pay with _____, your banking information remains separate from your individual purchase, thus ensuring if the card number is stolen, hackers _____ or _____.

10. Your social media presence defines your digital footprint to the point where companies are looking to use your social media identity to _____ and _____ to tackle identity fraud in the near future.

Reading Material

Ways to Protect Your E-commerce Site from Hacking and Fraud

Hackers are stealing credit card and other sensitive information from e-commerce sites. To protect (and reassure[1]) your customers, it's imperative[2] to know how to protect your e-business and your sensitive customer data. E-commerce and security experts share their tips on how you can prevent fraud and hacking and keep your site safe.

1. Choose a Secure E-commerce Platform

"Put your e-commerce site on a platform that uses a sophisticated object-orientated programming language[3]," says Shawn Hess, software development manager, VoIP Supply.

---

1 reassure   v. 使……安心，使……恢复信心，打消……的疑虑
2 imperative   adj. 紧急的，必要的
3 object-orientated programming language   面向对象的编程语言

"We've used plenty of different open source[1] e-commerce platforms in the past and the one we're using now is by far the most secure," Hess says. "Our administration panel is inaccessible[2] to attackers because it's only available on our internal network and completely removed from our public facing servers. Additionally, it has a secondary authentication that authenticates users with our internal Windows network."

2. Use a Secure Connection for Online Checkout, and Make Sure You Are PCI Compliant

"Use strong SSL (Secure Sockets Layer) authentication for Web and data protection," says Rick Andrews, technical director, Trust Services, Symantec.

"It can be a leap of faith for customers to trust that your e-commerce site is safe, particularly when Web-based attacks increased 30 percent last year. So it's important to use SSL certificates "to authenticate the identity of your business and encrypt the data in transit[3]," Andrews says. "This protects your company and your customers from getting their financial or important information stolen." Even better: "Integrate the stronger EV SSL (Extended Validation Secure Sockets Layer[4]), URL green bar and SSL security seal so customers know that your website is safe."

"SSL certificates are a must for transactions," Hess agrees. "To validate our credit cards we use a payment gateway that uses live address verification services right on our checkout," he says. "This prevents fraudulent purchases by comparing the address entered online to the address they have on file with their credit card company."

3. Don't Store Sensitive Data

"There is no reason to store thousands of records on your customers, especially credit card numbers, expiration dates and CVV2 (card verification value 2) codes," says Chris Pogue, director of Digital Forensics and Incident Response at Trustwave.

"In fact, it is strictly forbidden[5] by the PCI Standards," Pogue says. He recommends[6] purging old records from your database and keeping a minimal amount of data, just enough for charge-backs[7] and refunds. "The risk of a breach[8] outweighs the convenience for your customers at checkout," he says. "If you have nothing to steal, you won't be robbed[9]."

4. Employ an Address and Card Verification System

"Enable an Address Verification System[10] (AVS) and require the Card Verification Value (CVV) for credit card transactions to reduce fraudulent charges," says Colin O'Dell, lead Magento developer for Unleashed Technologies.

1　open source　　开放源码，开源
2　inaccessible　　*adj.* 不能访问的
3　in transit　　传输中的
4　Extended Validation Secure Sockets Layer　　扩展验证安全套接字层
5　forbidden　　*adj.* 禁止的，严禁的
6　recommend　　*v.* 推荐，介绍，劝告
7　charge-backs　　退款
8　breach　　*n.* 违背，破坏　*v.* 打破，突破
9　rob　　*v.* 抢夺，抢掠，剥夺
10　Address Verification System　　地址验证系统

5. Require Strong Passwords

"While it is the responsibility[1] of the retailer to keep customer information safe on the backend[2], you can help customers help themselves by requiring a minimum number of characters and the use of symbols or numbers," says Sarah Grayson, senior marketing manager for the Web Security Group at McAfee. "Longer, more complex logins will make it harder for criminals to breach your site from the frontend[3]," she says.

6. Set Up System Alerts for Suspicious Activity

"Set an alert notice for multiple and suspicious transactions coming through from the same IP address," advises Deric Loh, managing director at digital agency Vault Labs. Similarly, set up system alerts for "multiple orders placed by the same person using different credit cards, phone numbers that are from markedly[4] different areas than the billing address and orders where the recipient name is different than the card holder name".

7. Layer Your Security

"One of the best ways to keep your business safe from cybercriminals[5] is layering your security," says Grayson. "Start with firewalls, an essential aspect in stopping attackers before they can breach your network and gain access to your critical information." Next, she says, "add extra layers of security to the website and applications such as contact forms[6], login boxes and search queries." These measures "will ensure that your e-commerce environment is protected from application-level attacks like SQL (Structured Query Language[7]) injections and cross-site scripting."

8. Provide Security Training to Employees

Employees "need to know they should never e-mail or text sensitive data or reveal[8] private customer information in chat sessions[9] as none of these communication methods is secure," says Jayne Friedland Holland, chief security officer and associate general counsel at technology firm NIC Inc.

"Employees also need to be educated on the laws and policies that affect customer data and be trained on the actions required to keep it safe," Holland says. Finally, "use strict written protocols and policies to reinforce[10] and encourage employees to adhere to mandated security practices".

9. Use Tracking Numbers for All Orders

"To combat chargeback fraud, have tracking numbers for every order you send out," advises Jon West, CEO, AddShoppers, a social commerce platform for retailers. "This is especially

---

1 responsibility　　*n.*　责任, 职责
2 backend　　*n.*　后端
3 frontend　　*n.*　前端
4 markedly　　*adv.*　显著地, 明显地
5 cybercriminal　　*n.*　网络犯罪分子, 网络罪犯
6 contact form　　　联系表格
7 Structured Query Language　　结构化查询语言
8 reveal　　*v.*　展现, 显示, 揭示, 暴露
9 session　　*n.*　会话
10 reinforce　　*v.*　加强, 增援, 补充, 修补, 加固

193

important for retailers who drop ship."

10. Monitor Your Site Regularly, and Make Sure Whoever Is Hosting It Is, too

"Always have a real-time analytics tool," says Punit Shah, director of Marketing at online jeweler My Trio Rings. "It's the real-world equivalent of installing security cameras in your shop. Tools like Woopra or Clicky allow you to observe[1] how visitors are navigating and interacting with your website in real time, allowing you to detect fraudulent or suspicious behavior," he says. "With tools like these we even receive alerts on our phones when there is suspicious activity, allowing us to act quickly and prevent suspicious behavior from causing harm[2]."

Also, make sure whoever is hosting your e-commerce site "regularly monitors their servers for malware, viruses and other harmful[3] software," says Ian Rogers, SEO and Web developer, Mvestor Media, an SEO and website design company. "Ask your current or potential Web host if they have a plan that includes at least daily scanning[4], detection and removal of malware and viruses on the website."

11. Perform Regular PCI Scans

"Perform regular quarterly PCI scans through services like Trustwave to lessen the risk that your e-commerce platform is vulnerable[5] to hacking attempts," advises West. "If you're using third-third-party downloaded software like Magento or PrestaShop, stay on top of new versions with security enhancements," he says. "A few hours of development time today can potentially save your entire business in the future."

12. Patch Your Systems

"Patch[6] everything immediately, literally the day they release a new version," says Kyle Adams, chief software architect for Junos WebApp Secure at Juniper Networks. "That includes the Web server itself, as well as other third-party code like Java, Python, Perl, WordPress and Joomla, which are favorite targets for attackers."

"Breached sites are constantly[7] found running a three-year-old version of PHP[8] or ColdFusion from 2007," says Pogue. So it's critical you install patches on all software: "Your Web apps, Xcart, OSCommerce, ZenCart and any of the others all need to be patched regularly."

13. Make Sure You Have a DDoS Protection and Mitigation[9] Service

"With DDoS attacks increasing in frequency, sophistication and range of targets, e-commerce sites should turn to cloud-based DDoS protection and managed DNS[10] services to provide

---

1 observe   v.   观察, 观测
2 harm   v. & n. 伤害, 损害
3 harmful   adj. 有害的, 伤害的
4 scanning   v.   扫描
5 vulnerable   adj. 易受攻击的
6 patch   n. & v. 修补, 打补丁
7 constantly   adv. 不变地, 经常地, 坚持不懈地
8 PHP (Hypertext Preprocessor)   超文本预处理器
9 mitigation   n.   缓解, 减轻, 平静
10 DNS (Domain Name Server)   域名服务器

transactional capacity to handle proactive mitigation and eliminate the need for significant investments in equipment, infrastructure and expertise," says Sean Leach, vice president of Technology, Verisign.

"The cloud approach will help e-commerce businesses trim operational costs while hardening their defenses to thwart even the largest and most complex attacks," he argues. "In addition, a managed, cloud-based DNS hosting service can help deliver 100 percent DNS resolution, improving the availability of Internet-based systems that support online transactions and communications."

14. Consider a Fraud Management Service

"Fraud does happen. And for merchants, the best resolution is to make sure you are not holding the bag when it does," says Bob Egner, vice president of Product Management at EPiServer, a .NET content management and e-commerce product company. "Most credit card companies offer fraud management and chargeback management services. This is a practical approach to take because most security experts know there is no such thing as 100 percent safe."

15. Make Sure You or Whoever Is Hosting Your Site Is Backing It Up, and Has a Disaster[1] Recovery Plan

"Results from a recent study by Carbonite revealed businesses have big gaps[2] in their data backup[3] plans—putting them at risk for losing valuable information in the instance of power outage[4], hard drive[5] failure or even a virus," says David Friend, CEO of Carbonite. So to make sure your site is properly protected, back it up regularly—or make sure your hosting service is doing so.

参 考 译 文

电子商务零售商网站安全的基础

对于电子商务零售商来说，网站安全是在线业务成功的基石。为什么？因为人们只想把他们的钱和他们的业务给他们可以信任的公司和组织。

如果零售商的网站不安全，那么所有其他营销和内部努力就不会带来结果。在这里，我们提出一些基本的安全准则，供所有电子商务零售商使用，以确保他们的网站是一个安全、成功的线上目的地。

1. PCI 合规性

PCI 安全标准委员会是一个全球性组织，旨在开发、增强和维护支付账户的安全标准。其创始成员包括美国运通、Discover 金融服务、JCB 国际、万事达卡和维萨公司。

该组的成员共同提出了一套安全要求，称为支付卡行业数据安全标准（PCI DSS），所有处理、存储或传输信用卡信息的商家必须遵守。很好的理由在于：这些指南确保所有存储的

---

1 disaster　　n. 灾难
2 gap　　n. 缺口，裂口，差距
3 backup　　n. 备份　v. 做备份　adj. 备份的，支持性的
4 power outage　　停电
5 hard drive　　硬盘

信用卡数据都受到保护，敏感信息在整个交易过程中是安全的。

许多公司通过使用标记化来满足这些指南。

在应用于数据安全性时，标记化是用不具有外在或可利用意义或价值的非敏感等价物（称为令牌）替换敏感数据元素的过程。当敏感信息（如信用卡号码中的数字）被非敏感信息或令牌替换时，将无法读取。这是加密数据的有效方法，因为它非常安全：标记化信息只能在严格的安全控制下被分解才能恢复敏感数据，并且令牌和支付卡数据的存储必须符合PCI标准，包括使用强加密。

保持PCI兼容性并确保所有存储的信用卡数据以这种方式完全标记化，大大降低了这种敏感信息被盗和使用的风险。保持这些数据安全对所有在线零售商来说都非常重要。如果持卡人的数据被盗，他们的信用可能受到负面影响，他们可能失去可信度、金钱甚至他们的业务。

2. SSL 证书

每个PCI强制使用SSL证书，确保通过互联网发送的敏感信息也是加密和安全的。当零售商或网站访问者通过互联网发送信息或数据时，它在到达其目标服务器之前要经过多个计算机。在此链中的任何一点，如果未使用SSL证书加密，它就可能会被盗。

证书如何工作？它实质上是保证所有敏感信息（包括密码、信用卡信息和用户名）对于除目的地服务器之外的每个人都不能读，从而保护所有通信免受窃听和盗窃。

SSL证书对于电子商务零售商尤其有价值，这不仅仅是为了安全原因，而且还能建立与网站访问者和潜在客户的信任。获取SSL证书本质上验证了实体的凭据，证明他们所说的身份属实并且他们的网站对访问者是安全的。

请务必注意要求中的变化。例如，最近从SHA-1加密更改为SHA-2加密，以确保你的公司保持合规。

3. 使用 HTTPS

带有安全套接字层的超文本传输协议，即HTTPS，是一种用于通过网络传输数据的协议。在创建数据的所有页面上应该使用HTTPS而不是HTTP。这里的问题又都是关于加密的。使用HTTP，信息不加密——相反，它是作为纯文本发送的，这意味着任何人都可以拦截它并读取已发送的内容。

此外，许多客户知道这种不安全性，并倾向于避免使用HTTP的电子商务网站。这意味着随着时间的推移，继续使用HTTP可能会伤害零售商的安全性及其业务。

然而，重要的是要注意，并不是网站的每一页上都有HTTPS。为什么？如果零售商试图将其用于每一个页面，这将减慢网页加载速度，并且可能会影响其业务。HTTPS应该仅用于收集和存储数据的页面，以便客户觉得可以安全地发送其信息。这意味着可以跳过首页、"关于我们"等页面。

4. DoS 和 DDoS 保护

DoS（拒绝服务）和DDoS（分布式拒绝服务）保护工作能防止拒绝服务和分布式拒绝服务的攻击。

在这两种攻击中，攻击者试图阻止合法用户访问信息或服务，其使用的方法是让访问量泛滥、使目标系统的带宽过载并阻止合法请求的传达。

尽管两种攻击的工作方式相同，但其主要区别在于DoS攻击者通常使用单个计算机和互联网连接，而 DDoS 攻击者使用多个连接的设备，使信息泛滥更严重，更难中止。

有许多方法可以防止 DoS 和 DDoS 攻击。最简单和最昂贵的方法是购买更多的带宽。假设在这些攻击期间，他们试图淹没你的空间。如果你有大量的空间，攻击者将更难以淹没你。但是，这是一个很不切实际的解决方案，尤其是对于 DDoS 攻击，因为攻击太大了，无法战胜。

然而，还有更廉价和有效的其他方法来减轻攻击。例如，设置有效且配置良好的防火墙可以防止此攻击流量到达你的计算机。

5. 使用防火墙

顾名思义，防火墙是一个硬件或软件系统，它基本上作为两个或多个网络之间的墙或网关。它允许授权的流量访问网络或系统，并能阻止未授权的或潜在的恶意流量，就像一个实际的墙。

防火墙本质上保护网络外部对内部的访问——即来自其他网络的攻击，或者来自网络上的威胁（如后门和 DDoS 攻击）。由于电子商务网站有很多入站流量，他们需要防火墙来保护自己免受恶意入侵。

有许多类型的防火墙，但是对于在线零售商来说两个非常有效的防火墙是应用网关和代理防火墙。两者用作两个或更多网络之间的中间程序，意味着进入的流量不能直接访问零售商的网络。

6. 应用网关

使用应用网关，有两条通信线路：一条在你的计算机和代理之间，另一条在代理和目标计算机或网络之间。它本质上是一个检查点，所有的网络信息必须停下接受检查。通过使用这个中间点，应用程序网关帮助隐藏和保护你的网络，并且只允许已经授权的流量（或数据包）进入。

7. 代理防火墙

代理防火墙是最安全的。为什么？像应用网关一样，代理充当中间连接。然而，他们更进一步。不是直通连接到你的网络，而是在代理防火墙启动一个新的网络连接。这意味着在系统之间没有直接的连接，使攻击者更难发现和进入你的网络。

尤其要注意的是，它必须正确配置防火墙以便使其有效。这是什么意思？防火墙不会自动知道哪些流量是恶意的，他们需要用这些信息来配制。然后确保防火墙的建立者配置得当，以便让所有正确的信息通过。

通过掌握所有这些安全措施，在线零售商可以有效地建立其客户的信任和自己公司的信誉。

Unit 11

Text A

Mobile Commerce

The phrase "mobile commerce" was originally coined in 1997 by Kevin Duffey at the launch of the Global Mobile Commerce Forum, to mean "the delivery of electronic commerce capabilities directly into the consumer's hand, anywhere, via wireless technology". Many choose to think of Mobile Commerce as meaning "a retail outlet in your customer's pocket".

扫一扫，听课文

Mobile commerce is worth US$230 billion, with Asia representing almost half of the market, and has been forecast to reach US$700 billion in 2017. According to BI Intelligence in January 2013, 29% of mobile users made a purchase with their phones. Walmart estimated that 40% of all visits to their Internet shopping site in December 2012 was from a mobile device[1]. Mobile commerce made up 11.6 percent of total e-commerce spending in 2014, and is forecast to increase to 45 percent by 2020, according to BI Intelligence.

1. Products and Services Available

(1) Mobile Money Transfer

A money transfer system called MobilePay has been operated by Danske Bank in Denmark since 2013. It has gained considerable popularity with about 1.6 million users by mid-2015. Another similar system called Vipps was introduced in Norway in 2015.

Mobile Automated Teller Machine (ATM) is a special type of ATM. Most ATMs are meant to be stationary, and they're often found attached to the side of financial institutions, in stores, and in malls. A mobile ATM machine, on the other hand, is meant to be moved from location to location. This type of ATM is often found at special events for which ATM service is only needed temporarily. For example, they may be found at carnivals, fairs, and parades. They may also be used at seminars and workshops when there is no regular ATM nearby.

---

1 A mobile device (or handheld computer) is a small computing device, typically, small enough to hold and operate in the hand and having an operating system capable of running mobile apps. These may provide a diverse range of functions. Typically, the device will have a display screen with a small numeric or alphanumeric keyboard or a touchscreen providing a virtual keyboard and buttons (icons) on-screen. Many such devices can connect to the Internet and interconnect with other devices such as car entertainment systems or headsets via Wi-Fi, Bluetooth or Near Field Communication (NFC). Integrated cameras, digital media players, mobile phone and GPS capabilities are common. Power is typically provided by a lithium battery.

(2) Mobile Ticketing

Tickets can be sent to mobile phones using a variety of technologies. Users are then able to use their tickets immediately by presenting their mobile phone at the ticket check as a digital boarding pass. Most of users are now moving towards this technology. Best example would be IRCTC where ticket comes as SMS to users.

(3) Mobile Vouchers, Coupons and Loyalty Cards

Mobile ticketing technology can also be used for the distribution of vouchers, coupons, and loyalty cards. These items are represented by a virtual token that is sent to the mobile phone. A customer presenting a mobile phone with one of these tokens at the point of sale receives the same benefits as if they had the traditional token. Stores may send coupons to customers using location-based services[1] to determine when the customer is nearby.

(4) Content Purchase and Delivery

Currently, mobile content purchase and delivery mainly consists of the sale of ring-tones, wallpapers, and games for mobile phones. The convergence of mobile phones, portable audio players, and video players into a single device is increasing the purchase and delivery of full-length music tracks and video. The download speeds available with 4G[2] networks make it possible to buy a movie on a mobile device in a couple of seconds.

(5) Location-Based Services

The location of the mobile phone user is an important piece of information used during mobile commerce or m-commerce transactions. Knowing the location of the user allows for location-based services such as:

- local discount offers;
- local weather;
- tracking and monitoring of people.

(6) Information Services

A wide variety of information services can be delivered to mobile phone users in much the same way as it is delivered to PCs. These services include:

- News.
- Stock quotes.
- Sports scores.
- Financial records.
- Traffic reporting.
- Emergency alerts.

---

1 A Location-Based Service (LBS) is a software-level service that uses location data to control features. As such LBS is an information service and has a number of uses in social networking today as information, in entertainment or security, which is accessible with mobile devices through the mobile network and which uses information on the geographical position of the mobile device.

2 4G is the fourth generation of wireless mobile telecommunications technology, succeeding 3G. A 4G system must provide capabilities defined by ITU in IMT advanced. Potential and current applications include amended mobile web access, IP telephony, gaming services, high-definition mobile TV, video conferencing, and 3D television.

Customized traffic information, based on a user's actual travel patterns, can be sent to a mobile device. This customized data is more useful than a generic traffic-report broadcast, but was impractical before the invention of modern mobile devices due to the bandwidth requirements.

(7) Mobile Banking

Banks and other financial institutions use mobile commerce to allow their customers to access account information and make transactions, such as purchasing stocks, remitting money. This service is often referred to as mobile banking, or m-banking.

(8) Mobile Brokerage

Stock market services offered via mobile devices have also become more popular and are known as Mobile Brokerage. They allow the subscriber to react to market developments in a timely fashion and irrespective of their physical location.

(9) Auctions

Over the past three years mobile reverse auction[1] solutions have grown in popularity. Unlike traditional auctions, the reverse auction (or low-bid auction) bills the consumer's phone each time they place a bid. Many mobile SMS commerce solutions rely on a one-time purchase or one-time subscription; however, reverse auctions offer a high return for the mobile vendor as they require the consumer to make multiple transactions over a long period of time.

(10) Mobile Browsing

Using a mobile browser—a World Wide Web browser on a mobile device—customers can shop online without having to be at their personal computer. Many mobile marketing apps with geolocation capability are now delivering user-specific marketing messages to the right person at the right time.

2. Influence on Youth Markets

Mobile media is a rapidly changing field. New technologies, such as WiMax[2], act to accelerate innovation in mobile commerce. Early pioneers in mobile advertising include Vodafone, Orange, and SK Telecom.

Mobile devices are heavily used in Korea to conduct mobile commerce. Mobile companies in Korea believed that mobile technology would become synonymous with youth life style, based on their experience with previous generations of Koreans. "Profitability for device vendors and carriers hinges on high-end mobile devices and the accompanying killer applications[3]," said Gibran Burchett.

3. Payment Methods

Consumers can use many forms of payment in mobile commerce, including:

1) Contactless payment for in-person transactions through a mobile phone (such as Apple Pay

---

1 A reverse auction is a type of auction in which the roles of buyer and seller are reversed. In an ordinary auction (also known as a forward auction), buyers compete to obtain goods or services by offering increasingly higher prices. In a reverse auction, the sellers compete to obtain business from the buyer and prices will typically decrease as the sellers underbid each other.

2 WiMAX (Worldwide Interoperability for Microwave Access) is a family of wireless communication standards based on the IEEE 802.16 set of standards, which provide multiple physical layer (PHY) and Media Access Control (MAC) options.

3 In marketing terminology, a killer application (commonly shortened to killer app) is any computer program that is so necessary or desirable that it proves the core value of some larger technology, such as computer hardware, gaming console, software, a programming language, software platform, or an operating system. In other words, consumers would buy the (usually expensive) hardware just to run that application. A killer app can substantially increase sales of the platform on which it runs.

or Android Pay). In a system like EMV, these are interoperable with contactless credit and debit cards.

2) Premium-rate telephone numbers[1], which apply charges to the consumer's long-distance bill.

3) Mobile-Operator Billing allows charges to be added to the consumer's mobile telephone bill, including deductions to pre-paid calling plans.

4) Credit cards and debit cards.

① Some providers allow credit cards to be stored in a phone's SIM card or secure element.

② Some providers are starting to use Host Card Emulation[2], or HCE (e.g. Google Wallet and Softcard).

③ Some providers store credit card or debit card information in the cloud; usually in tokenized. With tokenization[3], payment verification, authentication, and authorization are still required, but payment card numbers don't need to be stored, entered, or transmitted from the mobile device.

5) Micropayment[4] services.

6) Stored-value cards[5] often used with mobile-device application stores or music stores (e.g. iTunes).

4. App Design for M-commerce

Interaction Design and UX design has been at the core of the m-commerce experience from its conception, producing apps and mobile web pages that create highly usable interactions for users. However, much debate has occurred as to the focus that should be given to the apps. In recent research, it was demonstrated that within Fashion M-commerce apps the degree that the app helps the user shop (increasing convenience) was the most prominent function. It was also showed that shopping for others was a motivator for engaging in m-commerce apps with great preference for close integration with social media.

New Words

coin	v.	杜撰，创造
forum	n.	论坛

---

1 Premium-rate telephone numbers are telephone numbers for telephone calls during which certain services are provided, and for which prices higher than normally are charged. Unlike a normal call, part of the call charge is paid to the service provider, thus enabling businesses to be funded via the calls. While the billing is different, calls are usually routed the same way they are for a toll-free telephone number, being anywhere despite the area code used.

2 Host Card Emulation (HCE) is the software architecture that provides exact virtual representation of various electronic identity (access, transit and banking) cards using only software. Prior to the HCE architecture, NFC transactions were mainly carried out using secure elements.

3 Tokenization, when applied to data security, is the process of substituting a sensitive data element with a non-sensitive equivalent, referred to as a token that has no extrinsic or exploitable meaning or value.

4 A micropayment is a financial transaction involving a very small sum of money and usually one that occurs online.

5 A stored-value card is a payments card with a monetary value stored on the card itself, not in an external account maintained by a financial institution. Stored-value cards differ from debit cards, where money is on deposit with the issuer, and credit cards which are subject to credit limits set by the issuer. Another difference between stored-value cards and debit and credit cards is that debit and credit cards are usually issued in the name of individual account holders, while stored-value cards may be anonymous, as in the case of gift cards. Stored-value cards are prepaid money cards and may be disposed when the value is used, or the card value may be topped up, as in the case of telephone calling cards or when used as a fare card.

wireless	*adj.*	无线的
pocket	*n.*	衣袋，口袋
	v.	装……在口袋里
	adj.	袖珍的，小型的
forecast	*n. & v.*	预测，预报
estimate	*v. & n.*	估计，估价，评估
considerable	*adj.*	相当大(或多)的，值得考虑的，相当可观的
popularity	*n.*	普及，流行
stationary	*adj.*	固定的
carnival	*n.*	嘉年华，狂欢节，节日，联欢
fair	*n.*	展销会，商品交易会，集市
parade	*n.*	游行
seminar	*n.*	研究会，讨论发表会
workshop	*n.*	车间，工场
voucher	*n.*	凭证，凭单，<美>优惠购货券
content	*n.*	内容，容量，目录，满足
ring-tone	*n.*	铃声
convergence	*n.*	集合，集中
location	*n.*	位置，场所，特定区域
emergency	*n.*	紧急情况，突然事件
pattern	*n.*	式样，模式，样品
broadcast	*n.*	广播
	v.	广播，播送，播放
impractical	*adj.*	不切实际的
bandwidth	*n.*	带宽
brokerage	*n.*	经纪人之业务，回扣
irrespective	*adj.*	不顾的，不考虑的，无关的
auction	*n. & v.*	拍卖
browser	*n.*	浏览器
geolocation	*n.*	地理定位
accelerate	*v.*	加速，促进
pioneer	*n.*	先驱，倡导者，先锋
synonymous	*adj.*	同义的
profitability	*n.*	收益性，利益率
micropayment	*n.*	微支付，小额支付
conception	*n.*	观念，概念
motivator	*n.*	促进因素，激发因素
preference	*n.*	偏爱，优先选择

Phrases

gain considerable popularity	非常受欢迎
mobile device	移动设备
on the other hand	另一方面
a variety of	多种的
digital boarding pass	数字登机牌，数字登机证
move towards	走向，接近
loyalty card	（商店的）积分卡，购物卡
location-based service	基于位置的服务
stock quote	股票报价
remit money	汇款，划拨款项
stock market	股票市场
mobile reverse auction	移动反向拍卖
personal computer	个人计算机（缩写为 PC）
killer application	杀手级应用
premium-rate telephone number	额外收费电话号码
stored-value card	储值卡

Abbreviations

ATM (Automated Teller Machine)	自动柜员机
IRCTC (Indian Railway Catering and Tourism Corporation)	印度铁路餐饮和旅游公司
4G (Fourth Generation of Wireless Mobile Telecommunications Technology)	第四代移动通信技术
SIM (Subscriber Identification Module)	客户识别模块
HCE (Host-Based Card Emulation)	基于主机的卡模拟
UX (User eXperience)	用户体验

Exercises

[Ex. 1] Answer the following questions according to the text.

1. When and by whom was the phrase mobile commerce originally coined? What did it mean?
2. What is the difference between most ATMs and a mobile ATM?
3. What can mobile ticketing technology also be used for?
4. What location-based services does knowing the location of the user allow for?
5. A wide variety of information services can be delivered to mobile phone users in much the same way as it is delivered to PCs. What services do they include?
6. What do stock market services offered via mobile devices allow the subscriber to do?
7. Why do reverse auctions offer a high return for the mobile vendor?
8. What are many mobile marketing apps with geolocation capability?
9. What did mobile companies in Korea believe?

10. What are the many forms of payment consumers can use in mobile commerce?

[Ex. 2] **Translate the following terms or phrases from English into Chinese and vice versa.**

1. loyalty card _____ 1. _____
2. mobile reverse auction _____ 2. _____
3. stored-value card _____ 3. _____
4. auction _____ 4. _____
5. bandwidth _____ 5. _____
6. 广播，播送，播放 _____ 6. _____
7. 微支付，小额支付 _____ 7. _____
8. 收益性，利益率 _____ 8. _____
9. 凭证，凭单，<美>优惠购货券 _____ 9. _____
10. 无线的 _____ 10. _____

[Ex. 3] **Translate the following passage into Chinese.**

Mobile Marketing and Advertising

In the context of mobile commerce, mobile marketing refers to marketing sent to mobile devices. Companies have reported that they see better response from mobile marketing campaigns than from traditional campaigns. The primary reason for this is the instant nature of customer decision-making that mobile apps and websites enable. The consumer can receive a marketing message or discount coupon and, within a few seconds, make a decision to buy and go on to complete the sale—without disrupting their current real-world activity.

For example, a busy mom tending to her household chores with a baby in her arm could receive a marketing message on her mobile about baby products from a local store. She can and within a few clicks, place an order for her supplies without having to plan ahead for it. No more need to reach for her purse and hunt for credit cards, no need to log in to her laptop and try to recall the web address of the store she visited last week, and surely no need to find a babysitter to cover for her while she runs to the local store.

Research demonstrates that consumers of mobile and wireline markets represent two distinct groups who are driven by different values and behaviors, and who exhibit dissimilar psychographic and demographic profiles. What aspects truly distinguish between a traditional online shopper from home and a mobile on-the-go shopper? Research shows that how individuals relate to four situational dimensions—place, time, social context and control determine to what extent they are ubiquitous or situated as consumers. These factors are important in triggering m-commerce from ecommerce. As a result, successful mobile commerce requires the development of marketing campaigns targeted to these particular dimensions and according user segments.

[Ex. 4] **Fill in the blanks with the words given below.**

directly	interface	billed	mobile	carriers
building	conditions	cash-out	deliver	wirelessly

1. Mobile Purchase

Catalog merchants can accept orders from customers electronically, via the customer's mobile device. In some cases, the merchant may even ___1___ the catalog electronically, rather than mailing a paper catalog to the customer. Consumers making ___2___ purchases can also receive value-add upselling services and offers. Some merchants provide mobile websites that are customized for the smaller screen and limited user ___3___ of a mobile device.

2. In-Application Mobile Phone Payments

Payments can be made ___4___ inside of an application running on a popular smartphone operating system, such as Google Android. Analyst firm Gartner expects in-application purchases to drive 41 percent of app store (also referred to as mobile software distribution platforms) revenue in 2016. In-app purchases can be used to buy virtual goods, new and other mobile content and is ultimately ___5___ by mobile carriers rather than the app stores themselves. Ericsson's IPX mobile commerce system is used by 120 mobile ___6___ to offer payment options such as try-before-you-buy, rentals and subscriptions.

3. Mobile ATMs

Mobile ATMs are usually self-contained units that don't need a ___7___ or enclosure. Usually, a mobile ATM can be placed in just about any location and can transmit transaction information ___8___, so there's no need to have a phone line handy. Mobile ATMs may, however, require access to an electrical source, though there are some capable of running on alternative sources of power. Often, these units are constructed of weather-resistant materials, so they can be used in practically any type of weather ___9___. Additionally, these machines typically have internal heating and air conditioning units that help keep them functional despite the temperature of the environment. Some operators are now looking for efficient ways to roll out and manage distribution networks that can support cash-in and ___10___. Unlike traditional ATM, SICAP Mobile ATMs have been specially engineered to connect to mobile money platforms and provide bank grade ATM quality. In Hungary, Vodafone allows cash or bank card payments of monthly phone bills. The Hungarian market is one where direct debits are not standard practice, so the facility eases the burden of queuing for the postpaid half of Vodafone's subscriber base in Hungary.

Text B

Mobile Marketing

Mobile marketing is marketing on or with a mobile device, such as a smart phone. Mobile marketing can provide customers with time and location sensitive, personalized information that promotes goods, services and ideas. In a more theoretical manner, academic Andreas Kaplan defines mobile

205

marketing as "any marketing activity conducted through a ubiquitous network to which consumers are constantly connected using a personal mobile device".

1. SMS Marketing

Marketing through cellphones' SMS (Short Message Service) became increasingly popular in the early 2000s in Europe and some parts of Asia when businesses started to collect mobile phone numbers and send off wanted (or unwanted) content. On average, SMS messages are read within four minutes, making them highly convertible.

Over the past few years SMS marketing has become a legitimate advertising channel in some parts of the world. This is because unlike e-mail over the public Internet, the carriers who police their own networks have set guidelines and best practices for the mobile media industry (including mobile advertising). The IAB (Interactive Advertising Bureau) and the Mobile Marketing Association (MMA), as well, have established guidelines and are evangelizing the use of the mobile channel for marketers. While this has been fruitful in developed regions such as North America, Western Europe and some other countries, mobile spam messages (SMS sent to mobile subscribers without a legitimate and explicit opt-in by the subscriber) remain an issue in many other parts of the world, partly due to the carriers selling their member databases to third parties. In India, however, government's efforts of creating National Do Not Call Registry have helped cellphone users to stop SMS advertisements by sending a simple SMS or calling 1909.

Mobile marketing via SMS has expanded rapidly in Europe and Asia as a new channel to reach the consumer. SMS initially received negative media coverage in many parts of Europe for being a new form of spam as some advertisers purchased lists and sent unsolicited content to consumer's phones; however, as guidelines are put in place by the mobile operators, SMS has become the most popular branch of the mobile marketing industry with several 100 million advertising SMS sent out every month in Europe alone.

2. Push Notifications

Push notifications were first introduced to smartphones by Apple with the Push Notification Service in 2009. For Android devices, Google developed Android Cloud to Messaging or C2DM in 2010. Google replaced this service with Google Cloud Messaging in 2013. Commonly referred to as GCM, Google Cloud Messaging served as C2DM's successor, making improvements to authentication and delivery, new API endpoints and messaging parameters, and the removal of limitations on API send-rates and message sizes. It is a message that pops up on a mobile device. It is the delivery of information from a software application to a computing device without any request from the client or the user. SMS and push notifications can be part of a well-developed inbound mobile marketing strategy.

According to mobile marketing company Leanplum, Android sees open rates twice as high as those on iOS. Android sees open rates of 3.48 percent for push notification, versus iOS which has open rates of 1.77 percent.

3. App-Based Marketing

With the increasingly widespread use of smartphones, app[1] usage has also greatly increased. Therefore, mobile marketers have increasingly taken advantage of smartphone apps as a marketing resource. Marketers will aim to increase the visibility of an app in a store, which will in turn help in getting more downloads. By optimizing the placement of the app usage, marketers can ensure a significant number of increases in download. This allows for direct engagement, payment, and targeted advertising.

Mobile App Development is benefiting various companies in order to maximize their profits. In the past couple of years the usage of mobile phones has increased at an astonishing rate. Most of the companies have slowly but surely acknowledged the potential that Mobile App possess in order to increase the interaction between a company and its target customers. While planning to invest in Mobile App for your business you must consider all the aspects of it. Always choose a reliable and experienced company to develop customized apps for your business as this would help to increase the chances of success of that App and minimize the chances of any technical glitches that might crop up. You must keep in mind that an App can prove to be a very beneficial element to promote your business on a vast level only if it is developed by efficient service provider.

4. In-Game Mobile Marketing

There are essentially three major trends in mobile gaming right now: interactive real-time 3D games, massive multi-player games and social networking games. This means a trend towards more complex and more sophisticated, richer game play. On the other side, there are the so-called casual games, i.e. games that are very simple and very easy to play. Most mobile games today are such casual games and this will probably stay so for quite a while.

Brands are now delivering promotional messages within mobile games or sponsoring entire games to drive consumer engagement. This is known as mobile advergaming or ad-funded mobile game.

In in-game mobile marketing, advertisers pay to have their name or products featured in the mobile games. For instance, racing games can feature real cars made by Ford or Chevy. Advertisers have been both creative and aggressive in their attempts to integrate ads organically in the mobile games.

Although investment in mobile marketing strategies like advergaming is slightly more expensive than what is intended for a mobile app, a good strategy can make the brand derive a substantial revenue. Games that use advergaming make the users remember better the brand involved. This memorization increases virality of the content so that the users tend to recommend them to their friends and acquaintances, and share them via social networks.

---

1 A mobile app is a software application designed to run on mobile devices such as smartphones and tablet computers. Most such devices are sold with several apps bundled as pre-installed software, such as a web browser, e-mail client, calendar, mapping program, and an app for buying music or other media or more apps. Some pre-installed apps can be removed by an ordinary uninstall process, thus leaving more storage space for desired ones. Where the software does not allow this, some devices can be rooted to eliminate the undesired apps.

5. Location-Based Services

Location-Based Services (LBS) are offered by some cell phone networks as a way to send custom advertising and other information to cell phone subscribers based on their current location. The cell phone service provider gets the location from a GPS chip built into the phone, or using radiolocation and trilateration based on the signal strength of the closest cell phone towers (for phones without GPS features). In the United Kingdom, which launched location-based services in 2003, networks do not use trilateration; LBS uses a single base station, with a "radius" of inaccuracy, to determine a phone's location.

Some location-based services work without GPS tracking technique, instead transmitting content between devices peer-to-peer[1].

6. Ringless Voice Mail

The advancement of mobile technologies has the ability to leave a voice mail message on a mobile phone without ringing the line. The technology was pioneered by VoAPP, which used the technology in conjunction with live operators as a debt collection service. The FCC has ruled that the technology is compliant with all regulations. CPL expanded on the existing technology to allow for a completely automated process including the replacement of live operators with pre recorded messages. By optimizing the technology, marketers can utilize the process to increase engagement of their product or service.

7. User-Controlled Media

Mobile marketing differs from most other forms of marketing communication in that it is often user (consumer) initiated (Mobile Originated, or MO) message, and requires the express consent of the consumer to receive future communications. A call delivered from a server (business) to a user (consumer) is called a Mobile Terminated (MT) message. This infrastructure points to a trend set by mobile marketing of consumer controlled marketing communications.

Due to the demands for more user controlled media, mobile messaging infrastructure providers have responded by developing architectures that offer applications to operators with more freedom for the users, as opposed to the network-controlled media. Along with these advances to user-controlled Mobile Messaging 2.0, blog events throughout the world have been implemented in order to launch popularity in the latest advances in mobile technology. In June 2007, Airwide Solutions became the official sponsor for the Mobile Messaging 2.0 blog that provides the opinions of many through the discussion of mobility with freedom.

Mobile advertising has become more and more popular. However, some mobile advertising is sent without a required permission from the consumer, causing privacy violations. It should be understood that no matter how well advertising messages are designed and how many additional possibilities they provide, if consumers do not have confidence that their privacy will be protected, this will hinder their widespread deployment. But if the messages originate from a source where the

---

1 Peer-to-Peer (P2P) computing or networking is a distributed application architecture that partitions tasks or workloads between peers. Peers are equally privileged, equipotent participants in the application. They are said to form a peer-to-peer network of nodes.

user is enrolled in a relationship/loyalty program, privacy is not considered violated and even interruptions can generate goodwill.

The privacy issue has become even more salient with the arrival of mobile data networks. A number of important new concerns emerged mainly stemming from the fact that mobile devices are intimately personal and are always with the user. The four major concerns are mobile spam, personal identification, location information and wireless security.

New Words

theoretical	*adj.*	理论的
ubiquitous	*adj.*	到处存在的，(同时)普遍存在的，泛在的
collect	*v.*	收集，聚集，集中，搜集
unwanted	*adj.*	不必要的，多余的，讨厌的
convertible	*adj.*	可改变的，可转换的
established	*adj.*	已制定的，确定的
evangelize	*v.*	宣传，传福音
fruitful	*adj.*	多产的，富有成效的
unsolicited	*adj.*	未被恳求的，主动提供的
Android	*n.*	安卓（操作系统）
successor	*n.*	继承者，接任者，后续的事物
improvement	*n.*	改进，进步
endpoint	*n.*	端点，终点
smartphone	*n.*	智能电话
astonishing	*adj.*	惊人的
glitch	*n.*	失灵，小故障
beneficial	*adj.*	有益的，受益的
aggressive	*adj.*	好斗的，有闯劲的，侵略性的
organically	*adv.*	有机地
expensive	*adj.*	花费的，昂贵的
substantial	*adj.*	坚固的，实质的，真实的，充实的
memorization	*n.*	记住
virality	*n.*	病毒式传播
acquaintance	*n.*	相识，熟人
subscriber	*n.*	订户
chip	*n.*	芯片
radiolocation	*n.*	无线电定位
trilateration	*n.*	三边测量(术)
inaccuracy	*n.*	不准确，有误差
respond	*v.*	回答，响应，做出反应
opinion	*n.*	意见，看法，主张，判断，评价

mobility	n.	移动性，机动性
permission	n.	许可，允许
violation	n.	违反，违背，妨碍，侵害
confidence	n.	信心
violate	v.	违犯，冒犯，干扰，违反，妨碍，侵犯
goodwill	n.	善意，亲切
salient	adj.	易见的，显著的，突出的
concern	n.	关心，关注
intimately	adv.	密切地

✍ Phrases

send off	寄出，发送出
on average	平均，普通
spam message	兜售消息，垃圾消息
National Do Not Call Registry	国家谢绝来电计划
Push Notification Service	推送通知服务
pop up	弹出，突然出现
target customer	目标客户
crop up	突然出现
real-time 3D game	实时三维游戏
multi-player game	多人游戏，多个玩家的游戏
casual game	休闲游戏
cell phone	蜂窝电话，手机
signal strength	信号强度
cell phone tower	手机信号塔，蜂窝电话塔
base station	基站，基地
voice mail	语音邮件
in conjunction with…	与……协力
differ from	不同
Mobile Originated	移动主叫，终端发起呼叫，缩写为 MO
Mobile Terminated	终端终止

✍ Abbreviations

IAB (Interactive Advertising Bureau)	(美国)互动广告局
MMA (Mobile Marketing Association)	移动营销协会
C2DM (Android Cloud to Device Messaging)	云端推送消息
GCM (Google Cloud Messaging)	谷歌云消息
API (Application Programming Interface)	应用编程接口
LBS (Location-Based Services)	基于位置的服务

GPS (Global Positioning System)　　　　　　全球定位系统
FCC (Federal Communications Commission)　　(美国)通信委员会

Exercises

[Ex. 5] Fill in the following questions according to the text.

1. Mobile marketing can provide customers with time and location sensitive, personalized information that promotes ＿＿＿＿, ＿＿＿＿＿＿ and ＿＿＿＿.

2. Over the past few years SMS marketing has become a ＿＿＿＿＿＿＿＿＿＿ in some parts of the world. This is because unlike e-mail over the public Internet, the carriers who police their own networks ＿＿＿＿＿＿ and ＿＿＿＿＿＿＿ for the mobile media industry (including mobile advertising).

3. SMS initially received ＿＿＿＿＿＿＿＿＿＿ in many parts of Europe for being a new form of spam as some advertisers ＿＿＿＿＿＿＿＿＿＿＿ to consumer's phones.

4. Push notifications were first introduced to smartphones by ＿＿＿＿＿＿＿ with ＿＿＿＿＿＿＿ in ＿＿＿＿＿＿.

5. According to mobile marketing company Leanplum, Android sees open rates ＿＿＿＿＿＿＿＿＿＿. Android sees open rates of ＿＿＿＿＿＿ for push notification, versus iOS which has open rates of ＿＿＿＿＿＿＿.

6. By optimizing the placement of ＿＿＿＿＿＿, marketers can ensure a significant number of increases in download. This allows for ＿＿＿＿＿＿, ＿＿＿＿＿＿, and ＿＿＿＿＿＿.

7. Most of the companies have slowly but surely acknowledged the potential that Mobile App possess in order to increase the interaction between ＿＿＿＿＿＿ and its ＿＿＿＿＿＿.

8. There are essentially three major trends in mobile gaming right now: ＿＿＿＿＿＿, ＿＿＿＿＿＿ and ＿＿＿＿＿＿.

9. Mobile marketing differs from most other forms of ＿＿＿＿＿＿ in that it is often user (consumer) initiated (Mobile Originated, or MO) message, and requires the express consent of the consumer to receive ＿＿＿＿＿＿.

10. The privacy issue has become ＿＿＿＿＿＿ with the arrival of mobile data networks. A number of important new concerns emerged mainly stemming from the fact that mobile devices are ＿＿＿＿＿＿ and are ＿＿＿＿＿＿. The four major concerns are ＿＿＿＿＿＿, ＿＿＿＿＿＿, location information and ＿＿＿＿＿＿.

Reading Material

Mobile Payment

Mobile payment (also referred to as mobile money, mobile money transfer, and mobile wallet) generally refer to payment services operated under financial regulations[1] and performed from or via a mobile device. Instead of paying with cash, cheque, or credit cards, a consumer can use a mobile

---

1　financial regulation　　金融管制，金融条例，财政法规

phone to pay for a wide range of services and digital or hard goods[1]. Although the concept of using non-coin-based currency systems has a long history, it is only recently that the technology to support such systems has become widely available.

There are four primary models for mobile payments:
- mobile wallets;
- card-based payments;
- carrier billing[2] (Premium SMS or direct carrier billing);
- contactless[3] NFC (Near Field Communication).

1. Mobile Wallets

Online companies like PayPal, Amazon Payments, and Google Wallet also have mobile options. Generally, this is the process:

1) First payment:
- User registers, inputs their phone number, and the provider sends them an SMS with a PIN[4].
- User enters the received PIN, authenticating[5] the number.
- User inputs their credit card info or another payment method if necessary (not necessary if the account has already been added) and validates payment.

2) Subsequent[6] payments:
- The user reenters[7] their PIN to authenticate and validates payment.

Requesting a PIN is known to lower the success rate (conversion) for payments. These systems can be integrated with directly or can be combined with operator and credit card payments through a unified mobile web payment platform.

2. Card-Based Payments

A simple mobile web payment system can also include a credit card payment flow allowing a consumer to enter their card details to make purchases. This process is familiar but any entry of details on a mobile phone is known to reduce the success rate (conversion) of payments.

In addition, if the payment vendor can automatically and securely identify customers then card details can be recalled for future purchases, turning credit card payments into simple single click-to-buy[8] giving higher conversion rates for additional purchases.

3. Carrier Billing

The consumer uses the mobile billing option during checkout at an e-commerce site—such as an online gaming site—to make a payment. After Two-Factor Authentication[9] involving a PIN and

---

1 hard good　　耐用品
2 carrier billing　　电信支付
3 contactless　　adj. 不接触的，遥控的
4 PIN (Personal Identification Number)　　个人身份号码
5 authenticate　　v. 鉴别，鉴定
6 subsequent　　adj. 后来的，并发的
7 reenter　　n. 重进入，再加入
8 click-to-buy　　点击购买
9 Two-Factor Authentication (also known as 2FA) is a method of confirming a user's claimed identity by utilizing a combination of different components. Two-Factor Authentication is a type of multi-factor authentication.

One-Time-Password[1] (often abbreviated as OTP), the consumer's mobile account is charged for the the purchase. It is a true alternative payment method that does not require the use of credit/debit cards or preregistration[2] at an online payment solution such as PayPal, thus bypassing banks and credit card companies altogether. This type of mobile payment method, which is extremely prevalent[3] and popular in Asia, provides the following benefits:

1) Secure——Two-factor authentication and a risk management engine prevents fraud.

2) Convenient——No pre-registration and no new mobile software is required.

3) Easy——It's just another option during the checkout process.

4) Fast——Most transactions are completed in less than 10 seconds.

5) Proven——70% of all digital content purchased online in some parts of Asia uses the Direct Mobile Billing method.

(1) Premium SMS[4] / Premium MMS[5]

In the predominant[6] model for SMS payments, the consumer sends a payment request via an SMS text message or an USSD[7] to a short code and a premium charge is applied to their phone bill or their online wallet. The merchant involved is informed of the payment success and can then release the paid for goods.

Since a trusted physical delivery address has typically not been given, these goods are most frequently digital with the merchant replying using a Multimedia Messaging Service to deliver the purchased music, ringtones, wallpapers[8] etc.

A Multimedia Messaging Service (MMS) can also deliver barcodes[9] which can then be scanned for confirmation of payment by a merchant. This is used as an electronic ticket for access to cinemas and events or to collect hard goods.

Transactional payments by SMS have been popular in Asia and Europe and are now accompanied[10] by other mobile payment methods, such as mobile web payments (WAP[11]), mobile payment client (Java ME, Android...) and Direct Mobile Billing.

---

1 One-Time-Password   一次性密码

2 preregistration   *n.* (办理正式手续前的)预先登记，预先注册

3 prevalent   *adj.* 普遍的，流行的

4 SMS (Short Message Service)   手机短信服务

5 MMS (Multimedia Messaging Service)   多媒体短信服务，即彩信

6 predominant   *adj.* 卓越的，主要的，突出的，有影响的

7 USSD (Unstructured Supplementary Service Data, 非结构化补充业务数据), sometimes referred to as "Quick Codes" or "Feature codes", is a protocol used by GSM cellular telephones to communicate with the service provider's computers. USSD can be used for WAP browsing, prepaid callback service, mobile-money services, location-based content services, menu-based information services, and as part of configuring the phone on the network.

USSD messages are up to 182 alphanumeric characters long. Unlike Short Message Service (SMS) messages, USSD messages create a real-time connection during a USSD session. The connection remains open, allowing a two-way exchange of a sequence of data. This makes USSD more responsive than services that use SMS.

8 wallpaper   *n.* 墙纸

9 barcode   *n.* 条形码

10 accompany   *v.* 陪伴，伴奏

11 WAP (Wireless Application Protocol)   无线应用协议

(2) Direct Carrier Billing

Direct carrier billing, also known as mobile content billing, WAP billing, and direct operator billing, requires integration with the mobile network operator. It provides certain benefits:

1) Mobile network operators already have a billing relationship with consumers, the payment will be added to their bill.

2) Provides instantaneous[1] payment.

3) Protects payment details and consumer identity.

4) Better conversion rates.

5) Reduced customer support costs for merchants.

6) Alternative monetization[2] option in countries where credit card usage is low.

One of the drawbacks is that the payout rate[3] will often be much lower than with other mobile payments options. Examples from a popular provider:

- 92% with PayPal;
- 85% to 86% with Credit Card;
- 45% to 91.7% with operator billing in the US, UK and some smaller European countries, but usually around 60%.

More recently, direct operator billing is being deployed in an in-app environment, where mobile application developers are taking advantage of[4] the one-click payment option that direct operator billing provides for monetising mobile applications. This is a logical alternative to credit card and Premium SMS billing.

In 2012, Ericsson and Western Union partnered to expand the direct operator billing market, making it possible for mobile operators to include Western Union Mobile Money Transfers as part of their mobile financial service offerings. Given the international reach of both companies, the partnership is meant to accelerate the interconnection[5] between the m-commerce[6] market and the existing financial world.

4. Contactless Near Field Communication

Near Field Communication (NFC)[7] is used mostly in paying for purchases made in physical stores or transportation services. A consumer using a special mobile phone equipped with a

---

1 instantaneous　　adj.　瞬间的，即刻的，即时的
2 monetization　　n.　货币化，当作货币
3 payout rate　　付费比率，支付率
4 take advantage of　　利用
7 interconnection　　n.　互连
6 m-commerce　　移动商务

7 Near-Field Communication (NFC) is a set of communication protocols that enable two electronic devices, one of which is usually a portable device such as a smartphone, to establish communication by bringing them within 4 cm (1.57 in) of each other.

NFC devices are used in contactless payment systems, similar to those used in credit cards and electronic ticket smartcards and allow mobile payment to replace/supplement these systems. NFC is used for social networking, for sharing contacts, photos, videos or files. NFC-enabled devices can act as electronic identity documents and keycards. NFC offers a low-speed connection with simple setup that can be used to bootstrap more capable wireless connections.

smartcard waves his/her phone near a reader module[1]. Most transactions do not require authentication, but some require authentication using PIN, before transaction is completed. The payment could be deducted from[2] a prepaid[3] account or charged to a mobile or bank account directly.

Mobile payment method via NFC faces significant challenges[4] for wide and fast adoption, due due to lack of supporting infrastructure, complex ecosystem[5] of stakeholders, and standards. Some phone manufacturers and banks, however, are enthusiastic[6]. Ericsson and Aconite are examples of businesses that make it possible for banks to create consumer mobile payment applications that take advantage of NFC technology.

NFC vendors in Europe mostly use contactless payment over mobile phones to pay for on- and off-street parking in specially demarcated[7] areas. Parking wardens may enforce the parkings by license plate[8], transponder[9] tags or barcode stickers[10]. First conceptualized in the 1990s, the technology has seen commercial use in this century in both Scandinavia and Estonia. End users benefit from[11] the convenience of being able to pay for parking from the comfort of their car with their mobile phone, and parking operators are not obliged to invest in either existing or new street-based parking infrastructures. Parking wardens maintain order in these systems by license plate, transponder tags or barcode stickers or they read a digital display in the same way as they read a pay and display receipt.

Other vendors use a combination of both NFC and a barcode on the mobile device for mobile payment, making this technique attractive[12] at the point of sale because many mobile devices in the market do not yet support NFC.

5. Others

(1) QR Code Payments

QR Codes 2D barcode are square bar codes. QR codes have been in use since 1994. Originally used to track products in warehouses, QR codes were designed to replace traditional (1D bar codes). Traditional bar codes just represent numbers, which can be looked up in a database and translated into something meaningful. QR, or "Quick Response" bar codes were designed to contain the meaningful info right in the bar code.

QR Codes can be of two main categories:

---

1 module *n.* 模块
2 deduct from 扣除
3 prepaid *adj.* 先付的，已支付的
4 challenge *n.* 挑战 *v.* 向……挑战
5 ecosystem *n.* 生态系统
6 enthusiastic *adj.* 热心的，热情的
7 demarcate *v.* 划分界线
8 license plate 牌照
9 transponder *n.* 收发机，询问机，转发器
10 sticker *n.* 张贴纸
11 benefit from 受益于
12 attractive *adj.* 吸引人的，有魅力的

- The QR Code is presented on the mobile device of the person paying and scanned by a POS[1] POS[1] or another mobile device of the payee[2].
- The QR Code is presented by the payee, in a static[3] or one time generated fashion and it's scanned by the person executing the payment.

Mobile self-checkout allows for one to scan a QR code or barcode of a product inside a brick-and-mortar establishment in order to purchase the product on the spot. This theoretically eliminates or reduces the incidence[4] of long checkout lines, even at self-checkout kiosks[5].

(2) Cloud-Based Mobile Payments

Google, PayPal, GlobalPay and GoPago use a cloud-based approach to in-store mobile payment. The cloud-based approach places the mobile payment provider in the middle of the transaction, which involves two separate steps. First, a cloud-linked payment method is selected and payment is authorized via NFC or an alternative method. During this step, the payment provider automatically covers the cost of the purchase with issuer linked funds. Second, in a separate transaction, the payment provider charges the purchaser's selected, cloud-linked account[6] in a card-not-present[7] environment to recoup[8] its losses on the first transaction.

参 考 译 文

移 动 商 务

"移动商务"这一词组最初是在1997年全球移动商务论坛上由凯文·达菲（Kevin Duffey）创造的，意思是"通过无线技术将电子商务能力直接传递到无论在哪里的消费者手中"。许多人认为移动商务是"客户口袋里的零售商店"。

移动商务价值2300亿美元，亚洲几乎占市场的一半，预计2017年将达到7000亿美元。根据BI智能2013年1月的报告，29%的移动用户使用手机购物。沃尔玛估计，2012年12月访问互联网购物网站的所有访问中有40%来自移动设备。根据BI智能报道，移动电子商务占2014年总的电子商务消费的11.6%，并预计到2020年将增加至45个百分点。

1. 可得到的产品和服务

（1）移动汇款

自2013年以来，丹斯克银行在丹麦开发了一个名为MobilePay的汇款系统。到2015年中期，该银行已经获得了大约160万用户的欢迎。另一个称为Vipps的类似系统于2015年在挪威推出。

---

1 POS (Point Of Sells)　电子收款机系统
2 payee　　*n.*　收款人，领款人
3 static　　*adj.*　静态的
4 incidence　　*n.*　发生率，影响范围
5 self-checkout kiosk　　自助结账亭
6 cloud-linked account　　云链接账号
7 card-not-present　　无卡交易
8 recoup　　*v.*　赔偿，补偿，扣除，补偿损失

移动自动柜员机（ATM）是一种特殊类型的 ATM。大多数 ATM 是固定的，并且它们通常放在金融机构、商店和商场的一侧。而移动 ATM 意在从一个位置移动到另一个位置。这种类型的 ATM 通常用于只要暂时 ATM 服务的特殊情形。例如，可以用于嘉年华、博览会和游行期间。当附近没有常规的 ATM 时，它们也可用于研讨会和讨论会期间。

（2）手机票务

可以使用各种技术把门票发送到手机中。然后用户能够立即使用他们的票，在检票时将其移动电话作为数字登记牌。大多数用户现在正在转向这种技术。最好的例子是 IRCTC，其中票据以 SMS 形式发送给用户。

（3）手机优惠购物券、优待券和会员卡

手机票务技术也可用于分发优惠购物券、优待券和会员卡。这些项目由发送到移动电话的虚拟代币表示。在销售点持有带这些代币的移动电话的客户与持有传统代币的客户享受同等待遇。商店可以使用基于位置的服务向客户发送优惠券以确定客户何时在附近。

（4）内容购买和交付

目前，移动内容购买和交付主要包括销售铃声、壁纸和手机游戏。将移动电话、便携式音频播放器和视频播放器融合到单个设备中增加了对完整音乐曲目和视频的购买和传送。4G 网络的下载速度让几秒钟内在移动设备上购买电影成为可能。

（5）基于位置的服务

移动电话用户的位置是在移动商务或移动商务交易期间使用的重要信息。知道用户的位置就能提供基于位置的服务。例如：

- 本地折扣优惠；
- 当地天气；
- 跟踪和监控人。

（6）信息服务

可以用与发送给个人计算机相同的方式将各种各样的信息服务发送给移动电话用户。这些服务包括：

- 新闻。
- 股票报价。
- 体育比分。
- 财务记录。
- 交通报告。
- 紧急警报。

基于用户的实际旅行模式的定制交通信息可以被发送到移动设备上。这种定制数据比一般的交通报告广播更有用，但由于带宽要求，在现代移动设备的发明之前是不切实际的。

（7）移动银行

银行和其他金融机构使用移动商务，允许他们的客户访问账户信息和进行交易，如购买股票、汇款。这项服务通常被称为移动银行。

（8）移动经纪

通过移动设备提供的股票市场服务也变得更受欢迎，被称为移动经纪。它们允许用户及时地对市场发展做出反应，而不管其地理位置如何。

（9）拍卖

在过去的三年中，移动反向拍卖解决方案越来越受欢迎。与传统拍卖不同，反向拍卖（或低出价拍卖）在每次出价时向消费者的手机发送账单。许多移动 SMS 商务解决方案依赖于一次性购买或一次性订阅；然而，反向拍卖为移动供应商提供高回报，因为他们需要消费者在长时间段内进行多个交易。

（10）移动浏览

使用移动浏览器——移动设备上的万维网浏览器——用户可以在线购物，而不必在个人计算机上操作。许多具有地理位置功能的移动营销应用程序现在可在适当的时间向适当的人提供面向特定用户的营销信息。

2. 对青年市场的影响

移动媒体是一个快速变化的领域。新技术（如 WiMax）用于加速移动商务的创新。早期移动广告的先驱包括沃达丰、奥兰治和 SK 电信。

韩国大量使用移动设备来进行移动商务。韩国的移动公司认为，根据前几代韩国人的经验，移动技术将成为青年人生活方式的代名词。"设备供应商和运营商的利润取决于高端移动设备和随之而来的杀手级应用，"纪伯伦·布查特（Gibran Burchett）说。

3. 付款方式

消费者可以在移动商务中使用多种付款方式，包括：

1）通过手机进行非接触式支付（如 Apple Pay 或 Android Pay）。在像 EMV 这样的系统中，这些可与非接触式信用卡和借记卡共同使用。

2）使用高费率电话号码，向消费者收取长途话费。

3）移动运营商计费允许将费用添加到消费者的移动电话账单中，包括扣除预付费呼叫计划。

4）信用卡和借记卡。

① 一些提供商允许将信用卡存储在手机的 SIM 卡或安全元件中。

② 一些提供商开始使用主机卡仿真，即 HCE（如谷歌电子钱包和软卡）。

③ 一些提供商在云中存储信用卡或借记卡信息，通常使用标记。使用标记化，仍然需要支付验证、认证和授权，但是不需要在移动设备中存储卡号，也不需要在移动设备上输入或发送支付信息。

5）小额支付服务。

6）存储值卡通常用于移动设备应用商店或音乐商店（如 iTunes）。

4. 移动电子商务的 App 设计

互动设计和用户体验设计一直是移动商务体验的核心，从它的概念、生产应用程序到移动网页都为用户创造高度可用的互动。然而，针对 App 有许多争论。最近的研究表明，在 Fashion M-commerce App 中，帮助用户购物（增加便利性）是最突出的功能。它还表明，为他人购物促进了移动商务 App 的使用，这些 App 与社交媒体结合紧密。

Unit 12

Text A

A Guide to Using CRM in E-commerce

1. What It Does

Originally, CRM was little more than an automated address book. A CRM app would keep track of the people who hadn't been contacted in a while, and send you reminders to reach out to them.

扫一扫，听课文

The next iteration of CRM focused more on its potential application in business. Salespeople quickly saw its potential for organizing leads and nurturing existing sales opportunities. Though CRM still dominates the sales space, the right CRM e-commerce app can help you with an array of critical tasks, with a scope broad enough to cover almost all aspects of your business:

- Acquiring leads through a variety of intake methods.
- Maintaining timely communication with all your customers and B2B partners.
- Conducting e-mail marketing campaigns and newsletters.
- Managing your social media channels.
- Keeping opportunities moving along your sales pipeline.
- Advanced reporting, to get a comprehensive view of your sales team, sales goals, marketing campaign effectiveness, seasonal trends, and more.
- Customer support / Help desk functionality.
- Data storage: localized knowledge base keeps pertinent customer information, support tickets, etc. in the cloud for near-instant access.

And that's just off the top of my head. In short, CRM for e-commerce covers just about everything from lead generation all the way through to a completed sale. Some CRM solutions even cross the grey area[1] between true CRM and Enterprise Resource Planning. ERP picks up where CRM leaves off; covering sales fulfillment and supply chain, and typically ending in customer re-engagement.

2. What to Get

Most e-commerce platforms (like Shopify, Volusion, and Bigcommerce) include some degree of CRM control. The depth of features offered will vary from cart to cart, and from one subscription

---

1 An area intermediate between two mutually exclusive states or categories, where the border between the two is fuzzy.

level to another.

If you are just starting out, be sure to determine which CRM and e-mail marketing features will be included in your chosen e-commerce platform. Don't over-buy just to get a ton of features! You can always upgrade your subscription (even in the middle of a contract) if your needs outstrip the features you signed up for.

If you are already well-established with your shopping cart platform, e-commerce CRM features may already be at your fingertips. If not, you can either upgrade your subscription level (if the features you need are available from your e-commerce software vendor), or you can easily integrate a third party solution.

When evaluating the many CRM e-commerce options out there, choose one that focuses on—you guessed it—actually managing your relationships with your customers. So many CRM apps in the market are geared towards the aforementioned sales pipeline, which is great, if that's what you need. But businesses which operate in the e-commerce space typically do not utilize a sales team to drive sales, making a Sales Pipeline Tracker a bit less relevant.

Instead, you should choose a CRM for your e-commerce business which emphasizes these targets:

- Acquiring customer data.
- E-mail marketing.
- Customer re-engagement (typically through loyalty programs[1]).
- Reporting and analytics on customer purchases, seasonal sales trends, etc.
- Customer support / Help desk functionality.
- Brand visibility.

In the next section, we'll look at how to hit these six e-commerce CRM targets.

3. What to Do

(1) Acquire Customer Data

The first, and hardest, part of using your CRM will probably be how you go about gathering useful data about your customers. There are a variety of ways you can do this, but perhaps the most effective way is to offer users the ability to create an account and log in to your site. This accomplishes several things at once and who doesn't love the efficiency of multitasking?

Offering your customer their own account on your site enables certain features which benefit them, and ultimately results in a ton of happy by-products which help you. It's a win-win! Though in full disclosure, it is not entirely without drawbacks. Enabling customer profiles from your e-commerce CRM App brings these benefits:

1) Customers will be able to maintain wish lists, get personalized loyalty rewards, shipment tracking, and streamlined checkout (with stored credit card information, shipping address, and order

---

[1] Loyalty programs are structured marketing strategies designed by merchants to encourage customers to continue to shop at or use the services of businesses associated with each program. These programs exist covering most types of business, each one having varying features and rewards schemes.

history), and a lot more, depending on the e-commerce and CRM apps you choose.

2) As a by-product, your CRM will be fed the most coveted data in Customer Info: e-mail address, regional location, name, purchase history, and possibly age and gender. These pieces of information will jumpstart your CRM like nothing else, allowing you to develop the most precise and effective marketing strategies. Over time, you'll be able to:
- See which marketing efforts were most successful.
- Create upsell[1] strategies tailored to each individual customer.
- Recover sales from abandoned carts.
- Re-engage customers who haven't visited you recently.

Enabling customer profiles from your e-commerce CRM app brings these drawbacks:

Since this is the best way to acquire customer data, it is an increasingly common practice. The end result for the user is that they'll have far too many accounts to manage among all the various places they shop, and may be loath to start one more account. Each account generates (from the customer's point of view) a ton of spam e-mails. Certain customers may simply choose Guest Checkout rather than create a new account, or they may register with a "spam e-mail account" which they exclusively use to sign up for things. Thus, any spam will go completely unseen by the customer.

(2) E-mail Marketing

This is where CRM really proves its worth. The axiom "it takes money to make money" is a nearly immutable law of business; so wherever business owners can cut costs, it's money in the bank. Marketing costs can really add up when you include print, postage, and promotions, but all of those costs are made virtually nil when your CRM can automate mass-email campaigns. And when each of those e-mails can be custom-tailored to each customer, you can see how this beats the socks off of mass-mailers cluttering the USPS floor.

With the dovetail of CRM and e-commerce, your customer can be given unprecedented individual attention. If Sally Shoebuyer hasn't been back to your online store in a while, your CRM can automatically send her an email when you have run a promotion on shoes. Or if Billy gets distracted mid-purchase, your CRM e-commerce platform can send him a reminder to come back and finish buying those t-shirts he wanted.

(3) Customer Re-engagement

The possibilities go on. You can have your CRM automatically serve your customers with:
- newsletters;
- notifications about the loyalty points they've accrued;
- notifications about price changes on items in their wish lists;
- seasonal sales;

---

1 Upselling is a sales technique whereby a seller induces the customer to purchase more expensive items, upgrades or other add-ons in an attempt to make a more profitable sale. While it usually involves marketing more profitable services or products, it can be simply exposing the customer to other options that were perhaps not considered. (A different technique is cross-selling in which a seller tries to sell something else.) In practice, large businesses usually combine upselling and cross-selling to maximize profit.

- personal coupon codes;
- blog snippets, local event invitations, or any other value-added info;
- as many calls to action as you can dream up to bring them back to your site.

(4) Reporting and Analytics

In both e-commerce and CRM, it's easy to get a bird's eye view of everything that happens in your retail domain. Want to see all the items customers have bought more than once? No problem. Need to see which promotions helped the most during last year's seasonal low tide? You got it. The ability to drill down into the specific details you need to see is easy.

(5) Customer Support / Help Desk Functionality

Customer support is often an afterthought, or worse, totally overlooked. Your e-commerce business lives or dies by the reputation you build for yourself, and nothing affects that reputation like excellent or awful customer service.

CRM to the rescue. Not only will happy customers be invited back to your store through your marketing efforts, but unsatisfied customers may yet be appeased if their problems can be resolved. Your CRM app will streamline this process. Support tickets can be flagged with varying levels of urgency so highest priority issues can be quickly resolved. Additionally, a customer's entire history can be at your fingertips; your interactions with them will be informed by their order history, communication history with your agents, and any other information that you can track. You might never need to tell your customers "I don't know".

(6) Brand Visibility

With something as simple as an e-mail or a post to social media, your brand stays fresh in the mind of your existing and potential customers.

I can't tell you how many great websites I've seen and assumed I'd remember, only to have them drowned out by a sea of vendors vying for my attention. Had I been able to follow them on Facebook, I'd be much more likely to revisit them in the future when I see their posts.

4. Conclusion

Is the combination of CRM and e-commerce starting to sound like a magic bullet?

It certainly can be, if implemented well. Like most things, what you get out of it depends on what you put into it. A halfhearted attempt to tack CRM onto your e-commerce business will yield small results. But if you invest well, CRM has the potential to streamline your workflow, broaden your marketing, and shine up your brand's reputation, all without narrowing your profit margins.

New Words

reminder	n.	通知单，提示信
iteration	n.	迭代，反复，重述，循环
salespeople	n.	售货员，店员
nurture	v.	培育，养育，滋养，培植
scope	n.	范围
aspect	n.	方面

intake	n.	入口，进口
pipeline	n.	管道，传递途径
pertinent	adj.	有关的，相干的，恰当的，中肯的
re-engagement	n.	诺言，重新雇用
accrue	v.	积累，增加，获得
outstrip	v.	超过
fingertip	n.	指尖，指套
aforementioned	adj.	上述的，前述的
emphasize	vt.	强调，着重
gathering	n.	聚集，收款
accomplish	v.	完成，达到，实现
multitask	n.	多任务
	v.	使多任务化
by-product	n.	副产品，意外结果，副作用
win-win	n.	双赢
covet	v.	垂涎，觊觎
start	v.	出发，起程，开始，着手，起动，发动
upsell	n.	向上销售，追加销售
loath	adj.	不情愿的，勉强的
axiom	n.	公理，格言，原理
immutable	adj.	不变的，永恒的
custom-tailor	v.	定制，定做
dovetail	v.	与……吻合
unprecedented	adj.	空前的，前所未有的
distracted	adj.	心烦意乱的
snippet	n.	片断，摘录
value-added	adj.	增值的
afterthought	n.	事后的考虑或想法，事后聪明，事后再想起，后来添加的东西
excellent	adj.	卓越的，极好的
awful	adj.	可怕的，糟糕的
rescue	v. & n.	援救，营救
appease	v.	安抚，缓和，满足
resolved	adj.	下定决心的，断然的
flag	n. & v.	标记
halfhearted	adj.	不认真的，不热心的，半心半意
workflow	n.	工作流

✎ Phrases

address book	通讯录，通讯簿

little more than	和……无差别，和……一样
keep track of	记录，追踪，与……保持联系
reach out to sb.	与某人接触
an array of	许多，大量
lead generation	线索产生，引导产生
get a comprehensive view of	全面了解
sales team	销售团队
sales goal	销售目标
marketing campaign effectiveness	营销活动的有效性
seasonal trend	季节性变化趋势
customer support	客户支持
help desk	帮助台功能，技术支持；客户服务
off the top of one's head	眼下能想到的
in short	简而言之
grey area	灰色地带
pick up	捡起，获得
be at one's fingertips	触手可及，在弹指间，手到拈来，轻而易举地完成
leave off	停止
supply chain	供应链
third party solution	第三方解决方案
loyalty program	会员积分奖励计划
full disclosure	财务事项的充分公布，充分披露
wish list	心愿单
shipment tracking	货运跟踪
streamlined checkout	简化结账
like nothing else	出类拔萃，与众不同，独一无二
abandoned cart	废弃的购物车
exclusive use	专用
beat the the socks off	彻底击败
loyalty point	忠诚积分，会员积分
dream up	空想出，构思，创造，设计
low tide	低潮，低落期
support ticket	支持请求
drown out	淹没
magic bullet	灵丹妙药，妙招
vying for	争夺

Abbreviations

ERP (Enterprise Resource Planning)　　　企业资源计划

USPS (United States Postal Service)　　　美国邮政管理局

Exercises

[Ex. 1] Answer the following questions according to the text.

1. What would a CRM app keep track of?
2. What does CRM for e-commerce cover?
3. What do most e-commerce platforms (like Shopify, Volusion, and Bigcommerce) include?
4. What are the six e-commerce CRM targets mentioned in the text?
5. What will the first, and hardest, part of using your CRM probably be?
6. What is where CRM really proves its worth?
7. What happens if Sally Shoebuyer hasn't been back to your online store in a while?
8. How can you have your CRM automatically serve your customers?
9. What does your e-commerce business live or die by?
10. What potential does CRM have if you invest well?

[Ex. 2] Translate the following terms or phrases from English into Chinese and vice versa.

1. abandoned cart　　　　　　　　1. _____
2. customer support　　　　　　　2. _____
3. keep track of　　　　　　　　　3. _____
4. loyalty point　　　　　　　　　4. _____
5. loyalty programs　　　　　　　5. _____
6. 货运跟踪　　　　　　　　　　　6. _____
7. 供应链　　　　　　　　　　　　7. _____
8. 第三方解决方案　　　　　　　　8. _____
9. 心愿单　　　　　　　　　　　　9. _____
10. 增值的　　　　　　　　　　　 10. _____

[Ex. 3] Translate the following passage into Chinese.

The consequences of e-commerce on logistics are little understood, but some trends can be identified. As e-commerce becomes more common, it is changing physical distribution systems.

The conventional retailing supply chain coupled with the process of economies of scale (larger stores, shopping malls) is being challenged by a new structure. The new system relies on large warehouses located outside metropolitan areas from where a vast number of small parcels are shipped by vans and trucks to separate online buyers. This spatially disaggregates retailing distribution, and reverses the trend towards consolidation that had characterized retailing (larger stores and larger distribution centers). Still, when online shopping reaches a large volume, parcel delivery companies have the opportunity to create economies through the consolidation of loads.

In the conventional retailing system, the shopper was bearing the costs of moving the goods from the store to home, but with e-commerce this segment of the supply chain has to be integrated in the freight distribution process. The result potentially involves more packaging and more tons-km of freight transported. Traditional distribution systems are thus ill fitted to satisfy the logistical needs of e-commerce, especially in urban areas.

[Ex. 4]   Fill in the blanks with the words given below.

| flexible | coverage | purchase | deliveries | location |
| chain | emergence | distribution | conventional | traveling |

Retail Logistics and E-commerce

Logistics is being impacted by e-commerce, particularly by its business to consumer segment. In a conventional retailing supply chain, customers are responsible to __1__ their goods at the retailer's location; they are assuming the "last mile" in freight distribution by __2__ to the store and back. For bulky purchases such as appliances and furniture, retailers offer local deliveries for their customers. Because __3__ is an important dimension of retailing, significant costs are assumed by the retailer to retain such an accessible location (e.g. rent), which defines its market area (its customer base). These costs are reflected in the final costs of a good which is assumed by the consumer. The retailer maintains a level of in-store inventory (in the form of stocked shelves) which is replenished by regional __4__ centers where goods from a wide range of suppliers are stored. The most efficient retailers have a network of stores and distribution centers, some of which operate on the cross-docking principle. The __5__ of e-commerce has changed the relationships between customers and retailers (e-retailers):

- Actors. In some cases, entirely new e-retailers have emerged, but the adoption of an online strategy by __6__ retailers has also been very significant. In the emerging distribution system, the e-retailer is at the same time a retailer and a distribution center; an e-fulfillment center.
- Locations. The locational choice is much more __7__ , permitting the use of lower cost locations that would not have been considered otherwise as suitable for retail. Large e-retailers can maintain a network of distribution centers to optimize their market __8__ and service regional markets from specific distribution centers.
- Purchasing. Customers are virtually interfacing with a store and the orders are shipped through postal and/or parcel services, which take care of home deliveries. Figuratively, the customers are directly linked to the supply __9__ since their action of ordering a product reaches directly the distribution center.
- Deliveries. The deliveries are now the responsibility of the e-retailer, a move away from standard retailing where the customer took charge of the goods as soon as they were purchased.
- Tracking. Customers want accurate time-in-transit information for the various shipping options such as next day __10__ . This challenges the distribution industry to implement information systems to track parcels as well as vehicles.

Text B

Reverse Logistics in E-commerce

In e-commerce, setting up and planning on reverse logistics in e-commerce is undoubtedly a requirement. You could go about fine tuning and perfecting your e-commerce logistics yourself, but it is highly recommended to seek out experts who have experience in not only effective logistics technology with e-commerce offerings for your freight and logistics, but also years of experience in setting up logistics management, including reverse logistics.

扫一扫，听课文

1. Reverse Logistics in E-commerce Is No Longer a HOPE to Have But a NEED to Have

It's no secret that an experience delivered to a customer determines whether that customer will come back. This is true in pretty much any industry, but especially true in manufacturing and distribution where collaborative relationships between suppliers and customers in a B2B setting are vital for long term success.

Shippers who have set up online shopping carts must not only enhance the user experience prior to pressing the "buy" button but also focus on the post-purchase site experience to keep customer retention metrics at satisfactory levels.

This is where many who are now shipping products drop the ball. Often, once a freight shipper starts doing e-commerce logistics, they have a need to consider reverse logistics for the first time. By incorporating new strategies to optimize this process, shippers can increase customer retention and add new revenue streams to the direct business beyond the traditional brick and mortar channel.

Here are some key metrics to support the reverse logistics in e-commerce business case:

- 85% of customers say they will stop buying from a business if the returns process is a hassle (Harris Interactive).
- 95% of customers say that they will likely shop with a catalog or business again if the online returns process is convenient (Harris Interactive).
- 40% of shoppers don't buy online due to returns difficulty (Jupiter Research).
- Customers who have their complaint resolved quickly have a repurchase intention rate of 82% (McKinsey).

2. The Conclusion of the Framework to Set Up Reverse Logistics in E-commerce Strategy

Reverse logistics in e-commerce are an inevitable fact of online retail. As the depth of online product categories became apparent in the last three years, the importance of setting up a reverse logistics process as part of your e-commerce logistics strategy increases as well. Provide a bad returns experience and you undoubtedly reduce the chance of a customer coming back for a repeat purchase.

3. Receiving

Processing returned packages is a very challenging task. The key purpose for a detailed receiving process is to issue credits or permit product exchange. The key challenge is proper identification to ensure proper matching to the original order. Since customers are managing their own returns, there is considerable variation in the labeling and contents.

Your receiving team needs to inspect and validate:

1) Who has returned the freight?
2) What goods have been received?
3) The condition of the freight.
4) Does the freight match the original purchase?

Receiving is a labor intensive process. Many companies set up an "assembly line" for their team to quickly and efficiently process these inbound items. Considerable skills and training are often required in the areas of product identification and product handling rules.

The impact of good return instructions is clearly noticeable at this stage in the reverse logistics in e-commerce process. But despite the best efforts of your company, many customers will not follow the instructions, resulting in difficulties in identification and matching to issue a prompt credit. This, of course, leads to unhappy customers, even though it was caused by their inability to follow simple directions.

Your return processes need to accommodate all possible exceptions quickly and effectively. The receiving process of reverse logistics in e-commerce is full of exceptions and returned items that do not fit the standard rule set. If these exceptions are not handled quickly and effectively your receiving team has three problems:

1) The assembly line processing breaks down, since valuable time is wasted trying to specially handle one item, which slows down processing for the entire team and often leads to a backlog.

2) Items that need to be specially handled get set aside and delayed even further.

3) Customers will call for status updates. This creates more problems since someone must spend valuable time handling the trace requests to track down the goods and issue the credit.

Poor processes lead to backlogs and a stressful working environment for your receiving team. Good processes lead to fast turnaround times, fast credits and happy customers.

4. Issue Credit or Ship an Exchange Item

Once the freight has been received and validated by the receiving team, a credit can be issued or an exchange can be shipped.

Issuing credits can be very costly to your company if not performed well. Care must be taken to ensure your receiving team is properly matching the original items purchased, with the actual items returned. Since many shippers who have employed e-commerce strategies have big gaps in their receiving processes, items often go missing. As a result, the customer service people are often instructed to issue unvalidated credits upon customer request because they have no way of verifying if the customer really did return their freight.

Good receiving and credit processes can significantly reduce the workload for your customer service personnel who handle the status update calls and e-mails from customers looking for their credits.

5. Inspection and Sorting for Reverse Logistics in E-commerce

The main purpose of inspection and sorting is to stream the returned items to the path of highest selling price or recovery value. This process is often combined or is attached to the receiving process since it is a logical next step while the inbound goods are being handled.

At this stage, the customer goods have been received and their credits have been processed and satisfied. Now it is time to satisfy your corporate needs. This is best done by recovering the highest value possible from the returned goods.

Training and product knowledge are often important for the inspection and sorting process. It is a labor intensive process. The better your team understand the products, the faster they can make decisions on how to process the products and the greater the likelihood of them capturing a higher recovery for that item.

Processing the returned items is often set up in an assembly line format to enable easy separation of the product as it flows to the next stage. Processing is very dependent on the type of products being handled. Depending on the volumes you need to handle, several stages may be required to streamline the processing. Often similar products or items requiring similar processing are physically streamed and consolidated until there is enough volume to move it to the next stage (i.e. when a pallet is full). Sometimes tests or test equipment is used to determine how to stream an item.

Each returned item is often given a unique identification tag for tracing and gathering statistics on processing and disposition.

Products can be streamed according to their final destination, such as:

- Restock—unopened boxes can go straight back to new inventory.
- Repackaging for sale—open box goods in "as new" condition that can be resold on the e-commerce site.
- Return to vendor—to be returned to the original vendor where they were purchased for credit or exchange.
- Disposition—items that have value, but will not be re-sold at the e-commerce site.
- Scrap—damaged or obsolete goods.

6. Asset Recovery

Even though the customer did not want to keep the goods, these returned items need to be viewed as "assets". An asset has value and can be sold. The challenge is to find or recover the highest value for each item.

In order to recover the highest value, these returned "assets" are often handled as follows:

- Restock—little loss of value if processed quickly and the product is still current.
- Repackaging for sale—open box goods in "as new" condition can often be sold in a "clearance" area of your e-commerce site or moved to a local "bricks and mortar" branch. These "B" goods are often sold for slightly less than retail, but often higher than original cost.

This is often the best channel for these goods since handling is minimized, and turnaround time is quicker.
- Return to vendor—defective goods, warranty issues or vendor agreements often allow for return of goods. This channel often means you will recover full cost of the items, but the cost of handling must be considered. For instance if the goods are not defective, it may be more prudent to sell the goods for cost plus a margin on your site.
- Disposition—freight that you do not wish to resell on your site, often still hold considerable value. A number of great disposition sources and services now exist for just about any products in any condition.
- Scrap—almost nothing is scrap anymore. If you have a lot of it, someone is usually willing to buy it from you.

Careful attention to rapidly processing, sorting and resale of your returned "assets" is one of the best opportunities for profit in your reverse logistics in e-commerce operations.

7. Outsourcing Your Reverse Logistics and E-commerce Logistics

Many shippers do not view the handling and processing of reverse logistics in e-commerce or reverse logistics in general as a core competency. A number of companies have outsourced partners in one or more of the key reverse logistics areas such as transportation management, returned goods processing, e-commerce logistics technology, and services such as freight claims, accounting, and carrier relations.

It is important to understand the processes you need before you outsource, so you can define what needs to be done, how it needs to be done and how to measure success so you are able to effectively choose which partner can best fit your needs.

8. "Returning" to Profitability

Reverse logistics in e-commerce is a newly emerging area that is just starting to get the attention of senior management and shipper executives who are looking at or have already implemented an e-commerce channel. It is highly likely that your company has significant challenges in this area. Do not be afraid. You are not alone. This is a "New Frontier" and should be viewed as an excellent opportunity to improve your corporate profitability.

New Words

undoubtedly	adv.	毋庸置疑地，的确地
freight	n.	货物，船货，运费，货运
	v.	装货，使充满，运送
manufacturing	n.	制造业
	adj.	制造业的
collaborative	adj.	合作的，协作的
shipper	n.	托运人，发货人
enhance	v.	提高，增强
satisfactory	adj.	满意的

incorporate	*adj.*	合并的，一体化的
	v.	合并，使组成公司，混合
metrics	*n.*	指标，度量
repurchase	*v.*	重新买
	n.	买回
framework	*n.*	构架，框架，结构
inevitable	*adj.*	不可避免的，必然的
challenging	*adj.*	挑战性的
challenge	*n.*	挑战
	v.	向……挑战
inspect	*v.*	检查
unhappy	*adj.*	不幸福的，不快乐的，不适当的
inability	*n.*	无能，无力
accommodate	*v.*	适应
backlog	*n.*	没交付的订货，存货，储备
	v.	积压，存储
turnaround	*n.*	转变，转向
costly	*adj.*	昂贵的，贵重的
missing	*adj.*	不见的，缺少的，丢失的
workload	*n.*	工作量
update	*v.*	修正，校正，更新
satisfy	*v.*	满意，确保
separation	*n.*	分离，分开
streamline	*v.*	组织，使简单化
consolidated	*adj.*	整理过的，统一的
pallet	*n.*	货盘
statistics	*n.*	统计学，统计表
restock	*v.*	重新进货，再储存
unopened	*adj.*	没有打开过的
straight	*adv.*	直接地；马上；立刻
repackage	*v.*	重新包装
scrap	*v.*	扔弃，敲碎，拆毁
obsolete	*adj.*	荒废的，陈旧的
competency	*n.*	资格，能力

Phrases

reverse logistics	逆向物流
deliver to	转交，交付，传达
come back	回来，复原，恢复

post-purchase site	邮购网站
returns process	退换流程
Harris Interactive	哈里斯互动调查公司
Jupiter Research	朱庇特研究中心
McKinsey	麦肯锡公司
online retail	在线零售
repeat purchase	重复购买
original order	原订单
assembly line	流水线，装配线
be caused by…	由……引起
be full of	充满
break down	停顿，中止
slow down	(使)慢下来
turnaround time	周转时间
customer service	客户服务
recovery value	收回价值，更新价值，复原价值
at this stage	眼下，暂时
returned goods	退回的货物
sorting process	分类处理
unique identification tag	唯一识别标签
core competency	核心竞争力
transport management	运输管理
freight claim	货物赔偿的要求

Exercises

[Ex. 5] Fill in the following blanks according to the text.

1. In e-commerce, it is highly recommended to seek out experts who have experience in not only _____ with e-commerce offerings for your freight and logistics, but also _____ in setting up logistics management, including _____.

2. Shippers who have set up online shopping carts must not only _____ prior to pressing the "buy" button but also _____ to keep customer retention metrics at satisfactory levels.

3. According to _____, 85% of customers say they will stop buying from a business if the returns process is _____ and _____ say that they will likely shop with a catalog or business again if _____ is convenient. According to Jupiter Research, _____ of shoppers don't buy online due to _____.

4. Your receiving team needs to inspect and validate:
   1) _____?
   2) _____?

    3) _____.
    4) _____?
   5. Receiving is a _____ process. Your return processes need to accommodate _____ and _____.
   6. Poor processes lead to _____ and _____ for your receiving team. Good processes lead to _____, _____ and _____.
   7. Since many shippers who have employed e-commerce strategies _____ in their receiving processes, items often go missing. _____, the customer service people are often instructed to _____ upon customer request because they have no way of verifying if the customer really _____.
   8. The main purpose of inspection and sorting is to _____ to the path of highest selling price or _____. This process is often combined or is attached to _____ since it is a logical next step while _____ are being handled.
   9. In order to recover the highest value, these returned "assets" are often handled as follows: _____, _____, _____, _____ and _____.
   10. It is important to understand the processes you need before you outsource, so you can define _____, _____ and _____ so you are able to effectively choose which partner can best fit your needs.

Reading Material

Electronic CRM

1. What Is Electronic CRM?

   This concept is derived from e-commerce. It also uses net environment i.e., intranet[1], extranet[2] and Internet. Electronic CRM (Customer Relationship Management) concerns all forms of managing relationships with customers making use of Information Technology (IT). eCRM is enterprises using IT to integrate internal organization resources and external marketing strategies to understand and fulfill their customers needs. Comparing with[3] traditional CRM, the integrated information for eCRM intraorganizational[4] collaboration can be more efficient to communicate with customers from Relationship Marketing[5] (RM) to CRM: The concept of relationship marketing was first coined by Leonard Berry in 1983. He considered it to consist of attracting, maintaining and enhancing customer relationships within organizations. In the years that followed, companies were engaging more and more in a meaningful dialogue with individual customers. In doing so, new

---

1 intranet   *n.*   内联网
2 extranet   *n.*   外联网
3 compare with   与……比较
4 intraorganizational   *adj.*   组织内的
5 Relationship Marketing   关系营销

organizational forms as well as technologies were used, eventually resulting in what we know as CRM. The main difference between RM and CRM is that the first does not acknowledge the use of technology, where the latter uses IT in implementing RM strategies.

2. The Essence of CRM

The exact meaning of CRM is still subject of heavy discussions. However, the overall goal can be seen as effectively managing differentiated relationships with all customers and communicating with them on an individual basis. Underlying thought is that companies realize that they can supercharge profits[1] by acknowledging that different groups of customers vary widely in their behavior, desires, and responsiveness to marketing.

3. Major Differences between CRM and eCRM

(1) Customer Contacts

CRM—Contact with customer made through the retail store[2], phone, and fax.

eCRM—All of the traditional methods are used in addition to Internet, e-mail, wireless, and PDA[3] technologies.

(2) System Interface

CRM—Implements the use of ERP systems, emphasis is on the back-end.

eCRM—Geared more toward front end, which interacts with the back-end through use of ERP systems, data warehouses, and data marts[4].

(3) System Overhead (Client Computers)

CRM—The client must download various applications to view the web-enabled applications. They would have to be rewritten for different platform.

eCRM—Does not have these requirements because the client uses the browser.

(4) Customization and Personalization of Information

CRM—Views differ based on the audience, and personalized views are not available. Individual personalization[5] requires program changes.

eCRM—Personalized individual views based on purchase history and preferences. Individual has ability to customize view.

(5) System Focus

CRM—System (created for internal use) designed based on job function and products. Web applications designed for a single department or business unit.

eCRM—System (created for external use) designed based on customer needs. Web application designed for enterprise-wide use.

---

1 supercharge profit   超额利润
2 retail store   零售店
3 PDA (Personal Digital Assistant)   个人数字助理
4 data mart   数据集市，数据市场
5 individual personalization   个性化

(6) System Maintenance and Modification[1]

CRM—More time involved in implementation and maintenance is more expensive because the system exists at different locations and on various servers.

eCRM—Reduction in time and cost. Implementation and maintenance can take place at one location and on one server.

4. Why eCRM?

eCRM has the following advantages:

- Gather and combine customer information into a unified picture.
- Response faster and accurately.
- Build customer loyalty.

5. Strategy Components of eCRM

When enterprises integrate their customer information, there are three eCRM strategy components.

1) Operational. Because of sharing information, the processes in business should make customer's need as first and seamlessly[2] implement. This avoids multiple times to bother customers and redundant[3] process.

2) Analytical. Analysis helps company maintain a long-term relationship with customers.

3) Collaborative. Due to improved communication technology, different departments in company implement (intraorganizational) or work with business partners (interorganizational) more efficiently by sharing information.

6. Different Levels of eCRM

Foundational services. This includes the minimum necessary services such as website effectiveness[4] and responsiveness[5] as well as order fulfillment.

Customer-centered services. These services include order tracking[6], product configuration and customization as well as security/trust.

Value-added services. These are extra services such as online auctions and online training and education.

7. Steps to eCRM Success

Many factors play a part in[7] ensuring that the implementation any level of eCRM is successful. One obvious way it could be measured is by the ability for the system to add value to the existing business. There are four suggested implementation steps that affect the viability of a project like this:

- Developing customer-centric strategies.

---

1 modification   n. 更改，修改，修正
2 seamlessly   adj. 无缝地
3 redundant   adj. 多余的
4 effectiveness   n. 效力，效果
5 responsiveness   n. 响应性
6 order tracking   订单跟踪
7 play a part in   在……中起作用，与……有关，对……有影响

- Redesigning[1] workflow management systems.
- Re-engineering work processes.
- Supporting with the right technologies.

8. What Is Included in a Successful eCRM?

- Knowledge Management. Acquisition of information about the customer. What actions to take as a result of this knowledge.
- Database Consolidation[2]. Re-engineering the business process around the customer. All interactions with customers recorded in one place.
- Integration of Channels and Systems. Respond to customers through their channel of choice e-mail, phone, chat line, etc.
- Technology and Infrastructure. Organization and scalability of technology must be able to handle increased volume of customers.
- Change Management. More than a change in technology is required. Change in attitude and philosophy is key. Product centric focus vs. customer centric focus.

9. One Subset of Electronic CRM—Mobile CRM (mCRM)

One subset of Electronic CRM is Mobile CRM (mCRM). This is defined as "services that aim at nurturing customer relationships, acquiring or maintaining customers, support marketing, sales or services processes, and use wireless networks[3] as the medium of delivery to the customers."

There are three main reasons that mobile CRM is becoming so popular:

The first is that the devices consumers use are improving in multiple ways that allow for this advancement. Displays are larger and clearer and access times on networks are improving overall. Secondly, the users are also becoming more sophisticated. The technology to them is nothing new so it is easy to adapt[4]. Lastly, the software being developed for these applications has become worthwhile[5] and useful to end users.

There are four basic steps that a company should follow to implement a mobile CRM system. By following these and also keeping the IT department, the end users and management in agreement, the outcome[6] can be beneficial for all.

Step 1—Needs analysis phase. This is the point to take your times and understand all the technical needs and desires for each of the users and stakeholders. It also has to be kept in mind that the mobile CRM system must be able to grow and change with the business.

Step 2—Mobile design phase. This is the next critical phase that will show all the technical concerns that need to be addressed. A few main things to consider are screen size, device storage and security.

Step 3—Mobile application testing phase. This step is mostly to ensure that the users and

---

1　redesign　　　v. & n.　重新设计
2　consolidation　　n.　整合，合并
3　wireless network　　无线网络
4　adapt　　v.　使适应
5　worthwhile　　adj.　值得做的，值得出力的
6　outcome　　n.　结果，成果

stakeholders all approve of the new system.

Step 4—Rollout[1] phase. This is when the new system is implemented but also when training on the final product is done with all users.

Advantages of mobile CRM include:

- The mobile channel creates a more personal direct connection with customers.
- It is continuously active and allows necessary individuals to take action[2] quickly using the information.
- Typically it is an opt-in only channel which allows for high and quality responsiveness.
- Overall it supports loyalty between the customer and company, which improves and strengthens relationships.

参 考 译 文

电子商务中使用 CRM 的指南

1. 它做什么

最初，CRM 只是一个自动通信录。CRM app 会记录一段时间没有联络过的使用者，并给他们发送提醒信息。

下一代的 CRM 迭代更侧重于其在业务中的潜在应用。销售人员很快看到了组织客户和培养现有销售机会的潜力。尽管 CRM 仍然主导着销售领域，但是好的 CRM 电子商务 app 可以帮助完成一系列关键任务，其范围足以涵盖业务的几乎所有方面：

- 通过各种入口方法获取潜在客户。
- 与所有客户和 B2B 合作伙伴保持及时沟通。
- 开展电子邮件营销活动和业务通信。
- 管理社交媒体渠道。
- 保持沿销售渠道前进的机会。
- 高级报告，以便全面了解销售团队、销售目标、营销活动效果、季节趋势等。
- 客户支持/服务台功能。
- 数据存储：用本地化知识库在云中保存相关的客户信息、支持票证等，以实现即时访问。

这就是我眼下能够想到的。简而言之，电子商务 CRM 涵盖从发现线索到完成销售的整个过程。一些 CRM 解决方案甚至跨越了真正的 CRM 和企业资源计划之间的灰色区域。CRM 退出的地方 ERP 进入；涵盖销售实现和供应链，通常以客户重新参与为结束。

2. 获得什么

大多数电子商务平台（如 Shopify、Volusion 和 Bigcommerce）都包括一定程度的 CRM 控制。提供功能的深度包括从车到车以及从一个订阅级到另一个订阅级。

---

1 rollout   *n.* 首次展示
2 take action   采取行动

如果你刚刚开始，请务必确定选用的电子商务平台中包含哪些 CRM 和电子邮件营销功能。不要为了获得众多功能而过度购买！如果需求超过注册的功能，可以随时升级（即使在合同中也可以）。

如果你已经具有良好的购物车平台，则电子商务 CRM 功能可能已经在弹指间。如果没有，可以升级订阅级别（需要的功能可以从你的电子商务软件供应商那里得到），或者可以轻松地把第三方解决方案集成进来。

当评估多种可选的电子商务 CRM 方案时，选择一个实际上重点处理——你猜对了——与客户的关系的。市场上那么多 CRM app 面向上述销售渠道，这太棒了，如果这也是你的需要。但是，在电子商务领域运营的企业通常不利用销售团队来推动销售，这就降低了销售管道跟踪系统（Sales Pipeline Tracker）的相关性。

相反，应为你的电子商务业务选择一个强调以下目标的 CRM：
- 获取客户数据。
- 电子邮件营销。
- 客户再次参与（通常通过会员积分奖励计划）。
- 提供客户购买、季节性销售趋势等的报告和分析。
- 客户支持/服务台功能。
- 品牌知名度。

在下一节中，我们将讨论如何实现这六个电子商务 CRM 目标。

3. 做什么

（1）获取客户数据

使用 CRM 的首要也是最困难的部分可能是收集客户的有用数据。有多种方法可以做到这一点，但也许最有效的方法是为用户提供创建账户和登录到你的网站的能力。这样一次就完成几件事情，谁不喜欢事半功倍？

客户在网站上提供自己的账户可以实现某些功能，使他们受益，并最终产生大量有助于你快乐的副产品。这是一个双赢！虽然充分公开，但它也不是完全没有缺点。电子商务 CRM app 会带来以下好处：

1) 客户将能够维护心愿单，获得个性化积分奖励、货运跟踪和简化的结账（有存储的信用卡信息、送货地址和订单历史记录）等，这取决于你选择的电子商务和 CRM app。

2) 作为副产品，你的 CRM 将获得客户信息中最令人垂涎的数据：电子邮件地址、地区位置、名称、购买历史，可能还有年龄和性别。只要有这些信息就能快速启动你的 CRM，让你开发出最精确和有效的营销策略。随着时间的推移，你将能够：
- 看到哪些营销活动最成功。
- 为每个客户量身定制销售提升策略。
- 使购物车中废弃的销售项得以恢复。
- 重新吸引最近没有造访过你的客户。

电子商务 CRM app 也有以下缺点：

由于这是获取客户数据的最佳方式，这是一种越来越常见的做法。对用户来说，最终结果是，他们在所有不同购物处有太多的账户要进行管理，可能不愿意再开一个账户。（从客户的角度）每个账户都会生成大量的垃圾邮件。某些客户可能只是选择访客结账，而不是创建一个新账户，或者他们可以注册一个他们专门用于注册购物的"垃圾邮件账户"，这样客户将完全看不到任何垃圾邮件。

（2）电子邮件营销

这就是 CRM 真正证明它价值的地方。"花钱赚钱"是一个几乎不变的商业法则；因此只要企业主可以削减成本，那就是他稳赚的。印刷费、邮费和促销费都会真正地增加营销成本，但是当 CRM 可以自动化大规模进行电子邮件营销时，所有这些成本就几乎为零。当可以为每个客户量身定制电子邮件时，可以看到这让那些拥挤在 USPS 里面的邮递员手足无措。

把 CRM 和电子商务相结合，你的客户就可以获得前所未有的个人关注。如果购买 Sally 牌鞋子的人有一段时间没有回到你的网店，CRM 就可以在鞋子促销时自动向她发送电子邮件。或者如果 Billy 在购买期间离开，CRM 电子商务平台就会提醒他，回来购买他想要的 T 恤。

（3）客户重新参与

可能性继续。可以让 CRM 自动为客户提供：

- 业务通信；
- 通知他们积累的积分；
- 当他们心愿单中的货物价格变化时就发通知；
- 季节性销售；
- 个人优惠券代码；
- 博客摘录、本地活动邀请或任何其他增值信息；
- 采取你能想到的一切行动，把客户带回到你的网站。

（4）报告和分析

在电子商务和 CRM 中，可以轻松地查看零售领域中发生的一切。想看到客户重复购买的物品吗？没问题。要看看哪些促销活动在去年的季节性低潮时帮助最大吗？放心吧，没问题！要深入查看特定的详细信息也是很容易的。

（5）客户支持/服务台功能

客户支持通常是事后的想法，或者更糟的是，完全被忽视。电子商务业务的生死由你自己建立的声誉而定，并且客户服务的优劣影响你的声誉。

CRM 帮助解决问题。通过你的营销努力不仅可以让满意的客户回到商店，也可以让不满意的客户感到欣慰——如果他们的问题可以解决。CRM 应用程序会简化此过程。支持请求可以按照紧急程度标记，这样最高优先级的问题可以很快解决。此外，你可以信手拈来客户的完整历史，你能通过其订单历史记录与他们互动、与代理沟通以及跟踪任何其他信息。你也许永远不需要告诉你的客户"我不知道"。

（6）品牌可见性

有了像电子邮件或社交媒体这样简单的东西，可以让品牌在现有和潜在客户的头脑中保持新鲜。

我不能告诉你我见过多少了不起的网站，并假设我会记得，只是它们被淹没在一大批争夺我注意力的供应商之中。如果我能够在 Facebook 上关注它们，当我看到它们的帖子时，我就更有可能再次访问它们。
4. 结论

CRM 和电子商务的组合开始听起来像灵丹妙药了吗？

如果实施得很好，它当然可以。像大多数东西一样，种瓜得瓜，种豆得豆。半心半意地将 CRM 与电子商务业务相结合，将产生小的结果。但是，如果你投资得好，CRM 有可能简化工作流程、扩大营销、提升品牌声誉，而并不会削减你的利润空间。

Unit 13

Text A

Benefits of Big Data for E-commerce Companies

Online retailers are using big data to create a better shopping experience, boost customer satisfaction and generate more sales.

If you have been reading the news, you probably saw the story on how Target was aware of a young woman's pregnancy before her father did. It turns out that when a woman starts shopping for products such as nutritional supplements, cotton balls and unscented beauty products, there is a good chance that she is pregnant.

A lot of people feel uncomfortable at the idea of retailers knowing so much about their lives and habits. However, big data is about improving the experience that shoppers have when they make a purchase online, increasing the satisfaction rate of customers and generating higher profits. This is a huge innovation for retailers and we are only just getting started.

This is how big data benefits e-commerce companies.

1. Deliver Something More Valuable

Amazon uses advanced tools to constantly adjust pricing. This retailer can compare pricing data from competitors and automatically adjust the price of its own products. Some prices changes more than ten times a day. With the right web platforms and plugins it's easy. Dynamic pricing means that companies can no longer compete by simply offering the lowest price. There is now more than ever a real need to offer something more than value, which means retailers have to develop a good reputation and become the go-to option when a shopper wants a low price and a good experience.

2. Deliver More Personalized Interactions

Amazon is well-known for using big data to make product recommendations to shoppers. If you have ever shopped on Amazon, you have probably noticed the "Customers who bought this item also bought" section. Adding this simple feature to product pages actually resulted in a 30% sales increase when the feature was originally implemented. This is a simple way to help shoppers find more products and to get people to spend more time on a shopping site.

I sell custom menswear online and we are currently working on creating a database with information on men's body measurements and their fashion preferences. Our goal is to be able to provide a shopper with products that fit their measurement once they enter their height and weight even though we are unable to measure the individual. The purpose of this feature is to make finding the right clothes easier for the customer and help them find the right tailor-made item.

3. Track People's Preferences

Big data's primary use for marketers is in microtargeting[1]. The bigger your data, the smaller you can target, and the more potentially crucial details about your customers you'll receive. Credit card companies, for example, have found some strange and fascinating correlations when it comes to who's likely to pay and who's not. People who buy anti-scuff pads for their furniture have been found to be some of the most reliable bill-payers. An insight into their cautious personalities, perhaps?

Bringing in more information about your customers can also bring to light information and metrics you may have never thought to track. It can also tell you what kind of treatment certain segments of customers prefer to receive, and what other products they may be interested in. One familiar use of big data is in "Recommendation Engines" like the one Amazon uses to suggest things that you might be interested in based on your viewing history.

For example, companies like SAS offer services that let you create customer profiles that will help you deliver much more personalized experiences to certain blocks and demographics of customers. They also offer marketing automation services so that they can handle a lot of the complications of implementing the data they collect for you. Quantcast, too, has a free tool that taps into big analytics data to give you some interesting information about your userbase.

According to NewVantage Partners founder John Barth, "there's a phase of analytics that's exploration and discovery...The phase in which you don't understand it, the discovery phase, is where big data is useful."

4. Make Accurate Predictions

Gathering data on shopper's measurements and their fashion preferences allows us to offer a better experience for our visitors. However, we can also use this information to determine which styles, cuts and even fabrics and colors are popular. This helps us keep the right products in stock and negotiate the best rates possible with our tailors and suppliers.

Companies can, for instance, use social media to keep an eye on trends that are relevant to their industry. This is a good way to get an idea of what people are buying. The well-known record label EMI uses data from many third-party sites and apps to get a comprehensive picture of how people listen to music and buy music in order to make better predictions regarding demand and to create more relevant advertising campaigns.

5. Reduce the Shopping Cart Abandonment Rate

Cross-device tracking, also known as re-targeting can be used to reduce your shopping cart

---

1 Microtargeting (also called micro-targeting or micro-niche targeting) is a marketing strategy that uses consumer data and demographics to identify the interests of specific individuals or very small groups of like-minded individuals and influence their thoughts or actions. An important goal of a microtargeting initiative is to know the target audience so well that messages get delivered through the target's preferred communication channel.

abandonment rate[1]. The e-commerce platform eBay found that shoppers usually do research from three to five different devices before they make a purchase. Big data can be used to record the different steps of the buying journey and to deliver relevant content to Internet users before they complete a purchase.

6. Provide Customers with a Better Experience

Internet users are not necessarily comfortable about retailers knowing about their private lives, but the truth is that big data will improve the experience shoppers can expect from retailers. Big data is, for instance, being used by CNA and other companies to look for possible frauds and protect the identity of shoppers. Credit card fraud can be prevented in real time thanks to information gathered from live transactions, geodata and social feeds.

The fact that a retailer knows some intimate details about your life can seem odd, but big data is really beneficial for companies and shoppers. Retailers can no longer focus on competing on prices alone since they have the tools necessary to creating a more pleasant, personalized and seamless experience for shoppers.

New Words

experience	n.	体验
	v.	经验，经历
satisfaction	n.	满意，满足
generate	v.	产生，制造
pregnancy	n.	怀孕
nutritional	adj.	营养的，滋养的
supplement	v.	补充，增补
	n.	营养品，补品；增补，补充，补充物
unscented	adj.	无气味的
pregnant	adj.	怀孕的
uncomfortable	adj.	不舒服的，不安的，不合意的
habit	n.	习惯，习性
innovation	n.	改革，创新
benefit	n.	利益，好处
	v.	有益于，有助于，受益
constantly	adv.	不变地，经常地
adjust	v.	调整，调节
competitor	n.	竞争者

---

1 In marketing, abandonment rate is a term associated with the use of virtual shopping carts. Also known as "shopping cart abandonment". Although shoppers in brick and mortar stores rarely abandon their carts, abandonment of virtual shopping carts is quite common. Marketers can count how many of the shopping carts used in a specified period result in completed sales versus how many are abandoned. The abandonment rate is the ratio of the number of abandoned shopping carts to the number of initiated transactions or to the number of completed transactions.

personalize	v.	使个人化，个性化设置，为个人特制，人格化
recommendation	n.	推荐，介绍，劝告，建议
menswear	n.	男服
microtargeting	n.	微目标，微定位
strange	adj.	陌生的，生疏的，前所未知的，奇怪的
fascinating	adj.	非常有趣的，迷人的，有极大吸引力的，使人神魂颠倒的
furniture	n.	家具，设备
personality	n.	个性，人格，人物
treatment	n.	对待，处理
complication	n.	复杂化，复杂因素
userbase	n.	用户群
exploration	n.	探索
discovery	n.	发现
fabric	n.	织品，织物，布，结构，构造
popular	adj.	流行的，受欢迎的
abandonment	n.	放弃
record	v.	记录
journey	n. & v.	旅行，旅程
geodata	n.	地理数据
intimate	v.	宣布，明白表示
	adj.	隐私的，亲密的
pleasant	adj.	令人愉快的，舒适的
seamless	adj.	无缝的，无漏洞的，流畅的

Phrases

big data	大数据
shopping experience	购物体验
turn out	结果是，被证明是
cotton ball	棉球，棉花球
beauty product	美容产品
at the idea of…	一想起……就
satisfaction rate	满意率
dynamic pricing	动态定价
anti-scuff pad	耐磨垫
shopping site	购物网站
bring in	生产，挣得，引进
bring to light	发现
be interested in…	对……感兴趣
recommendation engine	推荐引擎

tap into	利用，开发
abandonment rate	放弃率
geo-data	地理数据
social feed	社交媒体推送

Abbreviations

SAS (Statistics Analysis System)	统计分析系统公司
EMI (Electric and Musical Industries Ltd.)	百代唱片公司

Exercises

[Ex. 1] Answer the following questions according to the text.

1. What are online retailers using big data to do?
2. What does dynamic pricing mean?
3. What is Amazon well-known for?
4. What is big data's primary use for marketers?
5. What can bringing in more information about your customers do?
6. What does gathering data on shopper's measurements and their fashion preferences allow us to do?
7. What can we also use the information of shopper's measurements and their fashion preferences to do?
8. What does the well-known record label EMI use data from many third-party sites and apps to do?
9. What is cross-device tracking known as? What can it be used to do?
10. Why can retailers no longer focus on competing on prices alone?

[Ex. 2] Translate the following terms or phrases from English into Chinese and vice versa.

1. abandonment rate _____
2. be interested in… _____
3. big data _____
4. dynamic pricing _____
5. recommendation engine _____
6. 社交媒体推送 _____
7. 竞争者 _____
8. 利益，好处，有益于，受益 _____
9. 调整，调节 _____
10. 推荐，介绍，劝告，建议 _____

1. _____
2. _____
3. _____
4. _____
5. _____
6. _____
7. _____
8. _____
9. _____
10. _____

[Ex. 3] Translate the following passage into Chinese.

While many B2C companies use e-commerce platforms for direct sales, B2B organizations are also leveraging them to add transactional capabilities to their informational sites. In addition, the online experience is becoming more "consumerized," meaning that B2B buyers expect a retail-like customer experience—even when visiting non-retail sites. Cloud Solution Providers (CSPs) that focus solely on creating retail models are often not well-versed in B2B requirements which can be more complex. As a result, their offerings don't include B2B functions, such as easy entry of large orders and repeat orders, segmented product catalogues that are based on a client hierarchy and buying privileges, configure price quote capabilities and extended payment terms. IT leaders have an unprecedented number of CSPs from which to choose. However, they need to carefully evaluate ones that have experience meeting their industry-specific needs, whether it's B2B, B2C, or a combination of both.

IT leaders must also understand the pros and cons of cloud-based ownership models in order to select the right solution for their needs.

In addition to selecting a cloud-based e-commerce solution, IT leaders are tasked with choosing from a variety of ownership options. For example, an organization can use an Infrastructure-as-a-Service (IaaS) model to run its application package or custom e-commerce software. It can use a managed service provider to manage its applications or create custom e-commerce software on IaaS. Or the organization can subscribe to a Software-as-a-Service (SaaS) e-commerce application. Each of these options must be mapped back to the organization's financial resources and technology requirements. IT leaders also need to determine the features and functions they require for their organization's online selling initiatives. They should collaborate with an experienced CSP to develop a solution that supports their organization's long-term online sales objectives, and outlines current and future technology needs. Finally, IT needs to evaluate the Total Cost of Ownership (TCO) of their cloud model versus the traditional licensed approach for a pre-determined period of time to evaluate its ROI. The HOSTING team of cloud experts work with in-house application developers to design and build cloud-based e-commerce environments that can help organizations lower their costs and take advantage of new business opportunities.

[Ex. 4] **Fill in the blanks with the words given below.**

| advisers | benefits | evaluate | geographical | involved |
| solutions | cloud | integrated | implementing | investment |

The ability to lower costs, accelerate deployments and respond quickly to market opportunities and challenges are just a few reasons why so many IT leaders are leveraging cloud-based e-commerce applications. Given the variety of ____1____, IT leaders must research their options carefully in order to select the one that best meets their needs. Following are the top two impacts of ____2____ computing on e-commerce applications and steps IT leaders should take during their evaluation process.

1) Cloud-based e-commerce applications allow companies to respond quickly to market opportunities and challenges—as long as they engage IT.

It's easy for business leaders to focus on the ____3____ of cloud computing without considering the time and effort involved in ____4____ a viable solution. However, whatever cloud computing solution they select, the application will need access to customer data, product data, fulfillment systems and other operational systems in order to support e-commerce.

As we covered in our recent blog post, Cloud Computing Investments and the "New IT", today's IT staff is being tasked to serve as trusted business ___5___ to their organization's customers, partners and executives. Prior to an organization investing in a cloud solution, the IT team must clearly outline the business goals, objectives, costs and benefits. They should also review what systems and data must be ___6___ (i.e., fulfillment systems, customer service systems and customer and product data sources) in order to achieve the goals. Finally, IT should explain how failing to integrate other systems will impact overall business results.

2) Cloud-based e-commerce applications enable IT and business leaders to ___7___ new opportunities without large upfront investments.

With smaller capital expenditures (CapEx) needed to launch a site, combined with operational expenditures (OpEx) that are typically billed on a "pay as you go" basis, organizations can shift their business online with minimal ___8___ risk. A faster time to deployment allows them to streamline time-to-market for their products and services.

For companies looking to expand into new ___9___ regions or test an e-commerce business model with a new brand or product line, or as a Proof of Concept (POC), cloud-based e-commerce applications provide them with flexibility and scalability at a reasonable investment. However, it's important for IT to evaluate the total costs ___10___ in implementing a cloud solution, including: integration, customization requirements, migration costs, e-commerce seasonality and peak loads and scalability.

Text B

Cloud Computing and Its Effect on E-commerce

Cloud computing is a somewhat ambiguous concept that describes a blend of Software as a Service (SaaS), Infrastructure as a Service (IaaS), Platform as a Service (PaaS), grid computing (multiple computers working on a single application), and utility computing (pay for consumption) all bunched up in a package that should be more scalable, faster to implement, and less costly than traditional application and computing models.

1. What Is Cloud Computing?

Cloud computing is a type of Internet-based computing that provides shared computer processing resources and data to computers and other devices on demand. It is a model for enabling ubiquitous, on-demand access to a shared pool of configurable computing resources (e.g., computer networks, servers, storage, applications and services), which can be rapidly provisioned and released with minimal management effort. Cloud computing and storage solutions provide users and

247

enterprises with various capabilities to store and process their data in third-party data centers[1] that may be located far from the user—ranging in distance from across a city to across the world. Cloud computing relies on sharing of resources to achieve coherence and economy of scale, similar to a utility (like the electricity grid) over an electricity network.

Advocates claim that cloud computing allows companies to avoid up-front infrastructure costs (e.g., purchasing servers). It enables organizations to focus on their core businesses instead of spending time and money on computer infrastructure as well. Proponents also claim that cloud computing allows enterprises to get their applications up and running faster, with improved manageability and less maintenance, and enables Information Technology (IT) teams to more rapidly adjust resources to meet fluctuating and unpredictable business demand. Cloud providers typically use a "pay as you go" model. This will lead to unexpectedly high charges if administrators do not adapt to the cloud pricing model.

2. Perceived Benefits of Cloud Computing

Cloud computing offers three potential benefits:
- cost;
- flexibility/speed of implementation;
- scalability (sometimes called elasticity).

(1) Cost

Individual cloud users are supposed to save money because they don't have to purchase hardware, software or infrastructure and cloud computing costs are based on consumption.

The argument that cloud computing can save money is built around so-called peak usage. Imagine that your e-commerce website is busiest from November 1 to December 23 each year. During these peak periods, you require greater bandwidth, more computational power, and more data storage. But for the rest of the year your traffic requires just a third as much bandwidth etc.

In the traditional information technology model, you would purchase servers, frames, applications, etc. sufficient to handle your peak activity, leaving much of that capital hardware and software idle most of the year. But in a cloud you would theoretically only pay for the bandwidth, processing, or data storage you used.

(2) Flexibility

Cloud computing may be more flexible in terms of developing new applications or implementing custom applications because the cloud includes middleware (PaaS) to do your building on and loads of raw computing power to get things running in parallel.

(3) Scalability

Because users are not limited to one server or even one data center, cloud computing promises to be very scalable. For example, social media site Twitter recently went down, leaving hordes of microblogging addicts waiting to share their up-to-the-second status. And popular sites like Digg

---

[1] A data center is a facility used to house computer systems and associated components, such as telecommunications and storage systems. It generally includes redundant or backup power supplies, redundant data communications connections, environmental controls (e.g., air conditioning, fire suppression) and various security devices.

and Slashdot have both gone down for lack of bandwidth. But in cloud computing, an application should just be able to add more and more resources so that service is never interrupted. And when traffic wanes, so does the consumption of resources. The cloud-based application is perfectly scalable in theory.

3. Predicting Cloud Computing's Effect on E-commerce

So now let's get to where the rubber meets the proverbial road for e-commerce. How will cloud computing impact e-commerce in the near term? My opinion? At least 90 percent of e-commerce businesses will be using some form of cloud computing in the next five years.

Is that a bold statement? Am I overreaching to say that nine in ten online retailers will be participating in a cloud by 2014. No, not really. You see e-commerce has been migrating toward clouds for years.

Many (if not most) online merchants are already using some form of IaaS, PaaS, or SaaS. Consider that anyone with a hosted shopping cart has already moved beyond "traditional" computing to a web application that by our definition is a form of cloud computing. What's more, I believe that most e-commerce business owners that use licensed carts are paying for hosting services (i.e. IaaS), which is part of what cloud computing is.

So the move to cloud computing will simply mean that more and more e-commerce businesses will offload infrastructure, development, and software to the cloud—a trend that has been going on since before I opened my first store using Yahoo! Merchant Services.

In some ways, cloud computing is just a new way to describe what e-commerce businesses have already been doing.

4. Concerns about Cloud Computing

But cloud computing and even IaaS, PaaS, and SaaS do not come without significant concerns, and even cloud advocates can produce long lists of hurdles that the trend has yet address. For our purposes, I am going to focus on three: choice, custody, and cost.

(1) The Choice Problem for Cloud Computing

In spite of its promise, cloud computing will almost certainly limit customer choice, eliminate some potentially better solutions in favor of available solutions, and lock users into a particular providers.

Consider the example of hosted shopping carts or content management systems. While many of these are functional and easy to implement, they often lack the ability to integrate third-party solutions, and if they do allow such a thing, they require users to ask permission. They will limit that external solution.

For a specific example, try putting a content slider (like the free jFlow slider) on your hosted shopping cart. Can you? Some services won't allow it at all. If fact, can you even change the code on your hosted cart? Or are you required to use the templates provided?

Repeat this experiment with product image pan, tilt, zoom tools; third-party customer review solutions; and third-party analytics. Cloud computing, in this example, will limit your choices.

Also, don't be surprised if you cannot choose when your peak hours are. One of the promised benefits of cloud computing is that it is scalable, but some are already talking about "fairness" in the cloud. This means that if your business scales up too often—allegedly taking more than your fair share of the cloud—you could be throttled back. Sorry no scalability for you.

(2) The Custody Problem for Cloud Computing

There is a problem of who has custody of the data in cloud computing? Where will custom data, credit card data, your e-commerce business records, and personal data be stored? And if I am using multi-tenant software how easy will it be for other users to get my data?

To some extent, cloud computing will be protected by the same SSLs and protocols that have always protected e-commerce, but there is more room for trouble. As the cloud masks infrastructure and platforms, a sort of fog settles in and we can lose track of where data is being stored. For example, would you really want your customer data, including credit card data stored on a server in Turkmenistan?

In a cloud the users has no idea where the infrastructure is or how secure it is.

(3) The Cost Problem for Cloud Computing

In spite of its promise, cloud computing will actually cost some users more money. This is like IaaS, PaaS, and SaaS that can, in some circumstances, be more expensive than just owning or licensing your infrastructure, platform or software.

In fact, I would argue that more often than not using a licensed cart is less expensive than using a hosted one. Certainly there are other considerations, but I know of excellent licensed e-commerce solutions that cost less than $20 per month including basic payment processing fees and server space. Likewise having your own server is cheaper in the long term than using a hosting service.

New Words

ambiguous	*adj.*	不明确的
consumption	*n.*	消费，消费量
model	*n.*	模型，原型
	v.	模拟
configurable	*adj.*	结构的，可配置的
storage	*n.*	存储，贮藏，贮藏库
effort	*n.*	努力，成就
coherence	*n.*	一致
advocate	*n.*	提倡者，鼓吹者
	v.	提倡，鼓吹
proponent	*n.*	建议者，支持者
manageability	*n.*	易管理，易处理
fluctuate	*v.*	变动，波动，使动摇，使波动，使起伏
unexpectedly	*adv.*	出乎意料地，想不到地
perceive	*v.*	感知，感到，认识到
elasticity	*n.*	弹性

hardware	*n.*	(计算机的)硬件
imagine	*v.*	想象，设想
sufficient	*adj.*	充分的，足够的
middleware	*n.*	中间设备，中间件
interrupt	*v.*	中断
	n.	中断信号
proverbial	*adj.*	众所周知的，公认的
eliminate	*v.*	排除，消除
experiment	*n.*	实验，试验
	v.	进行实验，做试验
allegedly	*adv.*	依其申述
throttle	*v.*	扼杀
custody	*n.*	监管，保管
argue	*v.*	争论，辩论，说服

Phrases

cloud computing	云计算
a blend of	混合
grid computing	网格计算
utility computing	效用计算
bunch up	聚成一团，扎成一束
computing model	计算模型
third-party data center	第三方数据中心
peak usage	高峰用量
computational power	计算能力
in parallel	并行地，平行地
participate in	参加，参与，分享
in spite of	不管
in favor of	赞同，有利于
to some extent	某种程度上，（多少）有一点
in the long term	从长远观点来看
hosting service	托管服务

Abbreviations

SaaS (Software as a Service)	软件即服务
IaaS (Infrastructure as a Service)	基础设施即服务
PaaS (Platform as a Service)	平台即服务
IT (Information Technology)	信息技术

Exercises

[Ex. 5] Fill in the following blanks according to the text.

1. Cloud computing is a type of Internet-based computing that provides _____ and data to computers and _____. It is a model for enabling ubiquitous, on-demand access to a shared pool of _____.

2. The three potential benefits cloud computing offers are _____, _____ and _____.

3. Individual cloud users are supposed to save money because they don't have to purchase _____, _____ or _____ and cloud computing costs are based on _____.

4. In the traditional information technology model, you would purchase _____, _____, _____, etc. sufficient to handle your peak activity, leaving much of that capital hardware and software _____.

5. Cloud computing may be more flexible in terms of _____ or _____ because the cloud includes _____ to do your building on and loads of raw computing power to get things running in parallel.

6. According to the author, at least _____ of e-commerce businesses will be using some form of _____ in the next five years.

7. The move to cloud computing will simply mean that more and more e-commerce businesses will offload _____, _____ and _____ to the cloud.

8. In spite of its promise, cloud computing will almost certainly _____, _____ in favor of available solutions, and lock users into _____.

9. To some extent, cloud computing will be protected by _____ that have always protected e-commerce, but there is _____. As the cloud masks infrastructure and platforms, a sort of fog settles in and we can lose track of _____.

10. In spite of its promise, cloud computing will actually _____. Using a licensed cart is _____ than using a hosted one. Likewise having your own server is _____ than using a hosting service.

Reading Material

The Benefits of Cloud Computing to the E-commerce Industry

Within 10 years, 80% of all computing, storage, and e-commerce done worldwide may take place[1] in the cloud, predict analysts, in what's been termed the third phase of Internet computing in the modern era.

---

1 take place 发生

This paradigm[1] shift highlights 2010 as a watershed[2] year in the rising supremacy[3] of cloud computing and mobile devices in reshaping[4] where and how information (and applications) is accessed.

The first phase[5] of computing combined software and operating systems into one terminal allowing basic communication through devices such as e-mail. The second phase allowed the user to connect to the World Wide Web containing millions of websites, which in the mid-1990s saw Internet usage increase 100-fold in just two years. In the present third phase, everything will live in the cloud—including your data and software. Further, by 2020, there could be in excess of[6] 100 billion devices and sensors[7] accessing these remote data centers in the cloud. Only a small amount, approximately 1.4 billion, will be personal computers.

The progression away from the mainframe to personal computers is now being superseded by[8] the dual arrival of the Smartphone and cloud computing. In each step the underlying structure of computing has become more distributed. This has profound[9] implications for how consumers, vendors and suppliers will interact inside the e-commerce channel over the next decade.

1. Defining a Cloud Service

The term "cloud computing" has been hotly[10] contested, drawing both derision[11] and praise from different sectors of the I.T. community. At its core, the term refers to the outsourcing of data centers and application services to a remote provider under a pay-as-you-go[12] contract. This "metered" approach lowers costs and reduces complexity, simultaneously allowing the business to consume additional services "on-demand[13]".

This virtualization of server infrastructure—sharing one server as if it were several—allows for huge cost savings and economies of scale[14].

Hybrid[15] models are also possible whereby a business may build its own private cloud and temporarily access additional public cloud services if it so requires.

An example of this could include an e-commerce site, which leverages[1] further cloud services to deal with the effects of a successful social media campaign without having to upgrade its

---

1 paradigm   *n.*   范式
2 watershed   *n.*   分水岭
3 supremacy   *n.*   地位最高的人，至高，无上
4 reshape   *v.*   改造，再成形，采用新方针
5 phase   *n.*   阶段，状态
6 in excess of   超过，较……为多
7 sensor   *n.*   传感器
8 be superseded by   为……取代
9 profound   *adj.*   深刻的，意义深远的
10 hotly   *adv.*   热心地，激烈地
11 derision   *n.*   嘲笑
12 pay-as-you-go   随收随付制
13 on demand   按需，按要求
14 economy of scale   规模效益，因经营规模扩大而得到的经济节约
15 hybrid   *adj.*   混合的，杂种的

infrastructure.

However, the term cloud computing does have further meanings in addition to those defined above. These include Software as a Service (SaaS), Platform as a Service (PaaS), and Infrastructure as a Service (IaaS).

In simple terms, SaaS refers to an end user accessing a remote product or e-commerce service over the Internet. These could include a remote CRM such as Salesforce[2] or a data center offered by Amazon Web Services.

PaaS is geared towards developers who wish to deploy applications in the cloud and don't want to get involved with the server infrastructure. The Google apps store is an example of this.

The final version, IaaS, allows developers maximum interaction with the underlying server infrastructure including, but not limited to, deploying back-office applications[3] on that remote environment.

As of 2010 the SaaS model is the most dominant and widespread cloud variant in the marketplace.

2. Benefits to E-commerce

(1) Trust

One of biggest challenges[4] facing e-commerce pioneers[5] in the early days of the web turned out not to be a technical problem, but a human one: Trust.

It took time to build trust into their networks and establish a set of online credentials that made buyers feel comfortable initiating an online purchase.

With the advent of cloud computing, existing businesses and startups can immediately leverage the trust built into established cloud systems such as Google, Amazon and Salesforce. A business can now point out to its customer base that their technical platform is managed and secured by the best cloud engineers in the world.

(2) Cost Savings

Cost is generally one of the primary reasons for moving a business application or data center to the cloud. While there may be a low cost associated with developing and deploying an e-commerce application, the parallel need for hardware and bandwidth may turn out to be expensive.

Generally, a cloud-based initiative on a virtualized server may save a company 80% of the costs normally associated with a traditional e-commerce roll out[6].

(3) Speed

A company may be able to roll out an e-commerce application five times faster than before and begin selling immediately on the remote platform.

---

1 leverage　　v. 对……产生影响 n. 影响力，杠杆作用，优势，力量
2 Salesforce　它是创建于 1999 年 3 月的一家客户关系管理(CRM)软件服务提供商，总部设于美国旧金山，可提供随需应用的客户关系管理平台。
3 back-office application　　后台应用
4 challenge　　n. 挑战 v. 向……挑战
5 pioneer　　n. 先驱，倡导者，先锋
6 roll out　　铺开，全面推行

(4) Scalability

Often referred to as "elastic[1]", these cloud services allow a business to scale quickly and support seasonal spikes in demand or those triggered[2] by special promotions.

(5) Security

Securing applications, physical facilities and networks is a critical consideration. Many cloud vendors complete third-party certification, including ISO 27001 and SysTrust audits[3]. VI has been audited in for ISO 9001 and ISO 27001. Further security measures are implemented at the application, facility and network levels including data encryption, biometric screening of personnel and certification through third-party vulnerability assessment[4] programs.

(6) Interoperability[5]

The explosive growth in cloud e-commerce offerings in the next few years will also see an increase in the ability to share information between clouds and communities of clouds. Leading-edge cloud vendors will offer a standards-based framework, which allows programmatic access for users, partners and others who want to leverage additional functionality from within the cloud.

3. Conclusion

The term cloud computing is no longer an industry buzzword and signals a transformational[6] shift in how business data and e-commerce applications will be stored, accessed, shared, and transacted online.

In tandem[7], mobile applications and services will be provisioned from the cloud offering a myriad of ways for the end user to engage e-commerce operations.

The arrival of cloud computing is in many respects[8] equivalent to arrival of the Internet in the 1990s and fulfills the maxim prophesized by Google CEO, Eric Schmidt in 2006, when he declared "the network will truly be the computer".

参 考 译 文

大数据对电子商务公司的益处

在线零售商正在使用大数据来创造更好的购物体验，以提高客户满意度并产生更多的销售。

如果你一直在阅读新闻，可能看到了这样一个故事：Target 如何知道一个年轻女子怀孕了，而且比她的父亲知道得更早。事实证明，当一个女人开始购买诸如营养补品、棉球和无

1　elastic　　　　　　*adj.*　弹性的
2　trigger　　　　　　*v.*　引发，引起，触发
3　audit　　　　　　　*n.*　审计，稽核，查账　*v.*　稽核，查账
4　assessment　　　　*n.*　估价
5　interoperability　　*n.*　互用性，协同工作的能力
6　transformational　　*adj.*　转换的，变革的
7　in tandem　　　　　与……同时(发生)
8　in many respects　　在许多方面

味美容产品的时候,她很有可能怀孕了。

很多人对零售商知道自己那么多的生活和习惯感到不舒服。然而,大数据可以改善购物者在线购物体验,提高客户的满意度并产生更高的利润。这对零售商来说是一个巨大的创新,而且我们只是刚刚开始。

大数据如何使电子商务公司获得以下益处:

1. 交付更有价值的东西

亚马逊使用高级工具不断调整定价。该零售商可以比较竞争对手的价格数据,并自动调整自己产品的价格。有些价格每天变化十多次。使用合适的网络平台和插件,这很容易做到。动态定价意味着公司不能再只通过提供最低价格来竞争。现在比以往任何时候都更需要提供价格以外的东西,这意味着零售商必须建立良好的声誉,并在购物者需要低价格和良好的体验时成为首选。

2. 提供更多的个性化交互

亚马逊以使用大数据向购物者提供产品建议而闻名。如果你曾经在亚马逊购物,可能注意到"买了此商品的客户也买了"部分。最初将这个简单的功能添加到产品页面实际上增加了 30% 的销售额。这是一个简单的方法,能帮助购物者找到更多的产品,并让人们在购物网站上花更多的时间。

我在线销售定制男装,我们目前正在创建一个数据库,包括男士身体测量信息和他们的时尚偏好信息。我们的目标是,一旦顾客输入他们的身高和体重就能够提供尺寸适合的产品,即使我们无法量体。此功能的目的是更容易地为客户寻找到合适的衣服,并帮助他们找到正确的定制产品。

3. 跟踪人们的偏好

大数据对于营销人员的主要用途是微定位。数据越大,可以定位的范围越小,获得客户的潜在关键细节就越多。例如,当涉及谁可能支付,谁可能不支付时,信用卡公司发现了一些奇怪和非常有趣的相关性。发现为家具购买耐磨垫的客户是一些最可靠的付款人。也许洞察了他们的谨慎个性?

收集更多客户信息还可以带来信息和指标,这些信息和指标或许是你从未想过的。它还可以告诉你某些客户群体喜欢如何接待,以及他们可能感兴趣的其他产品。大数据的一个常见用法是"推荐引擎",比如亚马逊可根据查看过程建议你所感兴趣的商品。

例如,像 SAS 这样的公司提供的服务可以让你创建客户个人资料,帮助你为特定区域和特定客户提供更多个性化体验。他们还提供营销自动化服务,以便他们能够处理为你收集的许多复杂数据。Quantcast 也有一个免费的工具,可以利用大数据分析为你提供一些有关用户有趣的基本信息。

根据 NewVantage Partners 创始人约翰·巴特(John Barth)的说法:"有一个阶段的分析是探索和发现……你不明白的阶段,即发现阶段,大数据对其是有用的。"

4. 做出准确的预测

收集关于购物者的尺寸及其时尚偏好的数据让我们能为访客提供更好的体验。但是,也可以使用这些信息来确定哪些样式、裁剪甚至面料和颜色是受欢迎的。这有助于我们保持正确的产品库存,并与我们的裁缝和供应商谈判以获得最佳受益率。

例如,公司可以使用社交媒体来关注与其行业相关的趋势。这是了解人们购买内容的好方法。著名的唱片公司 EMI 使用来自多个第三方网站和应用程序的数据，全面了解人们如何听音乐和购买音乐，以便更好地预测需求，并创建更相关的广告活动。

5. 降低购物车放弃率

跨设备跟踪（也称重定向）可用于降低购物车放弃率。电子商务平台 eBay 发现，购物者通常在购买之前会从 3～5 个不同的设备中进行研究。大数据可用于记录购买历程的不同步骤，并在完成购买之前向互联网用户提供相关内容。

6. 为客户提供更好的体验

互联网用户不一定愿意让零售商知道他们的私人生活，但事实是，大数据将提高购物者在零售商处的购物体验。例如，大数据被 CNA 和其他公司用来寻找可能的欺诈和保护购物者的身份。从实时交易、地理数据和社交推送收集的信息有助于实时防止信用卡欺诈。

事实上，零售商知道一些你生活的私密细节看起来很怪异，但大数据对公司和购物者实际上是有益的。零售商不再能专注于竞争价格，因为他们有必要的工具，能为购物者创造一个更愉快、个性化和无缝的体验。